THE DIARY OF MARY BERG

The Diary of

Mary Berg

GROWING UP IN THE
WARSAW GHETTO

EDITED BY S. L. SHNEIDERMAN
NEW EDITION PREPARED BY
SUSAN LEE PENTLIN, PHD

ONEWORLD
OXFORD

A Oneworld Book

First published in America as *Warsaw Ghetto: A Diary* in 1945
Annotated, revised edition with a new introduction
Published by Oneworld Publications, 2007
Reprinted, 2007
This edition first published in trade paperback, 2009

ISBN 978–1–85168–585–1

Cover design by www.henrysteadman.com
Typeset by Jayvee Trivandrum, India
Printed in Great Britain by CPI Cox and Wyman

Oneworld Publications Limited
185 Banbury Road
Oxford OX2 7AR
England
www.oneworld-publications.com

The publishers would like to thank the United States Holocaust
Memorial Museum for permission to reproduce the photographs on pp.
15, 46, 65, 151, 170, 175, 224, 227, and the cover. The views or opinions
expressed in this book, and the context in which the images are used, do
not necessarily reflect the views or policy of, nor imply approval or
endorsement by, The United States Holocaust Memorial Museum.

The publishers would also like to thank the S. L. Shneiderman archives,
University of Tel Aviv, for providing the photographs and illustrations on
pp. ii, 25, 55, 63, 77, 84, 116, 125, 130, and the author photographs
on the cover; the James Fox archives (Stella Gumuchian Collection), for
providing the photograph on p. 220; and the Ghetto Fighters' Museum
for permission to reproduce the photographs on pp. 33 and 163. The
publishers have made every reasonable effort to identify and contact the
owners of the copyright to the photographs included in this book, and to
attribute copyright accordingly. Any errors are accidental and will be
corrected in future printings upon advice to the publisher.

CONTENTS

ILLUSTRATIONS

ACKNOWLEDGMENTS

I have been interested in and working with Mary Berg's diary since the mid-1980s. In the process, I have looked for, met and been helped by many people in the United States, Great Britain, Germany, Poland and Israel. Many have become friends. I would especially like to thank James A. Fox, former Editor-in-Chief of Magnum Photos in New York and Paris for thirty years, and retired photo curator and historian, for the time and effort he spent helping me to understand the Vittel internment camp. He met the Shneidermans in Paris at Magnum. Eileen Shneiderman's brother, the photographer David Seymour, was one of the founders of Magnum. I also appreciated the opportunity to interview Gutta Eisenzweig Sternbuch and David Kranzler in February 2006.

I want to give special thanks to Eileen and S. L. Shneiderman's children, Ben Shneiderman and Helen Sarid, and to Rochelle Saidel for their advice and encouragement, to Sylvia Glass's sons, Walter and David Goldfrank, and to Moira Hyle, the daughter of Norbert Guterman. I also want to thank: Alan Berger; Alice Eckhard; Anna and Tamas Adamik, Budapest; Batia Gilad, the Janusz Korczak Archive at the Ghetto Fighters' Kibbutz; Jenny Manuel, the American Jewish Archive; Krystyna Freijat, Secretary to Rev. Dr. Edward Puslecki, the General Superintendent of the United Methodist Church of Poland; Mark Shenise, of the General Commission on Archives and History, the United Methodist Church; Marianne Sandig, Berlin; Megan Lewis, USHMM Survivor Registry; Moishe Shubinsky, England; Monica

ACKNOWLEDGMENTS

Kulp, daughter of Gaither and Halina Warfield; Robert Giliank; Roman Zakharii; Ryszard Maczewski, Warsaw; Shelly Shapiro, Holocaust Friends and Survivors Education Center, Latham, NY; Serge and Beate Klarsfeld, Paris; Vanesa Chappell, Interlibrary Loan at Central Missouri State University; Central Missouri State University for the 1993 Faculty Research grant for research at the National Archives, and, as always, my husband Floyd C. Pentlin.

I want to remember my loving mother Jean Riddle (1919–2001), who wanted her children to learn how to think clearly, and my grandmother Addie Gillum Flanery (1893–1974), who was my English teacher in junior high and who had a deep appreciation and understanding of the English language. I also want to remember translators Norbert Guterman (1900–1984) and Sylvia Glass (1912–2006) for their efforts to bring this historical document to the public in 1945. I remember the interesting and lively telephone conversation I had with Sylvia Glass Goldfrank shortly before she passed away in January 2006.

As editor, I dedicate my work to the memory of S. L. Shneiderman, who played such a crucial role in ensuring that this important record of the Warsaw Ghetto was brought to public attention in 1944–5. He grasped its significance to the survival of the Polish Jews, and to history, working closely with Mary Berg and arranging for the diary's translation, serialization, and eventual publication in wartime New York. He was born in Kazimierz, Poland, in 1906 and died in Israel in 1996. I would also like to include in this dedication his wife and collaborator, Eileen Shneiderman, who was born Eileen Szymin in Warsaw, Poland in 1908 and passed away in Israel in 2004. Samuel Shneiderman lost his parents and two brothers and their families, eleven in all, in the ghetto of Opole, and Eileen Shneiderman her parents in the Otwock Ghetto. Together they formed an inspiring team as writers. They came to the United States in 1940, and devoted their lives to preserving the rich, cultural world of Polish Jews and the Yiddish language, which the Nazis attempted to destroy. I regret they did not live to see this diary come back into print.

SUSAN PENTLIN

PREFACE TO 1945 EDITION

Tell ye your children of it,
And let your children tell their children,
And their children another generation.

Joel, 1.3.

The walled Jewish quarters set up by the Nazis in Poland were intended to humiliate and torture the Jewish people. Today, these ghettos lie in ashes, after the Jews had converted them into citadels of resistance. In Warsaw, Bialystok, Bendzin, and Czestochowa, the Jews, men, women and children, armed with obsolete weapons, rose against the Nazi armored battalions. No ammunition was parachuted to these isolated fighters, not even during the Battle of Warsaw ghetto, which lasted for forty-two days. The heroic struggle and the sufferings of the Jews in the Polish ghettos constitute one of the most tragic and least known chapters of the war.

The term "ghetto" itself is a Nazi lie, for there can be no comparison between the Warsaw ghetto and others created by the Nazis in Poland, and the medieval ghettos, whose walls occasionally served as a protection to the Jews who lived within them. From the beginning, the modern ghettos served the enemy as death traps.

Paradoxically, the world that had given credence to the Nazi lies refused to believe in Nazi crimes. To this day there are "liberals" who refuse to believe that the Nazis have murdered almost four million Jews in Europe. They regard the revelations about gas chambers, crematoria, and bacteriological experiments performed on hundreds of thousands of Jews as products of anti-German propaganda.

The Nazis counted on this. They knew that the greater the crimes, the less credible they would appear.

People outside Poland had a completely false picture of the conditions within the isolated Jewish quarters in Poland. Abroad, it was imagined that the Jews were a mass of human beings apathetically awaiting slaughter. That this picture was erroneous, we learn from Mary Berg's diary, the first complete chronicle of the establishment and destruction of the Warsaw ghetto written by a witness without any political party bias.

At the beginning of the German occupation, the Jews themselves had no conception of the fate in store for them. They did their best to preserve their ways of life and, with them, the inevitable social distinctions which had prevailed before the occupation. Thus conditions in the ghetto naturally mirrored the life outside. In course of time, under the hardships of Nazi rule, solidarity among all classes of Jews grew. The Nazis deliberately squeezed into an area formerly occupied by about one hundred thousand people a heterogeneous group of six hundred thousand Jews from all the occupied territories. These Jews, of various cultures and ideas, flung into a pit of hunger, disease, and terror, succeeded in organizing a kind of community existence.

As would be true among any other groups, those who had reserves of cash or valuables managed to survive longer than the less fortunate. Underground trade with the so-called "Aryan" side continued, sometimes with the connivance of the Nazis themselves, who used these opportunities for acquiring valuables in return for worthless German marks. Through secret channels the Jewish fighting organizations got their meagre stores of arms; the funds for these arms came, to a considerable extent, from the wealthier Jews, some of whom paid willingly, while others contributed under pressure from the Jewish underground.

When Mary Berg was imprisoned in the Warsaw ghetto, she was barely sixteen years old. Events matured her quickly. As the daughter of an American citizen, she belonged to a tiny privileged group. The American flag on her lapel and another on the door of her apartment protected her like a talisman against the enemy. She was among those who suffered least, although, day after day, she was shaken by the tragedies of her schoolmates, neighbors, and family.

At some future time, we hope, chronicles hidden by writers in the ruins of the Warsaw ghetto will be discovered. Other survivors may be found to give additional testimony to this heroic episode of the war—heroic not only because of the death of so many martyrs, but because of their stubborn will to live a dignified life against fearful odds. For the time being, Mary Berg's diary is the only existing eye-witness record. She succeeded in bringing out her notes under the very noses of the Nazi officials, for after three years of looting, the Germans did not bother to search the few ghetto inhabitants who, as foreign citizens, finally left Warsaw. Originally the young girl wrote her notes in Polish, in abbreviated form. She rewrote them after her arrival in New York on the S.S. "Gripsholm." She was fifteen years old when she began her diary and twenty when she decided to have it published.

In preparing her manuscript for publication, I have made only those changes which were necessary to clarify details that would otherwise have been unintelligible for American readers. Almost all the names quoted in the diary are authentic; their bearers are either dead or out of danger. We have changed the names only of those persons whose fate is still uncertain or whose relatives might have been jeopardized if they had been named.

I wish to express my gratitude to Norbert Guterman who, in collaboration with Sylvia Glass, prepared the English version of *Warsaw Ghetto*.

S. L. SHNEIDERMAN

INTRODUCTION

> And it continued. Ten a day, ten thousand Jews a
> day. That did not last very long. Soon they took
> fifteen thousand. Warsaw! The city of Jews –
> the fenced in, walled-in city, dwindled, expired,
> melted like snow before my eyes.
>
> —from Yitzak Katzenelson's
> *The Song of the Murdered Jewish People*
> written 2–3–4 November 1943

On April 19, 1944, Mary Berg began her struggle to open American eyes to the Holocaust. On that day, a crowd of thousands gathered at the Warsaw Synagogue in New York and marched to City Hall in commemoration of the first anniversary of the Warsaw Ghetto Uprising. Heading the marchers was the Wattenberg family, Shya and Lena and their daughters Mary (Miriam) and Ann, who had escaped the terrible fate of so many European Jews and reached the United States just four weeks earlier. The marchers carried signs reading, "We appeal to the conscience of America to help save those Jews in Poland who can yet be saved," "Avenge the blood of the Polish ghetto" and "Three Million Polish Jews have been murdered by the Nazis! Help us rescue the survivors."[1]

The Wattenbergs had arrived in the United States in March 1944 as repatriates on the *SS Gripsholm*, an exchange ship leased by the U. S. Department of State from the Swedish American line. S. L. Shneiderman, a Yiddish journalist who had himself escaped Nazi Europe, had met Mary Berg, who was then nineteen years old, on the dock after the ship arrived. He learned she had brought a diary of her and her family's experiences in the Warsaw Ghetto with her, written in Polish in twelve small, spiral notebooks.

Shneiderman recalls in the preface to the 1983 Polish edition of the diary that:

> In a state of awe I read the tiny letters on the densely written pages of her notebooks. Afraid that the books might some day fall into the hands of the Nazis, Mary wrote her notes in a her own form of shorthand, using only initials for the people whose names she mentioned. She never used the word 'Nazi.' Instead, she wrote 'they.'

Nancy Craig, in a radio broadcast on station WJZ in New York, asked Mary how she had managed to bring her diary to the States. She replied, "I developed a sort of code of my own and wrote down the most important facts. Very simply I put them in my valise. Also I memorized all the important dates and names."[2] Soon after her arrival, Mary began to rewrite her notes in Polish.

Shneiderman worked closely with Mary for the next several months, deciphering the notebooks and asking her "to explain certain facts and situations which otherwise would have been puzzling not only for American readers but for readers through the world," apparently amending some spellings and perhaps adding some material. When she knew the persons mentioned had perished, she and Shneiderman changed the initials to full names. For the same reason, the author's surname was shortened to Berg to protect family and friends who might yet be alive in wartime Poland. In Pawiak, Mary had also begun rewriting parts of her diary. For these reasons, it is perhaps most accurate to call her published work "a diary memoir."

Shneiderman translated the Polish manuscript[3] into Yiddish, which he published, in serial form, in the *Der Morgen zshurnal*. He then hired Norbert Guterman, who was born in Poland, and Sylvia Glass, a graduate of Wellesley College, to translate the Polish version into English. Apparently, this version appeared in the *P.M.* newspaper in New York in serialized form, and in an abridged form in the *Jewish Contemporary Record*, in the fall of 1944. At about the same time, a German translation of the diary was translated by Mary Graf and appeared in the New York exile newspaper *Aufbau [Reconstruction]* from 22 September 1944 until 19 January 1945.[4]

In February 1945, Shneiderman published Mary Berg's full work, *Warsaw Ghetto: A Diary*, with L.B. Fischer in New York. Mary designed the original dust jacket portraying the brick wall marking the boundary of the Warsaw ghetto. In the foreword to a special edition of the diary, sponsored by the National Organization of Polish Jews, President Joseph Thon outlined Berg and Shneiderman's purpose in publishing the diary. He explained:

> The leaders of the United Nations have declared that they would resort to poison gas and bacteriological warfare only if the Germans used these inhuman methods first. The Germans have used these methods to slaughter millions of Jews in Treblinki, Majdanek, Oswiecim, and other camps. But even today the civilized world does not fully realize this fact. It is therefore our duty to make known the horrible truth, to publicize documents and eyewitness accounts that reveal it beyond any doubt.

Mary Berg's diary was published before the war was over, before people in the United States and abroad, and even the diarist herself, knew the enormity of the German crimes and the details of the Final Solution. Moreover, we should remember that as a witness to these crimes against humanity, Mary had arrived in New York before the summer of 1944, when the Hungarian Jews, the last of the European communities, were gassed at Auschwitz, and hope remained that the world's attention to their plight might lead to rescue.

Mary Berg was not the only witness of these events to testify in English before the end of the war. A few articles and pamphlets were published featuring eye-witness accounts between 1942 and 1943, and firsthand testimony was also included in a book on Polish Jewry in 1943.[5]

However, Mary Berg's diary was the first account to describe the events from the ghetto's establishment through to the first deportations that took place between July and September of 1942 to appear in English. It was also one of the first personal accounts to describe gas being used to kill the Jewish population at Treblinka. In a preface to the diary, Shneiderman pointed out that:

> At some future time, we hope, chronicles hidden by writers in the ruins of the Warsaw ghetto will be discovered. Other survivors may be found to give additional testimony to this heroic episode of the war... for the time being, Berg's diary is the only existing eye-witness record.[6]

Mary Berg's unique contribution was recognized in reviews during the winter of 1945. The *New Yorker* wrote: "This is a grim book, full of darkness and horror, and, because of the picture it gives of the courage and humanity of the people of the Warsaw ghetto, it is also a brave and inspiring one."[7] The *Kirkus Review* called it "a moving record of terrorism"[8] and the *New York Times* review recommended it as reading for everyone "without qualification."[9] *The Saturday Review* concluded that Berg's diary entries, "bear the imprint of sincerity and authenticity, and apparently are not 'glamorized' by editorial treatment."[10]

Soon after its publication in February 1945, the diary was translated into several foreign languages.[11] More recently, it has been the subject of a play, a piece of street theater, and featured in a 1991 documentary film, "A Day in the Warsaw Ghetto, A Birthday Trip to Hell."[12] It also appears as a source in the bibliography of many important works on the Holocaust available to students and scholars.[13]

Mary Berg's diary is unique for its authenticity, its detail and its poignancy, as well as for its early publication. Alice Eckhardt, a noted Christian theologian, wrote in 1995,

> Now with the ghetto's final fate known by all, the details of the community life that went on and even at times blossomed despite the dreadful conditions under which it existed become even more important for us to know. The unique factors that made it possible for this young woman to leave the ghetto just prior to its elimination give the book a vibrancy and at the same time a poignancy that is hard to match."[14]

Mary Berg was fifteen years old when the Germans attacked Poland, and her diary is that of a young girl. Like many child diarists, she was searching to find meaning in the cruelty she experienced. Like Anne Frank and others, she began her diary as a means to comfort and occupy herself. Later, it became an outlet for her and her friends. Alvin Rosenfeld in his work *A Double Dying*[15] concludes that diaries of the Holocaust written by children or young adolescents "seem almost to constitute a distinctive subgenre of the literature of incarceration."

She was with her family in the Warsaw Ghetto from its beginning in November, 1940 until a few days before the Great Deportation began on July 22, 1942. On July 17, 1942, they had been interned as American citizens in the Pawiak Prison, which stood inside the ghetto. From the windows of the prison, they witnessed the deportation of over 300,000 ghetto inhabitants. Several years later, Mary recalled watching many friends among "the aged men with gray beards, the blooming young girls and proud young men, driven like cattle to the Umschlagplatz on Stawki Street to their deaths."[16]

Shortly after midnight on January 18, 1943, the day the second *Aktion* began in the ghetto that was to lead to the first armed resistance the next day, Mary, her parents and her sister Ann were sent with other foreign internees to an internment camp in Vittel, France. Over a year later, they were selected for an exchange with German prisoners in the United States. They arrived in the United States aboard the *SS Gripsholm* on March 16, 1944.

Early in the occupation, Mary learned that the Germans would set a price on life and that those with wealth and privilege from before the occupation would have a better chance of survival. When the ghetto was established in Lodz, a schoolmate of Mary's came to Warsaw with, as Mary describes it, "bloodcurdling stories." Her family had managed to escape, she told her friend, by "bribing the Gestapo with good American dollars." Of course, Mary knew that only "the well-to-do Jews" could have easy access to foreign currency.

She realized that she was among the privileged. She explained, in her diary that those without privilege "have only a 10 per cent chance at most [to survive]." Later, she admitted with equal openness that, "Only those who have large sums of money are able to save themselves from this terrible life." Mary had grown up in a well-to-do home in Lodz. Her father owned an art gallery and traveled abroad to purchase works by European masters such as Poussin and Delacroix. She attended school in Lodz and her family could afford to spend six weeks in a health resort in the summer of 1939, and had relatives living in the United States.

She also had the insight to see that foreign citizens had a much better chance of survival. Jews with passports for neutral countries were exempt from having to wear the Jewish star and doing forced labor. When two friends obtained papers as nationals of a South American country, she commented: "No wonder many Jews try to obtain such documents; but not all have the means to buy them or the courage to use them."

Mary's mother, Lena, was born in New York on 1 May 1902, and was a citizen of the United States. When Lena was about twelve, she had moved to Poland with her Polish-born parents and an older brother and sister, who were also born in the States. Her younger brothers Abie and Percy were born after the family returned to Poland in 1914. When her parents and older siblings moved back to the States in the 1920s, Lena, a fashion designer, remained in Lodz with her younger brothers. She married Shya Wattenberg, a Polish citizen, who was a painter and an antique dealer.[17] They had two children, Mary and a younger daughter named Ann.

Under the Germans, her mother's status as an American citizen gave the whole family protection and privileges, even though Mary and her sister were born in Poland. When the mailman brought her mother a letter from the American consulate in December 1939, Mary reported that he "could not refrain from expressing his envy over the fact that we have American connections." On April 5, 1940, she noted, realistically, that "Polish citizens of Jewish origin have no one to protect them, except themselves." Later, she explained that her mother's visiting card on the door in Warsaw, indicating she was an American, was a "wonderful talisman against the German bandits who freely visit all Jewish apartments." This was so much so, that neighbors came to their apartment as soon as German uniforms came into view.

Although the Wattenbergs were refugees, they had managed to hold on to some money and valuables. They also received mail and packages from relatives in the States and Mrs. Wattenberg, as an American citizen, was permitted, at first, to leave the ghetto. When, in November 1940, the Germans officially closed the Jewish quarter in Warsaw as a ghetto, the Wattenbergs were fortunate to be able to remain in their apartment at

Sienna 41, on the corner of Sosnowa Street in the ghetto. It was included in the area referred to as the "Little Ghetto," at the southern border of the ghetto. The courtyard outside their windows opened onto the "Aryan" side of the ghetto where they could still see people walking around freely.

The "Little Ghetto" became the privileged quarter. Gutman points out that:

> Even though the ghetto adopted the slogan 'all are equal,' some people were 'more equal' than others, and this imbalance could be felt on the streets as well. Some streets, such as Sienna and Chlodna, were considered well-to-do sections. The apartments there were larger, the congestion lighter, and above all, the people relatively well fed. The streets were the addresses of the assimilated Jews... and rich Jews who had managed to hold on to a portion of their wealth.[18]

Mary was aware of this inequality and of the importance wealth played in the life of the ghetto.

Her knowledge of the corruptibility of the Judenrat is also clear from a later entry, after she and her family moved to an apartment at Chlodna 10, located right at the western ghetto gate, by the foot-bridge over Chlodna Street. She explained that:

> The well-to-do, who could afford to bribe the officials of the housing office, get the best apartments on this street with its many large modern houses. Chlodna Street is generally considered the 'aristocratic' street of the ghetto, just as Sienna Street was at the beginning.

Although Mary often seemed uncomfortable with the privileges and protection afforded her family, she also wanted to forget the horror all around her, and with the resilience of youth she adapted to life during the occupation. Wiszniewicz interviewed a ghetto survivor living in the United States a few years ago:

> People think the ghetto was like in the movies: con-stant, relentless terror. But it wasn't like that at all. We were always surrounded by terror, but we led normal lives right alongside it. Flirting went on in the ghetto, romances, concerts, theatrical perfor-mances. People went to a restaurant, while behind the restaurant somebody was dying. The normal and the abnormal intertwined repeatedly.[19]

This is the life that Mary describes on every page.

Many of her young friends from Lodz had also fled to Warsaw. During the summer of 1940, the principal of her Lodz gymnasium, Dr. Michael Brandstetter,[20] with a number of his teaching staff, started illegal classes in Warsaw. The students secretly met twice a week in the safety of the Watten-berg home so that they could finish their studies. School was only possible for the privileged, because students in the study-groups usually had to pay their teachers about thirty to forty zlotys a month.[21]

As the numbers of refugees increased and conditions grew more and more distressing, Jews in Warsaw began to establish a network of relief and self-help organizations in the Jewish quarter. Eager to make a contribution, Mary and eleven of her friends from Lodz founded a club to raise relief funds. Soon, at the request of a representative of the Joint Distribution Committee, they decided to put on a musical show. They called themselves the "Lodz Artistic Group" (Lodzki Zespol Artystyczny) or, in Polish, the LZA, whose letters appropri-ately, she felt, formed the word "tear."

One document recovered from the *Oneg Shabbat* archive refers to the "privileged" youth in the ghetto, mainly refugees from Lodz and neighboring towns, whom he disparagingly called the "golden youth." In her diary Mary describes going to the cafés on Sienna Street to sing, and to performances at the Feminina Theater with Romek, outings that stand in stark contrast to the starving youth and children in the ghetto. Even the LZA club, which was set up to raise funds for the poor, clearly brought the youth running it welcome relief from the horrors they saw all around them, as Mary reported that they "had a lively time" putting on their play, and were quite a hit. However, she remained sensitive to this inequality, and to the growing desperation in the ghetto. Just a few weeks earlier, she had noted a visit she made to a refugee home where she saw half-naked, unwashed children lying about listlessly. One child looked at her and said she was hungry. With character-istic candor, she confessed in her diary, "I am overcome by a feeling of utter shame. I had eaten that day, but I did not have a piece of bread to give to that child. I did not dare look in her eyes."

In another moving passage, she wrote about the "dreamers of bread" in the streets whose "eyes are veiled with a mist that belongs to another world." She explained that, "usually they sit across from the windows of food stores, but their eyes no longer see the loaves that lie behind the glass, as in some remote inaccessible heaven." In the same entry, she also expressed guilt about her privileges, concluding: "I have become really selfish. For the time being I am still warm and have food, but all around me there is so much misery and starvation that I am beginning to be very unhappy."

Abraham Lewin, a ghetto diarist who perished, described the huge contrasts between the better off inhabitants of the ghetto, and the many thousands who were suffering poverty, disease and starvation:

> The ghetto is most terrible to behold with its crowds of drawn faces with the color drained out them. Some of them have the look of corpses that

have been in the ground a few weeks. They are so horrifying that they cause us to shudder instinctively. Against the background of these literally skeletal figures and against the all-embracing gloom and despair that stares from every pair of eyes, from the packed mass of passers-by, a certain type of girl or young woman, few in number it must be said, shocks with her over-elegant attire... Walking down the streets I observe this sickly elegance and am shamed in my own eyes.[22]

As another *Oneg Shabbat* essayist reminded future historians, while these privileged youth lived comparatively well, "nevertheless they, too, were affected by wartime conditions which changed their lives in a negative way."[23]

Wealth and privilege in the ghetto influenced more than housing and education. Mary discovered they played a part in protecting the inhabitants from labor camp and helped secure the most desirable jobs. She clearly faced an inner, moral dilemma herself when in the fall of 1941, she learned that the Judenrat was offering practical courses in subjects like metallurgy and applied graphic arts near her home on Sienna Street.[24] The course was to last six months and the tuition was twenty-five zlotys. When she went to register, she found many friends among the almost six hundred applicants, all eager to escape labor camp.[25] Not surprisingly, there were only a few dozen openings.

She admitted to herself in her diary knowing that "pull" would play a large part in the selection of students. At first she "rebelled" against this, but when she realized she had little chance of being admitted, she "decided to resort to the same means." There was an additional selfishness in this decision, because she also admitted knowing that at the time girls were not threatened with labor camps as young boys were.

She had begun to accept the realities of bribes and pull a few months earlier. When the Judenrat established the Jewish Police force, she had explained, "more candidates presented themselves than were needed." She had then added, "A special committee chose them, and 'pull' played an important part in their choice. At the very end, when only a few posts were available, money helped, too... Even in Heaven not everyone is a saint." Since Mary's uncle Abie served in the police force, she probably knew of this at first hand.

Due to their pre-war social standing, education and wealth, many of Mary's relatives and friends were able to acquire positions of "privilege," thus enabling them to live much better than the average ghetto dweller and to survive at least a while longer. Most got their positions through the Judenrat. Although public opinion varied as to the integrity of the Judenrat, Ringelblum described the council as "hostile to the people" in his *Oneg Shabbat* notes.[26] Others, however, joined the Jewish Police, whom Ringelblum and other memoirists condemned outright, saying they "distinguished themselves with their fearful corruption and immorality."[27]

Later, Mary explained that her uncle Percy got a job with the Judenrat, picking up bricks in ruined buildings, but he lacked the "pull" to get a higher paying position as an overseer. On the other hand, she knew that her "boy friend" in the ghetto, Romek Kowalski, another "golden youth" from Lodz, had secured a position as an overseer for the construction of the ghetto wall, because he did have "pull." Kowalski was a relative of engineer Mieczslaw Lichtenbaum, the head of the wall construction commission formed by the Judenrat,[28] and of Marek Lichtenbaum, who became the head of the Judenrat after the Great Deportation.

After what she describes as a "struggle," which probably means bribes were required, her father got the coveted position of janitor in their apartment block. The Judenrat appointed janitors. They got a salary, free lodging, relief from community taxes and extra rations, as well as a pass from the Judenrat exempting them from forced labor. In Mary's words, "no wonder the job is hard to obtain." Also, Mary's sister Ann attended classes in sewing children's clothing, which were run by the Judenrat's Institute for Vocational Guidance and Training, known as the ORT.

Another acquaintance of Mary's, Heniek Grynberg, whose cousin Rutka was Ann's best friend, was a smuggler in the ghetto. He was apparently involved in the ghetto underworld, as he frequented the Café Hirschfeld with Gestapo agents. Mary notes, "He is one of the most successful people in this new business. This can be seen from his prosperous appearance and the elegant dresses worn by his wife and daughter." His main trade was to smuggle in anti-typhus serum which, of course, as typhus swept the ghetto, went to those who could pay high sums.

The Special Ambulance Service received particularly scathing criticism from Ringelblum, who regarded it as a front for selling cards and caps that afforded the holders valuable advantages, such as exemption from forced labor. It was run by the infamous mafia-style underworld in the ghetto known as the "Thirteen," which was widely feared to be a tool of the Gestapo. One of Mary's friends and a fellow member of the LZA, Tadek Szajer, was the son of a member of the "Thirteen," and himself a member of the Ambulance Service. He pursued her with youthful fervor, but she rejected his advances, noting that while others such as Romek Kowlaski had to work so hard to provide for their families, Tadek was always well fed and smartly dressed, and traveled everywhere by rickshaw. She suspected his father of doing business with the Nazis, and her decision not to see him any more suggested she understood what was happening, and wanted to take a moral stand.

In early 1942, Mary learned that U. S. citizens had been allowed to leave the ghetto and one acquaintance's father was interned in Germany. There were rumors in the ghetto of a prisoner exchange. A few weeks later, she noted that here "pull" and bribes could also be useful. She wrote in her diary, "Naturally, one must have some scrap of paper stating that at least one member of the family is a foreign citizen. My mother is lucky in this respect, for she is a full-fledged American citizen."

Later Mary's mother made contact with a Gestapo agent named "Z" who promised her help. Naively, Mary confessed to believing that "it seems that despite his position he has remained a decent man." More likely, money passed into his hands before he registered Mrs. Wattenberg with the Gestapo. A month later, Mary Berg and her family marched through the ghetto, with about seven hundred citizens of neutral, European and American countries, twenty-one of whom were Americans, to the Pawiak prison where they were interned.

When the Wattenbergs moved into the Pawiak prison, Mary parted not only from Kowalski and her many girl friends, but also from her mother's two younger, Polish-born brothers. Her Uncle Abie accompanied them to the prison gate. In parting, he asked her mother, "How can you leave me?" Later, in the relative safety of the internment camp in Vittel, Mary wrote in her diary, "we, who have been rescued from the ghetto, are ashamed to look at each other. Had we the right to save ourselves?... Here I am, breathing fresh air, and there my people are suffocating in gas and perishing in flames, burned alive. Why?"

On arrival at the Vittel internment camp in early 1943, the Wattenbergs and other internees from Pawiak could not at first believe that such a world of comparative normalcy existed any longer. Gutta Eisenzweig, who had shared a cell with Mary at Pawiak, writes in her recent memoir about her initial reaction, "I stood there in shock, for we had suddenly crossed the divide from hell to paradise... we had come to a serene atmosphere of Old World sumptuousness. The contrast was overwhelming."[29] Vittel was a showplace among the German internment camps in Europe, designed to reassure the International Red Cross that the internees were well-treated to help ensure the safety of Germans interned abroad.

The Vittel camp was based at a health spa in the Vosges Mountains of France. The internees had rooms in the hotels and some of the luxuries of the spa still were available. There was a hospital with kind inmate physicians such as Dr. Jean Levy, movies and entertainments, a few shops and a beautiful park they could promenade in during the day. With the help of Red Cross packages they received, no one was hungry. The American and British internees at Vittel had time enough to establish a social life. There were language classes and other courses available, concerts and entertainments. There were also contacts with the French resisitance, several hundred nuns, and internees like Sofka Skipwith who reached out to help the new arrivals from Warsaw.

Madeleine Steinberg, a British internee, has written her memoir about the Vittel camp. She recalls that Mary volunteered right away to help with the children at art classes and when they were playing. She also recalls that Mary was the first one to tell the other internees about life in the Warsaw ghetto and to explain why the children from Poland ran and hid in the cellar when they saw a German at Vittel.[30] The internees began to have hope once again. However, a few weeks after the Wattenbergs' departure for the *SS Gripsholm* exchange, most of the Polish internees who had been moved to the Hotel Beau Site outside the barbed wire surrounding the park were deported in two transports to Drancy, and a short time later, from there to Auschwitz, where they were gassed upon arrival.

In the Warsaw Ghetto, after the deportations in late summer 1942, the Jewish Fighting Organization and other political youth assassinated collaborators in the ghetto, including Jews who had worked with the Gestapo and made huge fortunes in business deals with the Germans and known

Gestapo informers.[31] Postwar reactions, especially among displaced survivors in Europe, against the Nazi perpetrators – including collaborators, those who were members of the ghetto councils, the ghetto police or *Kapos* in the camps – was, at first, determined. Some were tried in Occupied Germany and declared responsible for their actions.

Later, several much publicized cases against Jewish collaborators were tried in Israeli and German courts. However, "guilt" in a legal sense was often difficult to prove and to judge. Since the Germans' ultimate goal was to destroy the Jewish population, these collaborators were subordinated to the Germans' will, so the lines between cooperation and collaboration were often indistinct. The courts of public morality have also tended to judge these defendants with leniency, as people wonder what they might have done to save themselves or family members in similar circumstances, had they been tested.[32]

Questions my students often asked when they read Mary Berg's *Diary* were how she knew in Pawiak what was happening in the ghetto, and why she wrote that the victims at Treblinka were killed with steam. Although Mary was in Pawiak during the *Aktion* in 1942, the walls of Pawiak were transparent. She speaks of rumors that reached them through the prison guards and Polish police. She and the other internees at Pawiak also received letters from friends and family. Gutta Eisenzweig got detailed updates from Hillel Seidman, a community official. They also communicated with new internees and with ghetto inhabitations through the windows at Pawiak. Mary's writings also reflect what people knew at the time. Some of the first reports indicated that steam was being used to kill people at Treblinka. It was some time after people first escaped from Treblinka that Warsaw fully understood that the Germans were using carbon monoxide.

The images of suffering we see in headlines and on television screens today make our world, in fact, too similar to the world of Mary's girlhood experience. Young people today often lash out at the world to stop the killing. Holocaust scholars endeavor to do the same thing. They hope that educating future generations about the past will empower them to build a new world without hate. Mary's diary provides readers with an understanding of the Holocaust from an intense, personal perspective, and empowers readers to hope for a better future for the human family.

Marcel Reich-Reinicki explains in his recent memoir, in reference to his wife who escaped from the Umschlagplatz, "Whoever, sentenced to death, has at close quarters watched a train leaving for the gas chambers, remains marked for the rest of their lives."[33] Although Mary never passed through the Umschlagplatz, she watched as over 300,000 Jews marched by Pawiak prison in Warsaw on their way to their deaths at Treblinka. After she returned to the U. S., she learned that most of her friends and family in Europe had perished in the Holocaust, including over two hundred Jews at Vittel, her roommate Rosl Weingort, Adam Wentland and his sisters, Mrs. Tamara Schorr, the wife of the Grand Rabbi of Warsaw, and many others she knew. They were on the verge of freedom, but the world turned its eyes away and they were deported back to Poland where they died in the gas chambers of Auschwitz.

Mary began a new life in America and made an effort to leave the past behind her. When Nancy Craig asked her in early 1945 if she wanted to visit Poland again, she replied:

> No, I will never go back. America is my country now and I'm going to be a real American. It wouldn't be nice to go back to Poland and see only cemeteries... also my father's family has been killed... so have all our friends. After what we went through, I know what freedom really means... it means America. Just talking with you this morning over the radio... this is America.

While readers may conclude that Mary was "fortunate" in surviving, and assume that once in the United States she returned to the happiness of her early teenage years, most also understand that the lives of survivors of trauma, children perhaps most of all, are changed forever by persecution, the future altered by the horror, the losses and the choices they once had to make.

Until the early 1950s Mary Berg was a personality in New York, granting interviews and appearing on radio. Then she disassociated herself from the diary, saying she wanted to forget the past, and she disappeared from the public eye. It is not known if she found happiness in her adult years. We can only hope she was able to make a life for herself in the post-war world and find solace from past memories.

SUSAN PENTLIN

CHAPTER I

WARSAW BESIEGED

OCTOBER 10, 1939

Today I am fifteen years old.[1] I feel very old and lonely, although my family did all they could to make this day a real birthday. They even baked a macaroon cake in my honor, which is a great luxury these days. My father ventured out into the street and returned with a bouquet of Alpine violets. When I saw it I could not help crying.

I have not written my diary for such a long time that I wonder if I shall ever catch up with all that has happened. This is a good moment to resume it. I spend most of my time at home. Everyone is afraid to go out. The Germans are here.

I can hardly believe that only six weeks ago my family and I were at the lovely health resort of Ciechocinek, enjoying a carefree vacation with thousands of other visitors. I had no idea then what was in store for us. I got the first inkling of our future fate on the night of August 29 when the raucous blare of the giant loud-speaker announcing the latest news stopped the crowds of strollers in the streets. The word "war" was repeated in every sentence. Yet most people refused to believe that the danger was real, and the expression of alarm faded on their faces as the voice of the loud-speaker died away.

My father felt differently. He decided that we must return to our home in Lodz. In almost no time our valises stood packed and ready in the middle of the room. Little did we realize that this was only the beginning of several weeks of constant moving about from one place to another.

We caught the last train which took civilian passengers to Lodz. When we arrived we found the city in a state of confusion. A few days later it was the target of severe German bombardments. The telephone rang again and again. My father dashed from one mobilization office to another, receiving a different-colored slip of paper at each one. One day Uncle Abie, my mother's younger brother, rushed unexpectedly into our house to say goodbye before leaving for the front. He was ragged, grimy, and unshaven. He had no uniform; only his military cap and the knapsack on his shoulders marked him as a soldier. He had been making his way from one city to another, looking for his regiment.

We spent most of our time in the cellar of our house. When word came that the Germans had broken through the Polish front lines and were nearing Lodz, panic seized the whole population. At eleven o'clock at night crowds began to stream out of the city in different directions. Less than a week after our arrival from Ciechocinek we packed our necessities and set out once more.

Up to the very gates of the city we were uncertain which direction we should take—toward Warsaw or Brzeziny? Finally, along with most of the other Jews of Lodz, we took the road to Warsaw. Later we learned that the refugees who followed the Polish armies retreating in the direction of Brzeziny had been massacred almost to a man by German planes.

Among the four of us, my mother, my father, my sister, and I, we had three bicycles, which were our most precious possessions. Other refugees who attempted to bring with them things that had been valuable in the life they had left behind were compelled to discard them. As we advanced we found the highway littered with all sorts of objects, from fur coats to cars abandoned because of the lack of gasoline. We had the good luck to acquire another bicycle from a passing peasant for the fantastic sum of two hundred zlotys*, and we hoped it would enable us to move together with greater speed. But the roads were jammed, and gradually we were completely engulfed in the slow but steady flow of humanity toward the capital.

Mile after mile it was the same. The fields withered in the terrible heat. The gigantic cloud of dust raised by the vanguard of refugees swept over us, blotting out the horizon and covering our faces and clothes with successive layers of dust. Again and again we flung ourselves into the ditches on the side of the road, our faces buried in the earth, while planes roared in our ears. During the night huge patches of red flared up against the black dome of the sky. The fires of burning cities and villages rose all around us.

When we arrived in Lowicz, the city was one huge conflagration. Burning pieces of wood fell on the heads of the refugees as they forced their way through the streets. Fallen telephone poles barred our path. The sidewalks were cluttered with furniture. Many people were burned in the terrible flames. The odor of scorched human flesh pursued us long after we had left the city.

By September 9, the supply of food we had taken from home was used up. There was nothing whatever to be had along the way. Weak from hunger, my mother fainted on the road. I dropped beside her, sobbing wildly, but she showed no sign of life. In a daze, my father ran ahead to find some water, while my younger sister stood stock-still, as if paralyzed. But it was only a passing spell of weakness.

---

* One zloty, at normal (prewar) exchange rates, was worth about twenty US cents, or fifteen pence. One zloty = 100 groszy.

In Sochaczew we managed to get a few sour pickles and some chocolate cookies that tasted like soap. This was all we had to eat the entire day. Finding a drink of water was almost as difficult as procuring food. All the wells along the way were dried up. Once we found a well filled with murky water, but the villagers warned us not to drink from it because they were sure it had been poisoned by German agents. We hurried on in spite of our parched lips and aching throats.

Suddenly we saw a little blue plume of smoke rising from the chimney of a house at the side of the road. We had found all the other houses along the road deserted, but here was a sign of life. My father rushed in and returned with a huge kettle, but there was a strange expression on his face. In a trembling voice he told us what he had found, and for a while we could not bring ourselves to touch that precious water... He had found the kettle on a stove in which the fire was lit. Near by, on a bed, a man was lying with his face turned to the wall. He seemed to be sleeping peacefully, so my father called out to him several times. But there was no answer. Then he walked over to the sleeping peasant and saw that he was dead. The bed was full of blood. The window panes were peppered with bullet holes.

The kettle which we "inherited" from this murdered peasant became our faithful companion on the long road to Warsaw. As we neared the capital, we met the first German prisoners of war walking along the highway, led by Polish soldiers. This sight was encouraging to us, yet the Germans did not seem cast down by their condition. They wore elegant uniforms—they smiled insolently. They knew they would not be prisoners for very long.

We had our first taste of cooked food in Okecie, a suburb of Warsaw. A few soldiers in a deserted building shared their potato soup with us. After four days and nights of seemingly endless traveling, we realized for the first time how tired we were. But we had to go on. There was not a moment to lose, for as we left Okecie we saw men and women building barricades with empty streetcars and cobblestones torn up from the streets, in preparation for the siege of the capital.

In Warsaw we found women standing at the doorways of the houses, handing out tea and bread to the refugees who streamed into the capital in unending lines. And as tens of thousands of provincials entered Warsaw in the hope of finding shelter there, thousands of old-time residents of the capital fled to the country.

Relatives in the heart of Warsaw's Jewish quarter gave us a warm and hearty welcome, but constant air attacks drove us to the cellar during most of our stay with them. By September 12, the Germans began to destroy the center of the city. Once again we had to move, this time to seek better protection against the bombs.

The days that followed brought hunger, death, and panic to our people. We could neither eat nor sleep. At first, in a new home on Zielna Street, we knew real comfort. The owners had fled the city, leaving a clean apartment for our use. There was even a maid to give us hot tea, and for the first time since our flight from Lodz, we ate a real meal served on a table covered with a white cloth. It included herring, tomatoes, butter, and white bread. To get this bread my father had to stand for hours in a long line in front of a bakery. As he waited there, several German planes suddenly swooped down and strafed the people with machine guns. Instantly the line in front of the bakery dispersed, but one man remained. Disregarding the firing, my father took his place behind him. A moment later the man was hit in the head by a bullet. The entrance to the bakery shop was now free and my father made his purchase.

After this supper we listened to a broadcast in which an American reporter described the Nazi methods of warfare to his American listeners. "I stood in a field and from a distance saw a woman digging potatoes. Beside her was a little child. Suddenly a German plane swooped down, firing at the unarmed woman, who fell at once. The child was not hit. He

5

bent over his fallen mother and wept heartrendingly. Thus another orphan was added to the many war orphans of Poland. President Roosevelt!" he exclaimed in a deep voice, "I beg of you, help these mothers who are digging potatoes for their children; help these children whose mothers are falling on the peaceful fields; help Poland in her hour of trial!" But no help came...

Our house at 31 Zielna Street was next to the telephone building, which was a target for the German guns throughout the siege. Although struck by many shells, the lofty and solidly built structure was only slightly damaged and the telephone girls remained at their posts. Many houses nearby were destroyed, and again we had to spend our nights in the cellar. Then one of the bombs exploded in the front room of our apartment, and we were forced to return to the crowded home of our relatives.

Gradually the food supply of the city became exhausted. Now and then, depending upon which canning factory had been hit by the German bombs, various kinds of tinned goods were thrown on the market. Some days only sardines or pickles were to be had in the stores.

Our hunger for news was as great as our hunger for food. The only paper that still came out was the *Worker*, the organ of the Polish Socialist Party, which appeared in special editions. We admired the heroism of the editors and printers who, under the most difficult conditions, saw to it that the population was kept informed of events. They told us, for instance, that the British fleet had anchored at Gdynia. Very often the news printed in the *Worker* heartened us, but premature or falsely optimistic reports only deepened our disappointment later.

By September 20, the radio was silent and the water system had ceased to function. We began to feel as if we were on a desert island. I shall never forget September 23, the date of the Day of Atonement[2] in 1939. The Germans deliberately chose that sacred Jewish holiday for an intensive bombardment of the Jewish district. In the midst of this bombardment a strange meteorological phenomenon took place: heavy snow mixed with hail began to fall in the middle of a bright, sunny day. For a while the bombing was interrupted, and the Jews interpreted the snow as a special act of heavenly intervention: even the oldest among them were unable to recall a similar occurrence. But later in the day the enemy made up for lost time with renewed fury.

In spite of the danger, my father and a few other men who lived in our house went to the neighboring synagogue. After a few minutes one of them came running back, his tallith (prayer shawl) on his head, a prayer book in his hand, and so shaken that for some time he was unable to speak. A bomb had fallen upon the synagogue and many of the worshipers had been killed. Then, to our great joy, my father returned unharmed. White as chalk, and carrying his tallith crumpled under his arm, he told us that many of those who, only a moment before, had been praying at his side had been killed during the service.

That night hundreds of buildings blazed all over the city. Thousands of people were buried alive in the ruins. But ten hours of murderous shelling could not break the resistance of Warsaw. Our people fought with increased stubbornness; even after the government had fled and Marshal Rydz-Smigly[3] had abandoned his troops, men and women, young and old, helped in the defense of the capital. Those who were unarmed dug trenches; young girls organized first-aid squads in the doorways of the houses; Jews and Christians stood shoulder to shoulder and fought for their native land.

On the last night of the siege we sat huddled in a corner of the restaurant below our house. A few elderly Jews chanted Psalms in tearful voices. My mother had wrapped us all in thick blankets to protect us from the tiny splinters that filled the air. When she herself stuck out her head for a moment, she was hit on the forehead by a splinter of shrapnel. Her face was covered with blood, but her wound proved to be only a small scratch. We realized that our shelter was a firetrap, so we set out for Kozla Street to find safer quarters with our relatives, stumbling over the mutilated bodies of soldiers and civilians as we walked. We found only the skeleton of a house rising above a huge cellar packed full of people lying on the concrete floor. Somehow or other they made room for us. Beside me lay a little boy convulsed with pain from a wound. When his mother changed his dressing, one could see that a shell fragment was still embedded in his flesh and that gangrene had already set in. A little further on lay a woman whose foot had been torn off by a bomb. No medical aid was available for these people. The stench was unbearable. The corners were crowded with children wailing piteously. The grownups simply sat or lay motionless, with stony faces and vacant eyes. Hours went by. When daybreak came I was struck by the sudden stillness. My ears, accustomed to the crash of unceasing explosions, began to hum. It was the terrifying silence that precedes a great calamity, but I could not imagine anything worse than what we had already been through. Suddenly someone rushed into the cellar with the news that Warsaw had capitulated. No one stirred, but I noticed tears in the eyes of the grownups. I, too, felt them choking in my throat, but my eyes were dry. So all our sacrifices had been in vain. Twenty-seven days after the outbreak of the war, Warsaw, which had held out longer than any other city in Poland, had been forced to surrender.

As we came out of the cellar, we saw our ruined city in the clear September sun. Salvage crews were at work removing victims from the wreckage. Those who still showed signs of life were placed on stretchers and carried to the nearest first-aid stations. The dead were heaped upon carts and buried in the nearest empty ground—in the yard of a ruined house or an adjacent square. Soldiers were buried in public parks, and small wooden crosses were placed over their graves.

We returned to our own street. On the pavement lay the carcasses of fallen horses from which people were carving pieces of meat. Some of the horses were still twitching, but the hungry wretches did not notice; they were cutting the beasts up alive. We found the last place where we had stayed, the apartment on the Nalewki, intact except for broken window panes. But there was nothing to eat. The janitor invited us to join him in a dinner of duck and rice. Later I learned that this "duck" our janitor had caught was the last swan in the pond in Krasinski Park. In spite of the fact that this water was polluted by rotting human bodies, we felt no ill effects from that strange meal.

Some of the Polish soldiers hastily changed into civilian clothes. There were rumors that others had escaped across the border to Rumania and Hungary. We knew that one of my mother's brothers was with the Fifty-sixth Regiment, which had been entirely wiped out; of the other brother, we had no news at all.

That afternoon a cousin who lived on Sienna Street invited us to share her large apartment, in which she had stored a great deal of food. So we moved once again. It was a nightmarish journey. Common graves were being dug on all the squares. Warsaw looked like an enormous cemetery.

LODZ, OCTOBER 15, 1939

We are again in Lodz. We found our store and our apartment completely looted; the thieves had cut the larger pictures out of their frames. My father is miserable over the loss of the Poussin and the Delacroix[4] he bought in Paris for a considerable sum only a few weeks before the outbreak of the war. We have been here in Lodz for only two days, but we know now that it was a mistake to return here. The Nazis are beginning to intensify their acts of terrorism against the native population, especially the Jews. Last week they set fire to the great synagogue, the pride of the Lodz community. They forbade the Jews to remove the sacred books, and the "shames," or beadle, who wanted to save the holy relics was locked up inside the temple and died in the flames. My mother cannot forgive herself for having persuaded my father to bring us back here.

LODZ, NOVEMBER 1, 1939

We are planning to return to Warsaw. My father is already there ahead of us. He was forced to flee because one of our German[5] neighbors informed the Gestapo that he had hidden away some patriotic paintings of the great Polish painter, Matejko.[6] This neighbor often visited us in the past, and more than once borrowed money from my father. When the Gestapo came to look for the paintings, their ignoble informer was with them. Fortunately my father managed to hire a private car from an Aryan for the fifty-mile drive to Warsaw. This short trip cost him a fortune.

LODZ, NOVEMBER 3, 1939

Almost every day our apartment is visited by German soldiers who, under various pretexts, rob us of our possessions. I feel as if I were in prison. Yet I cannot console myself by looking out of the window, for when I peer from behind the curtain I witness hideous incidents like that which I saw yesterday:

A man with markedly Semitic features was standing quietly on the sidewalk near the curb. A uniformed German approached him and apparently gave him an unreasonable order, for I could see that the poor fellow tried to explain something with an embarrassed expression. Then a few other uniformed Germans came upon the scene and began to beat their victim with rubber truncheons. They called a cab and tried to push him into it, but he resisted vigorously. The Germans then tied his legs together with a rope, attached the end of the rope to the cab from behind, and ordered the driver to start. The unfortunate man's face struck the sharp stones of the pavement, dyeing them red with blood. Then the cab vanished down the street.

LODZ, NOVEMBER 12, 1939
Percy, my mother's younger brother, has returned from Nazi captivity. Only a miracle saved him from death. On the battle-field, seeing the approaching Nazis, and realizing that his unit had surrendered, he decided to commit suicide. As he was in a medical unit he had all sorts of drugs on his person; he swallowed thirty tablets of Veronal and fell asleep. He lay thus on the open field when suddenly a pouring rain began to fall. This awakened him. "I don't know how it happened," he told us, "but I suddenly began to vomit, and spat up almost all of the poison." He was too weak to move, and soon the Germans picked him up and placed him in a prison camp. The next day, with a comrade, he managed to get through the barbed-wire fence and, after wandering for a week in the so-called Kampinowska Forest, made his way to Lodz.

LODZ, NOVEMBER 23, 1939
Today Uncle Percy celebrated his wedding in secret. The Gestapo has officially forbidden Jews to marry, but in defiance of their order the number of Jewish marriages is increasing. It goes without saying that all the marriage certificates are antedated. Because of the dangers which surround us, all the engaged couples want to be together. Moreover, every-one wonders whether the Nazis will even let him live much longer.

To attend this wedding, we slunk one by one like shadows down the few blocks that separated us from the place of the ceremony. A guard stood at the door on the watch for Nazis, so that we could flee through another exit if necessary. The rabbi trembled while reciting the blessing. The slightest rustle on the staircase made us all rush to the door. The general mood was one of terror and apprehension. We all wept, and after the ceremony we left stealthily, again one by one.

More and more rumors are circulating to the effect that Lodz will be annexed to Germany and that the Jewish population will be locked up in a ghetto.[7] Jews are being kidnapped en masse and sent to various labor camps. The parents of my uncle's young wife have been sent off somewhere in the region of Lublin. One morning, as they went to work, they were seized by Nazi troops, thrown into a truck, and taken to the railroad station. Later we learned from someone who had escaped from their party that they had traveled in sealed wagons for several days without food. Exhausted and starved, they were unloaded in an open field and led to the little town of Zaklikow, joining several thousand other Jews brought there from other Polish cities. Poles, too, were transported from Lodz, chiefly the intellectuals, but not under such terrible conditions as the Jews.

LODZ, DECEMBER I, 1939
My father is at Bialystok, in Russian-occupied Poland. We breathed with relief when we learned this. There, at least, Jews are treated like everybody else, and have a chance to survive.

We are still constantly visited by our German "neighbors," railroad workers who live next door. Every time they come they ask for something, but their requests are really orders. Last week, for instance, they asked for pillows, pretending they had nothing to sleep on. A few days ago we had a visit from some high-ranking German officers who came to buy paintings. My mother told them that we had been robbed and had none to sell. They insisted, and began to rummage everywhere in the apartment. They found a little drawing and offered us a ridiculously small price for it. We had to accept the money in order to get rid of them.

Even more unpleasant was a visit from two drunken members of the Gestapo. They demanded objects that we did not possess. Our explanations did not satisfy them. At last my mother produced the papers proving her American citizenship. Then one of the drunks drew out his revolver and shouted: "Swear on Hitler's health that you're an American citizen or I'll shoot you on the spot!" But Jews have been forbidden to utter the Führer's sacred name. My mother asked whether an exception would be made in her case. The Nazi smiled and put his revolver back in its holster. After an unsuccessful search for the things he and his friend wanted, they left, clicking their heels and saluting the American flag that hung in the hallway.

LODZ, DECEMBER 15, 1939
The Nazis have banished the Jews from Piotrkowska Street, which used to be the main artery of Lodz, cutting through the entire city and dividing it into two equal parts. No Jew is allowed to live on this street or even to walk on it. The new German decree has thus created great hardships for many Jews. But the Germans are profiting from it; they are issuing special permits to the Jews to walk on Piotrkowska Street at five zlotys a permit.

LODZ, DECEMBER 18, 1939
The Germans have requisitioned our store and apartment. We are now living with our relatives on Narutowicz Street, near the high school I attend. This school is still functioning, although very few pupils attend the classes, because they are afraid to leave their homes. The cruelty of the Germans is increasing from day to day, and they are beginning to kidnap young boys and girls to use in their nightmarish "entertainments." They gather five to ten couples together in a room, order them to strip, and make them dance to the accompaniment of a phonograph record. Two of my schoolmates experienced this in their own home. Several Nazis entered their

apartment and, after a thorough search of all the rooms, forced the two girls into the parlor, where there was a piano. When their parents tried to accompany them, the Nazis struck them over the heads with clubs. Then the Nazis locked the parlor door and ordered the girls to strip. They ordered the older one to play a Viennese waltz and the younger one to dance. The sounds of the piano merged with the cries of the parents in the adjoining room. When the younger girl fainted in the midst of the dancing, the other sister began to cry for help at the window. This was too much for the Nazis, and they left. My schoolmates showed me the black and blue marks left on their bodies after their struggles with their tormentors.

WARSAW, DECEMBER 27, 1939
Last week we received a letter from the American consulate, summoning my mother to Warsaw. The mailman who brought us this letter could not refrain from expressing his envy over the fact that we have American connections. I left for Warsaw before my mother, thanks to a Gentile friend, the husband of a friend of my mother, who took me with him and passed me off as his daughter at the risk of his life. I am staying with him; at Christmas he also brought my sister from Lodz. We spend most of our time at home, venturing out only after nightfall to take short walks in front of the American embassy. Somehow we feel more secure in its shadow.[8]

WARSAW, JANUARY 5, 1940
My mother joined us only after New Year's Day. She told us that she had heard from father; he is getting along very well in Russia and has a job as curator of a museum in the Ukraine. He wants us to join him at once, but this is out of the question.[9] We are now staying in two small rooms at 41 Sienna Street,[10] where a cousin of ours also lives. Because this apartment block belongs to some Polish bank officials, the Germans have

allocated sufficient fuel for its maintenance. Thus we are protected from the terrible cold.

JANUARY 10, 1940

The Nazi-controlled Polish press has published unofficial reports that a ghetto is being planned for the Warsaw Jews. This report has aroused great bitterness among all our people, who have already been ordered to wear white armbands with the Star of David on them. For the time being, those whose Semitic appearance is not striking are not wearing these armbands; but in general all the Jews avoid showing themselves in the streets because of frequent attacks by Polish hooligans, who beat and rob every Jewish passer-by. Some Poles not blessed with Nordic features have also been molested by these hoodlums. For many days, a middle-aged Polish woman, wrapped in a long black shawl and holding a stick in her hand, has been the terror of Marszalkowska Street. She has not let a

Jews, wearing armbands, walk along a crowded street in the
Warsaw Ghetto

single Jew pass by without beating him, and she specializes in attacking women and children. The Germans look on and laugh. So far no Pole has protested against this. On the contrary, when a Jew happens to pass through a Gentile neighborhood, the inhabitants point him out to the Germans with the words: *"Oh, Jude!"*

The same Polish hooligans have also led the Nazis to the apartments of well-to-do Jews and have participated in looting in broad daylight. Protests were of no avail: the law does not protect the Jews.

MARCH 2, 1940

It seems that in Lodz the situation is even worse than here. A schoolmate of mine, Edzia Piaskowska, the daughter of a well-known Lodz manufacturer, who came to Warsaw yesterday, told us blood-curdling stories about the conditions there. The ghetto has been officially established, and her family succeeded in getting out at the last moment by bribing the Gestapo with good American dollars. The transfer of the Lodz Jews into the ghetto turned into a massacre. The Germans had ordered them to assemble at an appointed hour, carrying only fifty pounds of luggage apiece. At the same time, the Nazis organized extensive house searches, dragging the sick from their beds and the healthy from their hiding places, and beating, robbing, and murdering them. The quarter of Lodz which has been turned into the ghetto is one of the poorest and oldest sections of the city;[11] it is composed mostly of small wooden houses without electricity or plumbing, which formerly were inhabited by the poor weavers. It has room for only a few tens of thousands; the Germans have crowded three hundred thousand Jews into it.

The well-to-do Jews managed to escape the Lodz Ghetto by various means. Some bribed the Gestapo, like my friend's family; others smuggled themselves out in coffins. The Jewish cemetery is outside the ghetto, and it is possible to carry dead

persons there. Some people had themselves boarded up in cas-
kets, which were carried off with the usual funeral ceremonies.
Before reaching the cemetery, they rose from their coffins and
escaped to Warsaw. In one case the person locked in the coffin
did not rise up again: his heart had failed during that short and
ghostly trip.

MARCH 10, 1940
Today I witnessed an attack on an elderly Jewish woman by
Polish hooligans who hacked her with knives. Such incidents
are multiplying, and from all sides one can hear the cries of
helpless Jews. It is inconceivable that these Poles, forgetting
their own misfortunes, should persecute people even weaker
than themselves.

APRIL 5, 1940
The spring is beautiful, but we dare not go out into the streets.
Everywhere people, including women and children, are being
snatched up by the Germans and driven off to do hard labor. But
it is not so much the labor as the tortures to which the victims
are subjected that frighten us. Better-dressed Jewish women
have been forced to scrub the Nazis' headquarters. They are
ordered to remove their underclothes and use them as rags for
the floors and windows. It goes without saying that often the
tormentors use these occasions to have some fun of their own.

An interesting incident occurred with a Jewish woman who is
an American citizen. As a rule, the Nazis are careful to spare
foreigners, especially Americans, but this time they disregarded
the woman's protests and compelled her to scrub floors with
her expensive fur coat. After her ordeal the woman complained
to the American Consul, who demanded damages from the
German Governor, Frank. Without delay, this Jewish woman,
who had the luck to be an American citizen, received three thousand marks.[12] But Polish citizens of Jewish origin have no one to
protect them, except themselves. The moment the Germans

begin their manhunts, the Jewish passers-by signal to each other, and within a few moments the streets are emptied.

APRIL 17, 1940

Yesterday my father returned from Russia. We could hardly recognize him. He was unshaven, dressed in peasant garb, and looked like a gypsy who had just left some wild lair. He had smuggled himself across the so-called "green frontier"and was the only one of a group of thirty who managed to get through; the others were arrested and their fate is uncertain. He arrived in Warsaw on foot, walking by night and hiding in the woods during the day.

At first we could not understand why he had returned to the German hell at a time when so many people would have given everything they had to get across to the Soviet side. In Galicia[13] my father had been told by acquaintances that his family had gone to America, but when he telegraphed our relatives in America, they denied this report and gave him our Warsaw address. Powerless to send for us, he decided to return and share our bitter fate.

He told us interesting details about the so-called "Russian side." The Russians treat the civilian population much better than the Germans do; at least there is no religious discrimination. Many Jews have fled from German-occupied territory and entered Russia. A large percentage of them immediately joined the ranks of the Red Army, while others have gone to work in war factories. The greater part of them have accepted Russian citizenship. Those who refused to do this, whether they were Jews or Gentiles, were deported to Siberia.[14] The food situation is bad because the government rations are inadequate and there is no black market.

Wags circulate jokes about the Russian army. The Russian tanks, they say, have crews of a hundred men each—that is to say, one soldier is inside, and the other ninety-nine push the machine. The Russian soldiers are good-natured, although they can be cruel for patriotic reasons. Many women are in active service, especially in the air force. They wear the same uniforms as the men and have the same privileges. Many officers have their wives with them. No one would guess that the wide peasant skirts and headkerchiefs of these women are worn by highly intelligent individuals, most of them university graduates who hold important positions.

A curious incident took place in a Lwow theater. The wife of a Russian officer came to an evening performance dressed in a nightgown. This Russian woman, like all her sisters, had no idea of the European style of dressing. Even modest frocks seem luxurious to them. Elegant silk slips are unknown in Russia. This particular woman took a long pink nightgown for an evening gown, and was very hurt when her appearance was greeted with a wave of laughter.

Perhaps our jokes about the Russians are an unconscious expression of our disappointment over the fact that Russia is not at war with Hitler. Most of the inhabitants of Warsaw are certain, without knowing why, that a war between Hitler and Russia will break out sooner or later. This thought helps us to bear our ordeal.

APRIL 28, 1940

We have managed to obtain a separate apartment in the same house where we had been sharing rooms. My mother has tacked up her visiting card on the door, with the inscription: "American citizen." This inscription is a wonderful talisman against the German bandits who freely visit all Jewish apartments. As soon as German uniforms come into view at the outer door of our building, our neighbors come begging us to let them in so that they, too, can benefit from our miraculous sign. Our two little rooms are filled to the brim—for how could we refuse anyone? All of the neighbors tremble with fear, and with a silent prayer on their lips gaze at the two small American flags on the wall.

Jews who possess passports of neutral countries are not compelled to wear armbands or to do slave labor. No wonder many Jews try to obtain such documents, but not all have the means to buy them or the courage to use them. Two of my friends have acquired papers proving that they are nationals of a South American republic.[15] Thanks to these they can move freely around the city. They went boldly to the Gestapo headquarters at the Bruehl Palace to have these papers sealed with a swastika, and the German experts did not realize that they were forged. They can even go to the country to buy food. With such documents, they have at least a ninety per cent chance of survival—the other Jews have only a ten per cent chance at most.

MAY 20, 1940
We are following with despair the Nazi invasion of France. Two weeks ago my mother was informed by the American consulate in Berlin that her passport would be ready on a certain date. All the foreign consulates in Warsaw have been closed, and for several weeks my mother has been rushing around to all sorts of officials trying to obtain permission to visit the capital of the Third Reich.[16]

JUNE 16, 1940
My mother is back. Her trip was fruitless. Because of Italy's entry into the war, the Italian ports have been closed, and in addition a new decree has forbidden anyone to leave the Gouvernement General (the name given by the Germans to the administrative area of Poland, in which Warsaw is situated). My mother left Berlin on June 14, the day of the fall of Paris. The Nazi capital was jubilant, wallowing in a sea of swastikas.

JUNE 24, 1940
My mother's younger brother, Abie, is here, having escaped from a Hungarian internment camp for Polish officers. One of

reasons that he risked all the perils of escape was his fear that, as a Jew, he would be transferred to a concentration camp. He does not look like a Jew—he is tall, broad-shouldered, blond and blue-eyed—a real Nordic type. Thanks to his appearance, he had no difficulty in traveling from Hungary to Warsaw. At the beginning of his stay in the camp, his Polish companions-in-arms were unaware of his Jewish origin. When they learned about it, they began to persecute and threaten him, and finally denounced him to the Hungarian authorities. Such is the solidarity of the Polish officers with those who shared their struggle against the common enemy.

JULY 12, 1940
There is no ghetto here in Warsaw as in Lodz but, unofficially, there are boundaries that the Jews voluntarily refrain from crossing in order to avoid being hunted by the Germans or attacked by Polish hooligans. They feel safer within these unofficial boundaries. New loads of Jewish refugees keep arriving from little towns—they all think they will be safer in the capital and will have a better chance to make a living here than in their home towns. There is also a psychological reason for this movement—all the Jews want to be together. As a result of the influx there is a shortage of living quarters. At the same time, various social institutions have been requisitioning all the larger apartments for their own needs. Finally, an official regulation has prescribed that at least four persons must occupy each room. We have sublet one of our rooms to the R. family from Lodz. Mr. R. was one of the four or five Jewish experts on the manufacture of cloth, the leading industry of Lodz, whom the Germans employed at a salary of 6,000 zlotys a month. He was compelled to live in the factory outside the ghetto and could visit his family only once a week. Like the other few privileged Jews, he gave most of his earnings to the relief committee in the Jewish quarter. From the R.s we learned some details about the life of the Lodz Ghetto. The rations are three

ounces of bread a day, and all the inhabitants are compelled to work in military workshops manufacturing blankets and shoes with wooden soles. Religious services and marriages are forbidden. As a result of overcrowding and poor hygienic conditions, the narrow streets of the Baluty quarter are the scene of many epidemics. Only those who have large sums of money are able to save themselves from this terrible life.

Last week self-supporting popular kitchens began to function in Warsaw. One of these is close to us, at 16 Sienna Street.[17] A meal in such a kitchen consists of potato or cabbage soup and a tiny portion of vegetables. Twice a week one receives a tiny piece of meat which costs one zloty twenty groszy.

There are now a great number of illegal schools, and they are multiplying every day. People are studying in attics and cellars, and every subject is included in the curriculum, even Latin and Greek. Two such schools were discovered by the Germans some time in June. Later we heard that the teachers were shot on the spot, and that the pupils had been sent to a concentration camp near Lublin.[18]

Our Lodz school too has started its classes. The majority of the teachers are in Warsaw, and twice a week the courses are given at our home, which is a relatively safe spot because of my mother's American citizenship. We study all the regular subjects, and have even organized a chemistry and physics laboratory using glasses and pots from our kitchen instead of test tubes and retorts. Special attention is paid to the study of foreign languages, chiefly English and Hebrew. Our discussions of Polish literature have a peculiarly passionate character. The teachers try to show that the great Polish poets Mickiewicz, Slowacki, and Wyspianski[19] prophesied the present disaster. Everyone is repeating the famous quotation from Wyspianski's *Wedding:*

> Uncouth yokel, you had a golden horn.
> Now what is left you is only a rope.

The teachers put their whole heart and soul into their teaching, and all the pupils study with exemplary diligence. There are no bad pupils. The illegal character of the teaching, and the danger that threatens us every minute, fills us all with a strange earnestness. The old distance between teachers and pupils has vanished, and we feel like comrades-in-arms responsible to each other.

Textbooks are hard to get as their sale has been officially forbidden. We take notes on our professors' lectures and memorize them. Despite these extraordinary difficulties, our school has actually issued bachelors' diplomas. The examinations and graduation ceremonies took place in the apartment of our principal, Dr. Michael Brandstetter. It was in the afternoon, all the curtains were drawn and a guard of students was posted in front of the house. The pupils were examined separately by the teachers seated around a table covered with green cloth. Without exception, all of them passed the examination successfully. The diplomas were not issued by the Ministry of Education as in the old days, but by the board of the illegal school; they were typed on ordinary sheets of paper and bore the signatures of all the teachers. With tears in his eyes, the principal made the customary speech to the new bachelors who, like all the youth of Poland—particularly the Jewish youth—left the school without any prospect for the future, except to become slaves in a Nazi labor camp.

AUGUST 16, 1940
The population of the Jewish quarter has begun to organize its social life. Conditions are miserable and all sorts of ingenious ways have to be found to raise money and organize relief. House committees have been formed, and they gather each night in a different apartment to discuss urgent problems and to establish the amount of the contribution of each house to the central relief body of the Jewish community. The house committees also do educational work, stressing the struggle

against epidemics. The young people gather together once a week. The first part of the meeting is devoted to the discussion of scientific or literary questions, and the second part to entertainment—dancing to records. The receipts from these affairs are handed over to the relief organizations.

The young Jewish people of Lodz have founded a club for the purpose of raising relief funds. Harry Karczmar has been elected president and the charter members are Bolek Gliksberg, Romek Kowalski, Edek Wolkowicz, Tadek Szajer, Olga Szmuszkowicz, Edzia Piaskowska, Stefan Mandeltort, Misza Bakszt, Dolek Amsterdam, Mietek Fein and myself.

As soon as we were organized, a representative of the Joint Distribution Committee[20] appealed to us to arrange a show to raise funds for the refugees from Lodz. We went to work with enthusiasm to get a program together, and everyone tried to discover some talent in himself. Our president, Harry Karczmar, has a beautiful voice, and was asked to sing a solo number. The oldest among us, he is of medium height, with chestnut hair, and looks much older than his twenty-three years. He has suffered a great deal in his life. He broke a leg in a car accident and limps a little, and recently the doctors have discovered that he has symptoms of tuberculosis. Although he knows there is no way of curing him now, he is always cheerful and energetic. He practices a great deal and so forgets his sufferings.

His accompanist is Romek Kowalski, a dark nineteen-year-old boy of aristocratic appearance. His delicate face, with its deep dark eyes, classical nose, and red lips, has a childish expression. He bears the mark of that precocious war maturity which is characteristic of so many of us. It is really a psychological, rather than a biological, maturity. Romek is a good-natured boy, always ready to help others and marvelously gifted—he began to study the piano only a few months before the war and now plays almost like a virtuoso. He has a predilection for light music and adores jazz.

Romek Kowalski

Stefan Mandeltort, the youngest of our boys at only seventeen, is small and agile, and looks like a typical urchin of the Warsaw working-class suburbs. He recites charmingly and is to do a few impersonations.

Mietek Fein is a born tap dancer, tall, slender, blond, with a pale narrow face very much like Fred Astaire's, but more beautiful. He is twenty, an orphan, and has not even any distant relatives left alive. But he thinks very little of his unhappy situation; his mind is preoccupied with dancing.

Dolek Amsterdam, a tall, chestnut-haired lad, with a square, rather commonplace face, is phlegmatic by nature. He speaks only rarely, and then to agree with the others. He is very easily influenced, especially by Harry Karczmar. He has a well-trained voice. Our two other singers are Edek Wolkowicz and Bolek Gliksberg. Misza Bakszt makes a very good master of ceremonies. He does not even have to prepare his speeches, for he can improvise on the spur of the moment. Aged nineteen, he is a born critic, quick at repartée, and is very successful with all the girls. Olga Szmuszkewicz, whose father is in Palestine, has studied the piano since her childhood. She is still taking lessons with a well-known piano teacher, although her material situation is of the worst.

To my great surprise, my comrades have discovered that I have a voice. As an "American"—that is what I am called everywhere—I have been asked to sing a few light American songs. It is forbidden to use French or English in public, but we are ignoring these prohibitions.

Edzia Piaskowska and Tadeusz Szajer are the only members of our group without any gifts as performers, so they have assumed the task of looking for a place for the show.

Our little group is having a lively time and is finding preparations for the show absorbing, but one look outside the window is enough to wake us up to reality. At any given moment one can see tangible evidence of the terror that reigns in the city. The manhunt goes on without interruption. We always have to leave our meetings one by one. The girls go out first and make sure that no Nazis are around. If everything is quiet, they call the boys.

SEPTEMBER 11, 1940

Our first performance took place early this month at 5 Przejazd, in the Joint Distribution Committee office. Our success surpassed all expectations, and the receipts were considerable. We were immediately asked to give other performances, all of which were very successful. Our Lodz group is proud of making such a hit in Warsaw. Some of us are now quite famous with the Jewish population. Harry's voice fascinates all the girls, Stefan's witty introductions arouse stormy applause, and Olga is praised for her playing. As for myself, the most fantastic rumors are spread about me—this is Harry's work. People wonder whether it is really true that I know very little

Polish and that I performed in America. At every show I have to repeat my first song, "Moonlight and Shadow," several times. The other members of our group are also very popular. We call ourselves the "Lodz Artistic Group," or, as it is abbreviated in Polish, the LZA. This is curiously symbolic: the word "*lza*" in Polish means "tear."

At about the same time as we organized our group, a few cafés were opened on the Aryan side, where famous Polish artists who refused to perform in the Nazi-controlled theaters serve simultaneously as artists and waiters.

NOVEMBER 2, 1940

A persistent rumor is circulating that the Jewish quarter will soon be locked up. Some people say that this will be better for us, because the Germans will not dare to commit their crimes so openly and because we will be protected from attacks by Polish hooligans. But others, especially those among us who escaped from the Lodz Ghetto, are aghast: they have already tasted life in a secluded Jewish quarter under German domination.

CHAPTER II

THE GHETTO BEGINS

NOVEMBER 15, 1940

Today the Jewish ghetto was officially established. Jews are forbidden to move outside the boundaries formed by certain streets. There is considerable commotion. Our people are hurrying about nervously in the streets, whispering various rumors, one more fantastic than the other.

Work on the walls—which will be three yards high—has already begun. Jewish masons, supervised by Nazi soldiers, are laying bricks upon bricks. Those who do not work fast enough are lashed by the overseers. It makes me think of the Biblical description of our slavery in Egypt. But where is the Moses who will release us from our new bondage?

There are German sentries at the end of those streets in which the traffic has not been stopped completely. Germans and Poles are allowed to enter the isolated quarter, but they must not carry any parcels. The specter of starvation looms up before us all.

NOVEMBER 20, 1940

The streets are empty. Extraordinary meetings are taking place in every house. The tension is terrific. Some people demand that a protest be organized. This is the voice of the youth; our elders consider this a dangerous idea. We are cut off from the world. There are no radios, no telephones, no news-papers. Only the hospitals and Polish police stations situated inside the ghetto are allowed to have telephones.

The Jews who have been living on the Aryan side of the city were told to move out before November 12. Many waited until the last moment, because they hoped that the Germans, by means of protests or bribes, might be induced to counter-mand the decree establishing the ghetto. But as this did not come to pass, many of our people were forced to leave their beautifully furnished apartments at a moment's notice, and they arrived in the ghetto carrying only a few bundles in their hands.

Christian firms within the limits of the isolated Jewish quarter are allowed to remain temporarily if they have been there for at least twenty-five years. Many Polish and German factories are situated within the ghetto, and thanks to their employees we have a little contact with the outer world.

NOVEMBER 22, 1940
The ghetto has been isolated for a whole week. The red-brick walls at the end of the ghetto streets have grown considerably higher. Our miserable settlement hums like a beehive. In the homes and in the courtyards, wherever the ears of the Gestapo do not reach, people nervously discuss the Nazis' real aims in isolating the Jewish quarter. How shall we get provisions? Who will maintain order? Perhaps it will really be better, and perhaps we will be left in peace?

This afternoon all the members of our LZA group gathered at my home. We sat in a stupor and did not know what to undertake. Now all our efforts are useless. Who cares for the theater these days? Everyone is brooding over one thing and one thing only: the ghetto.

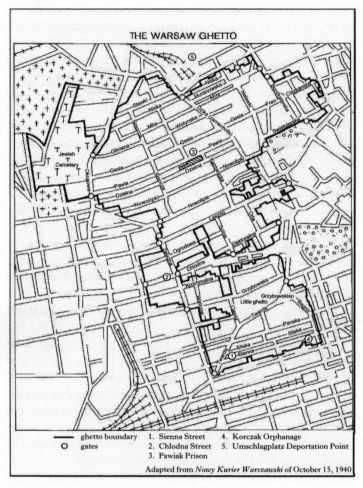

THE WARSAW GHETTO

——— ghetto boundary   1. Sienna Street   4. Korczak Orphanage
○   gates   2. Chlodna Street   5. Umschlagplatz Deportation Point
                       3. Pawiak Prison

Adapted from *Nowy Kurier Warszawski* of October 15, 1940

Map of the Warsaw Ghetto

DECEMBER 15, 1940

Life goes on. My mother, as an American, is still allowed to leave the gates of the ghetto. As she leaves, she shows her passport, and the Nazi guard salutes her with great respect as he returns this American document.

Recently my mother has made several such trips to do all sorts of errands for her friends. They are particularly appreciative when she can send letters abroad for them, because the post offices in the ghetto refuse such letters. As an American citizen, she can send out letters from the German post office without any special difficulty. Her passport is checked at the window—the name of the sender of the letter must be the same as that on the passport. I can imagine the surprise of people abroad when they see that letters from their closest relatives bear a stranger's name as the sender.

The relief office of the American colony in Warsaw is situated at 14 Mokotowska Street. Once a month, all American citizens receive a large package of foodstuffs for the sum of eleven zlotys—but its real value is three hundred, and it often contains articles that are unobtainable elsewhere at any price whatsoever.

The question of obtaining food is becoming ever more pressing. The official ration cards entitle one to a quarter of a pound of bread a day, one egg a month, and two pounds of vegetable jam (sweetened with saccharine) a month. A pound of potatoes costs one zloty. We have forgotten even the taste of fresh fruit. Nothing can be imported from the Aryan districts, although there is an abundance of everything there. But hunger and the desire for profit are stronger than all the penalties threatening smugglers, and smuggling is now gradually becoming an important industry.

Sienna Street, which forms one of the boundaries of the ghetto, is separated by walls only from the streets that cross it; the houses whose courtyards give on Zlota Street (Zlota is parallel to Sienna), the so-called "other side," are temporarily separated from the outer world by barbed wire. Most of the smuggling takes place here. Our windows face such a courtyard. All night long there is a commotion there, and by morning, carts with vegetables appear in the streets and the stores are filled with bread. There is even sugar, butter, cheese—of course for high prices, for people have risked their lives to get these things.

Sometimes a German sentry is bribed and a whole wagon full of all kinds of merchandise manages to get through the gates.

The Germans have demanded that the Jewish community administration take steps to stop the smuggling. They have also ordered that a Jewish militia be formed to help the Polish police in maintaining order in the ghetto. The community is trying to recruit two thousand able-bodied men between the ages of twenty-one and thirty-five. War veterans are given preference. A high educational standard is also required: a certificate from a school is the minimum.

DECEMBER 22, 1940
The Jewish police is an accomplished fact. More candidates presented themselves than were needed. A special committee chose them, and "pull" played an important part in their choice. At the very end, when only a few posts were available, money helped, too... Even in Heaven not everyone is a saint.[1]

The chief commissioner of this ghetto police is Colonel Szerynski, a converted Jew who was the police chief of Lublin before the war. Under him are three assistant commissioners: Hendel, Lejkin and Firstenberg, who together form the supreme police council. Then come the regional commandants, the district chiefs (the regions are divided into districts), and finally the ordinary policemen who perform routine duties.

Their uniform consists of a dark blue police cap and a military belt to which a rubber club is attached. Over the visor of the cap there is a metal badge bearing the Star of David and the inscription *Jüdischer Ordnungsdienst* (Jewish Order Service). On a blue ribbon around the cap, the policeman's rank is indicated by special signs: one round tin disk the size of a thumbnail for a policeman, two for a senior policeman, three for a district chief; one star for a regional commandant, two stars for the three assistant commissioners, and four for the commissioner himself.

Just like all the other Jews, the Jewish policemen must wear a white armband with the blue Star of David, but in addition, they wear a yellow armband with the inscription *Jüdischer Ordnungsdienst*. They also wear metallic badges with their numbers on their chests.

Among the duties of these new Jewish policemen are guarding the gates of the ghetto together with German gendarmes and Polish policemen, directing traffic in the ghetto streets, guarding post offices, kitchens and the community administration, and detecting and suppressing smugglers. The most difficult task of the Jewish police is the curbing of beggars—this actually consists in driving them from one street to

A Jewish policeman directing traffic at the intersection of Chlodna and Zelazna Streets in the Warsaw Ghetto

another, because there is nothing else to do with them, especially as their number is growing from hour to hour.

Central Police Headquarters, the so-called KSP,[2] are at 15 Ogrodowa Street; the five regional offices are on Twarda Street, Ogrodowa Street, Leszno Street, at Gesia near Nalewki, and near the Jewish cemetery.

I experience a strange and utterly illogical feeling of satisfaction when I see a Jewish policeman at a crossing—such policemen were completely unknown in pre-war Poland. They proudly direct the traffic—which hardly needs to be directed, for it consists only of rare horse-driven carts, a few cabs and hearses—the latter are the most frequent vehicles. From time to time Gestapo cars rush by, paying no attention whatsoever to the Jewish policemen's directions, and perfectly indifferent as to whether they run people over or not.

DECEMBER 24, 1940
Our second war Christmas. From my window, which faces the Aryan side, I can see Christmas trees lit up. But little pine trees were also sold in the ghetto this morning at exorbitant prices. They were smuggled in yesterday. I saw shivering people hurrying home with the little trees pressed to their chests. These were converts or first-generation Christians whom the Nazis regard as Jews, and whom they have confined in the ghetto.

DECEMBER 25, 1940
Today a new group of uniformed Jewish officials appeared in the ghetto. They belong to the special Commission for the Fight Against Speculators, whose task it is to regulate the prices of various articles. For some time this organization has functioned in secret, but now it is out in the open. These officials wear the same kind of cap as the Jewish policemen, but with a green band, and instead of the policemen's yellow armbands, they wear lavender armbands with the inscription, "Fight Against Speculators."

While the attitude of the Jewish population toward the Jewish policemen is cordial, these new officials are treated with marked reserve because they are suspected of being tools of the Gestapo. Their organization has been nicknamed "The Thirteen," because its office is at 13 Leszno Street. Its chief is Commissar Szternfeld and his main collaborators are Gancwajch, Roland Szpunt and the lawyer Szajer of Lodz.

There is another group of uniformed Jewish officials in the ghetto—the workers of the ambulance unit, who wear a blue band on their caps, and blue armbands. Still another is the black-clad corps of undertakers employed by private companies, among which the most popular are Pinkiert's, next to the community building on the Grzybowska, and Wittenberg's, directly across the street. Even to move into the next world is not very easy these days. Funerals are frightfully expensive, and a plot in the overcrowded Jewish cemetery is as precious as gold.

Meanwhile, life is being organized in the ghetto. Work helps one to forget everything, and it is not hard to get work here. A great number of workshops and factories have opened, making all sorts of articles that have never been manufactured in Warsaw before.

Our theatrical group has received several invitations to give performances in cafés. We also have our own hall, and intend to give regular shows two or three times a week in the afternoon. We have rented Weisman's dancing school on Panska Street, although it had an unsavory reputation before the war because the Warsaw underworld used to meet there. The inhabitants of the quarter once called this hall the "old joint." But now we have our own public, which will disregard the bad reputation of the hall and attend our shows no matter where they are given. Moreover, there is no better hall in the whole so-called Little Ghetto that lies between Sienna and Leszno Streets.

The way from the Little Ghetto to the Big Ghetto begins at the corner of Chlodna and Zelazna Streets. Only the roadway, separated from the rest of Chlodna Street by walls on each side, is considered part of the ghetto. In the middle of the street there is an exit to Zelazna Street. This exit is especially well guarded by a Nazi gendarme armed with a machine gun, and two policemen, one Jewish and one Polish.

JANUARY 2, 1941
Our New Year's shows unexpectedly drew an enormous audience. The hall was packed to capacity. Because December 31 happened to coincide with the last day of Chanukah, we had improvised a scene depicting the heroic fight of the Maccabees, which contained many timely hints. We lit eight candles on the stage. The audience applauded enthusiastically, and there was hardly a dry eye in the house.

All our matinees are a great success. Half of the receipts go to the refugee committee, for there is still an enormous flood of homeless refugees.

JANUARY 4, 1941
The ghetto is covered with deep snow. The cold is terrible and none of the apartments are heated. Wherever I go, I find people wrapped up in blankets or huddling under feather beds, that is, if the Germans have not yet taken all these warm things for their own soldiers. The bitter cold makes the Nazi beasts who stand guard near the ghetto entrances even more savage than usual. Just to warm up, as they lurch back and forth in the deep snow, they open fire every so often and there are many victims among the passers-by. Other guards who are bored with their duty at the gates arrange entertainments for themselves. For instance, they choose a victim from among the people who chance to go by, order him to throw himself in the snow with his face down, and if he is a Jew who wears a beard, they tear it off, together with the skin, until the snow is red with blood. When such a Nazi is in a bad mood, his victim may be the Jewish policeman who stands guard with him.

Yesterday I myself saw a Nazi gendarme "exercise" a Jewish policeman near the passage from the Little to the Big Ghetto on Chlodna Street. The young man finally lost his breath, but the Nazi still forced him to fall and rise until he collapsed in a pool of blood. Then someone called for an ambulance, and the Jewish policeman was put on a stretcher and carried away on a hand truck. There are only three ambulance cars for the whole ghetto, and for that reason hand trucks are mostly used. We call them rikshaws.[3]

JANUARY 10, 1941

Last night we went through several hours of mortal terror. At about 11:00 p.m. a group of Nazi gendarmes broke into the room where our house committee was holding a meeting. The Nazis searched the men, took away whatever money they found, and then ordered the women to strip, hoping to find concealed diamonds. Our subtenant, Mrs. R., who happened to be there, courageously protested, declaring that she would not undress in the presence of men. For this she received a resounding slap on the face and was searched even more harshly than the other women. The women were kept naked for more than two hours while the Nazis put their revolvers to their breasts and private parts and threatened to shoot them all if they did not disgorge dollars or diamonds. The beasts did not leave until 2:00 a.m., carrying a scanty loot of a few watches, some paltry rings, and a small sum in Polish zlotys. They did not find either diamonds or dollars. The inhabitants of the ghetto expect such attacks every night, but this does not stop the meetings of the house committees.

JANUARY 30, 1941

Today we held the inaugural meeting of the Youth Club of our block on Sienna Street. Similar clubs have been formed in all the streets of the ghetto.[4] We have elected as president

37

Manfred Rubin, an intelligent young German Jewish refugee, who came to Poland shortly before the war.

Engineer Stickgold greeted us in the name of the house committees of Sienna Street. He urged us to study as hard as possible and to share among ourselves not only our bread, but also our knowledge. Every member of our group at once began to prepare a subject for a talk.

FEBRUARY 5, 1941

There is panic among the inhabitants of Sienna Street, for the rumor has spread that the street will be cut off from the ghetto, allegedly because of the extensive smuggling that is carried on here. But this is certainly not the real reason, for the same is true of all the border streets, and if one street is cut off, the smuggling will simply move over to the next one. The Germans themselves are circulating rumors that Sienna Street will be left to the Jewish inhabitants if they pay a contribution. This must be the real reason for the threat—the Germans want to get a large sum of money out of the inhabitants of the ghetto.

Meanwhile, snow is falling slowly, and the frost draws marvelous flower patterns on the window-panes. I dream of a sled gliding over the ice, of freedom. Shall I ever be free again? I have become really selfish. For the time being, I am still warm and have food, but all around me there is so much misery and starvation that I am beginning to be very unhappy.

Sometimes I quickly snatch my coat and go out into the street. I gaze at the faces of the passers-by, blue with cold. I try to learn by heart the look of the homeless women wrapped in rags and of the children with chapped and frozen cheeks. They huddle together, hoping to find some warmth in each other. The street vendors stand in the gateways, offering candy and tobacco for sale. They carry small boxes slung over their shoulders. These boxes contain a few packages of cigarettes, and a handful of candy made without a grain of sugar and sweetened with saccharine.

Through a show window in a store I can see the reflections of various people. The spectacle is now familiar to me: a poor man enters to buy a quarter of a pound of bread and walks out. In the street he impatiently wrenches a piece off the gluey mass and puts it in his mouth. An expression of contentment spreads over his entire face, and in a moment the whole lump of bread has disappeared. Now his face expresses disappointment. He rummages in his pocket and draws out his last copper coins... not enough to buy anything. All he can do now is lie down in the snow and wait for death. Perhaps he will go to the community administration? It is no use. Hundreds like him are already there. The woman behind the desk who receives them and listens to their story is sympathetic. She smiles politely, and tells them to come back in a week. Each of them must wait his turn, but few of them will live through the week. Hunger will destroy them, and each morning another body of an old man with a blue face and clenched fists will be found lying in the snow.

What are the last thoughts of such people, and what makes them clench their fists so tautly? Surely their last glance was cast at the window of the store across the street from where they have laid themselves down to die. In that shop window they see white bread, cheese, and even cakes, and they fall into their last sleep dreaming of biting into a loaf of bread.

Every day there are more such "dreamers of bread" in the streets of the ghetto. Their eyes are veiled with a mist that belongs to another world... usually they sit across from the windows of food stores, but their eyes no longer see the loaves that lie behind the glass, as though in some remote, inaccessible heaven.

After I have taken a good look at all this, and my heart is full to the brim with grief, I return to my warm room where I can smell the appetizing odors of good food cooking. My dreams of freedom fade. I am hungry. Now my only wish is to fill my stomach.

FEBRUARY 15, 1941

One after another the ghetto streets have been shut off. Now only Poles are used for this work. The Nazis no longer trust the Jewish masons, who deliberately leave loose bricks in many places in order to smuggle food or to escape to the other side through the holes at night.

Now the walls are growing taller and taller and there are no loose bricks. The top is covered with a thick layer of clay strewn with glass splinters, intended to cut the hands of people who try to escape.

But the Jews still find ways. The sewer pipes have not been cut off, and through these openings they get in small bags of flour, sugar, cereal, and other articles. During dark nights, they also take advantage of holes made in the gates to bring in foodstuffs. The removal of one brick is sufficient. Special packages are prepared to fit these holes.

There are other ways, too. Many bombed houses are situated on the border between the ghetto and the other side. The cellars of these houses often form long tunnels that extend for three, four, or five houses. The greatest part of the smuggling is carried on through these tunnels. The Germans know this, but are unable to control the traffic.

Meanwhile, the Nazis are cutting out of the ghetto the larger and more modern apartment houses. A number of streets have been split in two: one side belongs to the ghetto, the other to the Aryan side. In the middle of the street there is barbed wire or a wall. We tremble lest the same thing be done with Sienna Street, where we live, because the most beautiful houses in the whole quarter are on that street.

FEBRUARY 17, 1941

The Jewish community administration is completing its preparations for a course in machine drawing, architecture, and graphic arts. I have registered for it. I received a type-written prospectus, which explains that the course is being opened by the special permission of the German authorities and is part of the general program for training locksmiths, electrotechnicians, and other artisans from among the young Jewish people who have no trade. We all realize that the Germans' real intention is to train workers for their war industries—workers who will work without wages.

The metallurgical and related courses will be given in the community building at 26 Grzybowska Street, and the courses in industrial drawing will be given at 16 Sienna Street, not far from my home. I shall not be exposed to the danger of walking many streets to get to school. The course will last six months, and the tuition fee is twenty-five zlotys a month. There are also a number of scholarships for poor but gifted pupils.

When I went to register, I saw many familiar faces, among them Mark Unger, my accompanist, and Manfred Rubin, the president of the Youth Committee of our block. There are almost six hundred candidates, although the number of vacancies is only a few dozen. Unfortunately, "pull" plays a large part in the selection of students. At first I rebelled against this, but when I realized that my chances of being admitted were slight, I finally decided to resort to the same means.[5]

FEBRUARY 20, 1941

Today I went to see a schoolmate from Lodz, Lola Rubin. I have a great admiration for her courage. This seventeen-year-old girl supports herself and her ten-year-old brother. Their parents remained in the Lodz Ghetto. Lola Rubin managed to get a forged birth certificate somewhere, under a Christian name, and, with the help of this magic piece of paper she makes a living. She often goes to the Aryan side, buys various little things that are now unobtainable in the ghetto, and resells them to her acquaintances at a good profit. Usually she crosses the demarcation line through the law courts building on Leszno Street, where both Jews and Gentiles are tried. One side of this building gives on

Ogrodowa and Biala Streets, which are next to the Aryan side. There she mingles with the Poles who come to the court building.

Lola has a little room, and receives many visitors. Today I met an interesting creature there, Mickey Mundstuck, a dwarf. He is twenty-four years old, comes from Leipzig, and speaks German and English. He told us his strange life story. At the age of eight he was taken to Hollywood by his father. He was a child prodigy and appeared in various moving pictures. In order to continue his career, Mickey had to remain a child, but since he was growing, his father decided to have him operated on to arrest his growth. But this proved of no avail. Other child prodigies appeared, and Mickey's film career came to an end. He left Hollywood, and returned to Germany in 1933. The Nazis had just seized power and sent his father to the concentration camp at Dachau, where he died. Mickey was left alone, and a few months ago was deported to Warsaw. Now he supports himself by teaching English.

FEBRUARY 25, 1941

I have been attending the course in graphic arts for the last three days. The atmosphere is pleasant. I feel as though every day I am visiting another world for a few hours, a world far removed from the ghostly life of the ghetto. The classes last from nine in the morning till two-thirty in the afternoon, and comprise both theoretical subjects and practical exercises. The theoretical subjects are history of art, history of architecture, history of costume design, and various branches of drawing, beginning with geometrical figures and ending with blueprints, ornamentation, and lettering.

The professors of drawing are Hilf, a Viennese artist, and Greifenberg, the well-known Warsaw designer. Geometry and history of architecture are taught by Engineer Goldberg, who built the most modern government buildings in Warsaw. He is particularly popular with the students.

The young people attending the course are of various ages; the youngest among them is fifteen, the oldest thirty. Some of them worked before the war as designers and some were even well known as painters. There are also a few graduate engineers. The majority are men, and there is good reason for this. Recently Jewish men have been rounded up en masse and sent to labor camps from which no one returns. The Germans now chiefly send people to the region of the Bug River where they use them to build fortifications near the Soviet border.

The students of the community courses are not sent to labor camps, but as soon as they graduate they are bound to report "voluntarily" to the German labor office. But who worries about what will happen in eight months? By then the war may be over. No wonder most of our students are men. The community is also in favor of this, because for the time being girls are not threatened with labor camps.

CHAPTER III

LIFE GOES ON

FEBRUARY 28, 1941

The shortage of bread is becoming more and more acute. One gets very little on the official ration cards, and on the black market a pound of bread now costs ten zlotys. All the bread is black and tastes like sawdust. White bread costs as much as fifteen to seventeen zlotys. On the Aryan side, prices are much lower. Many of our students come to class without having eaten anything, and every day we organize a bread collection for them.[1] The lot of our life models is even more tragic. Recently we have been drawing many portraits, and our favorite subject is "misery." Models are not lacking for that. They stand on line to earn a few pennies by posing for us. Often they fall asleep on the stand, and then, with closed eyes, they look like corpses.

The directors of our course pay two zlotys for two hours of posing, and we gather together a few small pieces of bread for each model. Yesterday our model was an eleven-year-old girl with beautiful black eyes. All the time we were working, the child shook with fever and we found it hard to draw her. Someone suggested that she be given something to eat. The little girl tremblingly swallowed only part of the bread we collected for her, and carefully wrapped the rest in a piece of newspaper. "This will be for my little brother," she said. "He waits at home for me to bring him something."

After that she sat quietly through the entire drawing period.

Once we were compelled to carry an old man out of the classroom; he had fainted from hunger and could not even finish the bread we gave him.

APRIL 4, 1941

The number of professional schools and courses in the ghetto is increasing. The ORT[2] organization has opened a special course for girls under the direction of Roma Brandes, the wife of the lawyer and Jewish Socialist leader who escaped abroad. These courses cover the following specialties: ladies' tailoring, children's clothes, glove-making, millinery, ladies' bags, and artificial flowers. The ORT has obtained two halls for these courses at 13 Leszno Street and 13 Nalewki Street. My sister Anna* has registered for the course in children's clothing. There are two classes, one in the morning and one in the afternoon, and a great number of girls attend them. They produce shoes for orphanages, where almost all the children are barefoot. Since leather is unobtainable, old felt hats are collected in the ghetto and brought to the school, where they are cleaned and turned into shoes of various kinds. For soles the students use two or three layers of felt or leather from old shoes given by well-to-do inhabitants of the ghetto for that purpose. The girls work willingly, because they know how many freezing little feet are waiting for the fruit of their labors, and no one wants to be paid for this work.

In general children receive a great deal of attention. In many houses there are special committees that help to provide for poor orphans. In our own house, a special kettle of soup is cooked every Friday for the Mattias Berson Children's Hospital[3] on

* Throughout the diary Mary Berg refers to her sister as both Anna and Ann.

45

Two destitute children beg on the pavement in the ghetto

Sienna Street. There are various other organizations for children. Particularly popular is the so-called Spoon Committee, which collects a spoonful of sugar or two spoonfuls of flour and gruel twice a week from each tenant in a given house. Potatoes, carrots, beets, cabbage, and other foodstuffs are also collected.

The youth circle of our house at 41 Sienna Street helps Dr. Janusz Korczak's Children's Home. Every day two of our members are appointed to make collections, and everyone, even those who themselves need help, willingly give to Dr. Korczak's little wards. The names of the contributors and their contributions are listed and posted in the doorway.

The children's homes now live almost exclusively on such collections, because the various community organizations must devote themselves to the thousands of homeless refugees who arrive daily in the ghetto.

APRIL 9, 1941
Our theatrical group is continuing its performances. It is now well known that every Monday the youth of the Little Ghetto

46

gathers together to see the shows of the LZA. We are now an old experienced company. In the beginning there were many such groups, but most of them did not last long.

At 16 Sienna Street, in the house where our courses in graphic arts take place, a new café, directed by Tatiana Epstein, has been opened. The waitresses are ladies of the best society. Famous artists give performances there, among them the virtuoso Wladislaw Spielman. In a few days, this café is going to run a contest for young talent. The prize is a week's contract as a performer in the café, at a good salary. I have entered my name among the competitors.

APRIL 14, 1941

Our show today was a great experience for me. I suggested that as a Passover number we should choose something from the Haggadah,[4] and, as I am the best student of Hebrew in our group, I was given the honor of reciting the curses. To a strongly rhythmic piano accompaniment, I thundered out the ten plagues that every Jew in the ghetto wishes upon the Nazis. The whole audience repeated the words after me, and together we silently wished that they should strike the new Egyptians as soon as possible... but meanwhile, the wrath of God is heavy upon His own chosen people.

APRIL 20, 1941

The café contest was a tremendous success, and during the three days it lasted the place was packed to the rafters. There were prizes for singing, dancing, recitation, and performance on instruments.

Stanislawa Rapel, a pupil of Janina Pruszycka, won the first prize for dancing. A six-year-old boy, a pupil of Wladislaw Spielman, received the first prize for piano. This little boy is a real genius and an accomplished virtuoso. I won the first prize for singing light jazz songs in English and, as usual, I was accompanied by Romek Kowalski.

47

The distribution of prizes took place in an atmosphere of tremendous excitement and enthusiasm. The jury that handed out the awards was composed of Wladislaw Spielman, Helena Ostrowska, the well-known singer, the editor Stefan Pomper, the wife of the architect Bela Gelbard, who is popular as a generous patron of the arts, and Tatiana Epstein, the owner of the café.

Artistic life is flourishing in the ghetto. On Nowolipie Street, a tiny Yiddish art theater called "Azazel" is functioning under the direction of the actress Diana Blumenfeld, Jonas Turkow's wife. On Nowolipki Street, which runs parallel to Nowolipie, the Cameral Theater gives performances in Polish. For the last four weeks they have been performing the popular comedy, *Dr. Berghof's Office Hours are from Two to Four*, by the Czech playwright, Polaczek.[5] The chief actors of this theater are Michal Znicz, Aleksander Borowicz, and Wladislaw Gliczynski.

The Femina Theater on Leszno Street is very successful. There one can see Aleksander Minowicz, Helena Ostrowska, Franciszka Man (who won first prize at an international dance contest), Kinelski, Pruszycka and her ballet, Noemi Wentland, and many other celebrities that no one knew—before the war—were Jewish. The Femina has a mixed repertory of revues and operettas. Recently it staged *Baron Kimmel*[6] and a revue in which pride of place was given to skits and songs about the Judenrat. There were biting satirical remarks directed against the ghetto "government" and its "ministers." These included many apt references to certain bureaucratic gentlemen of the community administration, but on the whole, I felt that the attitude of this group was exaggerated and perhaps even unfair, especially with regard to the president of the community, Engineer Czerniakow, whose position is far from enviable.

True, Czerniakow often rides in a car to meet with Governor Frank,[7] but each time, he returns a broken man. He carries the heavy burden of responsibility for everything that takes place in the ghetto. For instance, as soon as the Germans discover that someone is circulating illegal newspapers, they take hostages from among the members of the community administration, which they have deliberately expanded and which now includes the most prominent personalities. These people display extraordinary pride and courage and often pay for it with their lives. All this is surely not an appropriate subject for satire.

President Czerniakow lives at 26 Elektoralna Street. I often come to this house because a friend of mine lives there, but I have never met the president on the stairs or in the street. He seldom goes out, for he is entirely absorbed by his heavy tasks. It is not easy to visit him; one has to pass a number of secretaries and receptionists at barred windows and go through various offices. Often a private citizen has to wait for three weeks before getting to see the president. In the meantime, the desired interview loses its meaning, and the would-be petitioner gives up his turn.

I have had occasion to see President Czerniakow during his visits to our school. He is a tall, stout man with a broad steadfast face. He is always clad in black and wears glasses. He has a sharp but mild look. I have never seen him smile, but this is quite natural considering his heavy responsibilities. To have to deal with the Germans every day and, at the same time, to bear with the complaints and reproaches of a starving, embittered and distrustful population—such a task is certainly not enviable. I am not surprised that he is always so gloomy.

Whenever Czerniakow visits our school, he is accompanied by Engineer Jaszunski, the director of the community's network of schools. Jaszunski is almost as tall as Czerniakow, wears a goatee and has thick eyebrows that make his mild face look even milder. He is a man of wide knowledge and shows great interest in our work.

When they come, they inspect the portraits, drawings, modern lettering patterns, blueprints for buildings, and technical drawings. We hardly realize the great progress we have made within a short time. I myself did not know how to hold a pencil when I entered the school, yet I have learned a great deal during these last two months.

APRIL 27, 1941

Today the Germans paid another visit to our school. Recently they have been coming more and more often. As soon as their gray car enters our street and we see through the window a group of officers in yellow SA uniforms with red armbands and swastikas getting out, there is a great bustle in our class. The teachers pull the best work of the pupils from their files. We hurriedly put on our armbands, which must be worn even over dresses and sweaters. Everything is quickly put in order. God forbid that the Germans should find even a scrap of paper on the floor.

They march in insolently with a firm tread. A deathlike silence prevails in the room. Engineer Goldberg, our teacher, who has an excellent knowledge of German, greets the visitors. He answers all their questions and shows them the best drawings. The Germans are not interested in the illustrations, nor in the architectural blueprints; they devote most of their attention to the technical drawings, upon which they dwell at length and which they criticize in detail. Before leaving, they inspect our armbands, and if they find one that is a little bit crumpled, they scold and threaten to close the school. As soon as the gray car leaves we sigh with relief and resume our work.

MAY 20, 1941

On the other side of the barbed wire, spring holds full sway. From my window I can see young girls with bouquets of lilac walking on the Aryan part of the street. I can even smell the tender fragrance of the opened buds. But there is no sign of spring in the ghetto. Here the rays of the sun are swallowed up by the heavy gray pavement. On a few window sills, long, scrawny onion stalks, more yellow than green, are sprouting. Where are my lovely spring days of former years, the gay walks in the park, the narcissus, lilac, and magnolia that used to fill my room? Today we have no flowers, no green plants.

This is my second spring in the ghetto. In the vegetable

wagons in the streets one sees only dirty turnips and last year's carrots. Next to them are wagons full of stinking fish—tiny little fish in a state of decay. A pound of them costs one zloty. These fish now constitute the most important article of food in the ghetto. It is the only one that the Germans allow to be sold freely. Of course, meat, chicken, and even a real carp for the Sabbath are to be had. The bazaar on Leszno Street has everything one's heart desires—but chicken costs twenty zlotys a pound. Kosher meat and fish are even more expensive; only those who have a large cash reserve can afford such luxuries, and very few such people remain in the ghetto.

The community kitchens are still open and there one can get a dish of soup, consisting of hot water with a potato swimming in it, for thirty groszy. The community administration also has a kitchen for its own employees where soup with gruel is served, but this costs one zloty.

The food section of the community administration is headed by Abraham Gepner. He controls the various factories that have recently opened up in the ghetto to manufacture foodstuffs, among them "honey" and marmalade. This marmalade is made of carrots and beets sweetened with saccharine. The "honey" is made of yellow-brown molasses. The only virtue of this product is its natural sweetness. But a piece of bread with such honey is far beyond the reach of most people.

There is another aspect of the ghetto—new cafés and expensive grocery stores have appeared, where everything can be had. On Sienna and Leszno Streets, women are seen in elegant coats and dresses fashioned by the best dressmakers. The ghetto even has its own styles. Most women wear long jackets without collars or lapels, so-called "French blazers," and full skirts. The hats are mostly small, round, and very high. High cork heels, too, are very fashionable. The most stylish colors are gray and dark red. When the weather is good, dresses of French silk printed with big flowers are seen.

The fashionable crowd meets at the Café Sztuka (Art) on

Leszno Street, the most popular establishment in the ghetto. At elegantly set tables, to the sound of a brilliant orchestra, the high society of the ghetto disports itself. Just as they did before the war, they gossip and discuss the latest fashions. The singer, Vera Gran, who is tremendously successful, is to be heard here. There are many other cafés on Leszno. Wladislaw Spielman plays at the Café Pod Fontanna (Under the Fountain).

In the Little Ghetto on Ogrodowa Street, a garden café, called "Bajka" (Fairy Tale) has been opened. The tables are outside and there is a little grass and two trees. This café covers the site of a completely bombed-out house. To one side stands a wall with burned window openings. This is an excellent backdrop. Near by is a "beach"—a piece of ground on which a few deck chairs have been placed. For two zlotys one can bask in the sun here for an entire day. Bathing suits are obligatory, apparently in order to create the atmosphere of a real beach.

The places formerly occupied by bombed houses are used for various purposes to extend the living space of the ghetto. In this respect, the recently formed Toporol Society[8] shows a great deal of energy. The aim of this society is to popularize gardening among the people. All the free plots of land have been requisitioned by the community and handed over to the Toporol. Hundreds of young boys and girls are working the plots on which bombed buildings stood, both in the courtyards and on the streets.

Apart from that, the German authorities permit a large group of volunteer farm workers to leave the ghetto every day to cultivate the fields outside the city. The work affords the young people of the ghetto the opportunity to breathe a little fresh air. Most members of these groups are young Zionists who believe that, by some miracle, they will succeed in getting to Palestine. For that reason they are glad to gain experience as farm workers.[9]

I look with a feeling of pride at these ranks of boys and girls who march along the ghetto streets, returning from work outside. All of them are tanned by the sun and refreshed by the free air they have breathed in the fields beyond the city. From their knapsacks protrude red radishes and golden young carrots. Every one of them carries a loaf of fresh bread received from the peasants. Officially it is forbidden to bring bread in from the outside, but in this case, the Germans let it pass because they need the manpower of these young people.

The Toporol is trying to have as many vegetables as possible planted in the ghetto. The first radishes grown in the soil of the ghetto have appeared on the market. These local vegetables facilitate the sale of the greens that are smuggled in. Here and there one sees small quantities of spinach on the carts, and in some showcases, even the lordly asparagus has appeared at eight zlotys a pound. And there are large numbers of young onions at twenty groszy a bunch. They are planted in pots and boxes, on roofs and on window sills, in all sorts of odd corners.

JUNE 5, 1941
A new means of transportation has appeared in the ghetto. Through the windows of our school on Sienna Street this morning, I saw the first horse-drawn trolley car pass by. One of our older teachers remarked facetiously that he must be growing younger—suddenly his days of childhood, when Warsaw had only horse-drawn trolleys, are coming back. I was not born at that time, and the only thing I think of when I see these vehicles is the period of Napoleon.

These omnibuses of 1941 are called the Kohn-Hellers, after the names of the two partners, Kohn and Heller, who founded the omnibus corporation. They are wooden cars with windows and look like ordinary trolley cars, but the upper part is painted yellow, the lower blue, and in the middle there is a white Star of David with the inscription TKO (Polish abbreviation for Company of Omnibus Transportation). This vehicle moves on high wheels, and gives the impression of a gigantic yellow and blue armband. The driver and the conductor wear special dark uniforms. The price of a ticket is twenty groszy. Often the driver stops the omnibus in the middle of a trip to "refuel," that is to say, to water the two emaciated sweating mares, which can barely manage to drag the overcrowded car.

These omnibuses are a private enterprise and, aside from Kohn and Heller, there are a number of smaller shareholders, but it is said that the chief partners are the gentlemen of the Gestapo who gave permission for the undertaking.

Meanwhile, the ghetto walls are growing higher and higher. Barbed-wire fences are gradually giving place to red-brick walls.[10] At the spots where the Jewish quarter is separated from the Aryan side only by barbed wire, there are signs reading *Seuchensperrgebiet—Nur Durchfahr Gestattet*.[11] This is to warn the German soldiers against entering the forbidden zone, which is allegedly a hotbed of infectious diseases.

The Jewish community itself is forced to supply building materials for the ghetto walls. For this purpose, a special committee was formed by the Community Council, to which the name *Instandhaltung der Seuchensperrmauern* (maintenance of the wall against epidemics) was given. Engineer Mieczyslaw Lichtenbaum heads this committee. Workers are now being recruited to deliver bricks to the places where the walls are being completed. The committee takes the bricks from hopelessly bombed houses, and there are many to choose from. My young uncle, twenty-six-year-old Percy, works at gathering up these bricks from ruined buildings. This job is a dangerous one, yet the wages are only ten zlotys a day, hardly enough for two pounds of black bread. The overseers of the demolition workers get much better pay, but to become an overseer one must have "pull."

My friend Romek Kowalski has succeeded in obtaining such a job. Because of his unfortunate financial situation, he was forced to leave the drawing courses and look for employment. His father died during the siege of Warsaw, and he must now support his mother and his younger sister. As long as they had things to sell, they managed to get along, but now their jewels and furs are gone, and Romek must work. Fortunately,

Engineer Lichtenbaum is a relative of his, and thus Romek
had no difficulty in obtaining a job as an overseer.

His task is to see to it that the work of the others is done
quickly. Very often the bricks are taken from buildings on the
Aryan side. Then Romek takes his group of laborers past the
German sentry post at the ghetto wall and reports the number
of his workers to the Nazi guard. He is responsible for them, and
the full complement must be present when they return. He
must also see to it that no one smuggles anything into the ghetto.
Should anything be found on his workers he, like the smuggler
himself, is subject to the death penalty. He works twelve hours
a day, from seven in the morning till seven at night. When he
returns home he can barely drag his feet behind him.

Romek is bitter about this. His wish is to learn something,
to do something worthwhile with his life. He dreams of being
an architect, of building houses, not demolishing them as he

Romek Kowalski overseeing the building of the ghetto wall

does now. It is he who must find the material with which to wall up his brothers and himself in a living grave.

When Romek is not too tired, we go out for a walk in the evening. Now curfew rings at nine instead of at eight, as formerly. We walk down the hot streets on the melting asphalt, our spirits heavy, and our mood despondent. What can we hope for? If the war lasts another year, our strength will be exhausted. Those who still have a reserve of money will not have any a year hence. Some will go earlier, some later—there is no hope for anyone within the ghetto walls.

I try to repress these thoughts, but Romek says over and over, "I feel that I won't live to see the end of the war." In vain do I try to comfort him. He smiles bitterly at my words of cheer, points to the half-dead homeless people in the streets, and says, "In a few weeks you will see me among them." I try to divert him from such black thoughts, but at the bottom of my heart I know he is right.

From time to time we go to the theater. Last Sunday, we attended a matinee concert of Marysia Eisenstadt at the Femina. She is nineteen years old, brown-haired, of medium height and not particularly pretty, but she has an extraordinary voice, and is called the "nightingale of the ghetto." She is the daughter of the former choirmaster of the Tlomacki Street synagogue, who now directs the symphony orchestra of the ghetto. Although she began to appear in public only a few weeks ago, she has achieved tremendous popularity. At her first concert, which Romek and I attended, the enormous hall of the Femina was packed full. She sang a group of old French songs by Béranger, and Mozart's "Alleluia."[12] It was a pleasure to see her standing in the middle of the stage beside her father, who directed a twenty-man orchestra. The hall resounded with enthusiastic applause and she had to repeat several numbers. After the concert, she was presented with three or four bouquets of magnificent flowers that had probably been smuggled in from the Aryan side, because in the flower shops on Leszno Street roses and lilies are unobtainable.

CHAPTER IV

UNDERGROUND

JUNE 10, 1941

Today I found an illegal sheet between the leaves of the *Gazeta Zydowska* (Jewish Journal), the official ghetto newspaper. I suspect that the mailman himself stuck it there.

It is printed on fancy pink letter paper and contains news issued by the British Broadcasting Corporation and a warning against letting oneself be lured into working for the Germans.

The war news in this illegal sheet is very different from that published in the *Gazeta Zydowska* printed in Cracow with the permission of Governor Frank! But the readers of the official newspaper ignore the first page anyhow. This paper is read for its inside pages, which print valuable reports from the various segregated Jewish quarters throughout the Gouvernement General. Thus the *Gazeta Zydowska* is the only legal means of contact between the various ghettos. From the notes sent in by the Jewish Councils or Councils of Elders of the various communities, one can gather much important information about the living conditions, the number of refugees in the various cities, and the situation of the various relief organizations, hospitals, etc.

One of the most popular columns in the ghetto newspaper is the Letter Box, where various readers' questions concerning what is permitted and what is forbidden are answered. Usually the answer is "forbidden," but the readers keep on asking questions just the same.

The middle pages of the newspaper are devoted to literary works by Yiddish writers translated into Polish, and to original works by young writers who still flower within the narrow ghetto walls.

The last page even contains a section for advertisements, mostly of doctors, pharmacists, and tailors from Warsaw and Cracow. On the same page there is also a Lost Persons column, where parents inquire about their lost children and children about their vanished parents. This is the only means by which dispersed families can locate their loved ones.

The *Gazeta Zydowska* also has an editorial office in Warsaw, on Elektoralna Street. The paper has a large circulation, and every copy is read by hundreds of persons, because the Germans allow only a limited number of copies to be printed. This is the only legal newspaper for the three million Jews of Poland, and it is passed eagerly from hand to hand.

The people are even more interested in circulating the illegal press, which is published irregularly but constitutes the only source of accurate information about political events and the course of the war. From time to time my father brings home such a newspaper. Before trusting himself to give it to us, he locks the doors. He has pledged himself to hand it over the same day to another person whose name he refuses to reveal. Thus, these sheets move about from house to house.[1]

Within the ghetto there is, supposedly, more illegal activity than anywhere else in Poland. Not only the Jewish working-class parties, but also the PPS (Polish Socialist Party) have found out that it is easier to print their illegal publications and conceal their receiving and sending sets here. It is also said that many of the most active Polish Socialist militants live in the ghetto.

A search took place a few days ago in Sienna Street, at the corner of Sosnowa. The Nazis allegedly had come to requisition the furniture of a Jewish tenant, and while doing this, discovered a radio station. Later, the inhabitants of the block told us that during the whole previous day, a Nazi car had moved back and forth ceaselessly on the street until it finally stopped at the corner house and disgorged the Gestapo agents who made the search. Apparently this car belonged to the radio division of the Gestapo and was provided with a special detector for discovering secret radio stations.

All the male inhabitants of the house where the radio set was found were taken to prison, and most of them were shot on the spot. But secret radio stations continue to exist, underground bulletins continue to be published, and the Nazi threats and tortures do not frighten anyone. What is more, the underground movement is paying the Nazi and Polish traitors back in kind, as far as possible. The famous Polish moving-picture star, Igo Sym, who collaborated with the Nazis, was executed recently by the patriots. The Nazis posted red placards all over the city, promising a reward of ten thousand zlotys for the delivery of the "traitors." Meanwhile, a few hundred prominent Poles have been imprisoned as hostages and some of them have been shot.

JUNE 12, 1941

The ghetto is becoming more and more crowded due to a constant stream of new refugees. These are Jews from the provinces who have been robbed of all their possessions. Upon their arrival the scene is always the same: the guard at the gate checks the identity of the refugee, and when he finds out that he is a Jew, gives him a push with the butt of his rifle as a sign that he may enter our Paradise.

These people are ragged and barefoot, with the tragic eyes of those who are starving. Most of them are women and children. They become charges of the community, which sets them up in so-called homes. There they die, sooner or later.

I have visited such a refugee home. It is a desolate building. The former walls of the separate rooms have been broken down to form large halls, there are no conveniences, and the plumbing has been destroyed. Near the walls are cots made of boards and covered with rags. Here and there lies a dirty red feather bed. On the floor I saw half-naked, unwashed children lying listlessly. In one corner an exquisite little girl of four or five sat crying. I could not refrain from stroking her disheveled blond hair. The child looked at me with her big blue eyes, and said, "I'm hungry."

I was overcome by a feeling of utter shame. I had eaten that day, but I did not have a piece of bread to give to that child. I did not dare look in her eyes, and went away.

During the day the grownups go out to look for work. The children, the sick, and the aged remain lying on their cots. There are people from Lublin, Radom, Lodz, and Piotrkow—from all the provinces. All of them tell terrible tales of rape and mass executions. It is impossible to understand why the Germans allow all these people to settle in the Warsaw Ghetto, which already contains four hundred thousand Jews.

Mortality is increasing. Starvation alone kills from forty to fifty people a day, but there are always hundreds of new refugees to take their places. The community is helpless. All the hotels are packed, and hygienic conditions are horrific. Soap is unobtainable, and what is distributed as soap on our ration cards is a gluey mass that falls to pieces the moment it comes into contact with water. It makes one dirty instead of clean.

One of the plagues of the ghetto is the beggars, who continue to multiply. They are refugees who have no friends or relatives here, and for whom there is no place even in the terrible hostels established by the community. During the first few days after their arrival they look for work. At night they sleep in the doorways, that is to say, in the street. When they become exhausted and their swollen feet refuse to carry them any further, they sit down on the edge of the sidewalk or against a wall. They close their eyes and timidly stretch out a begging hand for the first time. After a few days they ask for charity with their eyes open. When hunger torments them even more fiercely, they begin to cry, and thus the so-called "rabid beggar" develops. Someone throws him twenty groszy or even half a zloty, but he cannot buy anything for such small sums.

Then these newly-born beggars begin to walk from door to door, asking whether there are any leftovers of soup or a few slices of stale bread in the house. The impatient host explains that he has nothing, that he must feed his own refugees—a sister with three children from the provinces and his wife's old mother. His home is in an uproar, he has to lodge three subtenants with their families, and, he thinks to himself anxiously, in addition to all that he must constantly open the door. How insolent the beggars have become! But the beggars go on their way from door to door, pleading, "Maybe something was left from your dinner? A few slices of stale bread? Or perhaps you need someone to take out your garbage?"

My mother has her two permanent refugees, compatriots from Lodz, who come every day for their main meal. One comes at noon, the other at night. I avoid entering the kitchen when they eat in order not to hurt their feelings. But every day I see similar respectable beggars with sunken faces and vacant eyes sitting on the stairs of our house and eating the leftovers that charitable and better-off housewives have given them. Very often after such a wonderful meal of a little gruel, beets, borscht, and other odds and ends, they fall asleep and are carried away by sweet dreams of full dishes of food and soft beds.

Today when I went to the courtyard I saw a tall, apparently well-dressed young man standing near the garbage can. He was one of those who, before the war in Poland, studied the humanities without having to worry about their daily bread. Suddenly, as though he realized he was being watched, he turned around, and I saw then that his coat was completely torn in front, and through his unbuttoned shirt I saw his hollow chest. He bent to pick up the paper bag that lay beside him, and quickly ran away. This young man had been rummaging in the garbage looking for some food. I had surprised him and he ran away ashamed.

Some time ago, a young boy who seemed to be about thirteen years old fainted in our doorway. One of the tenants brought him round and gave him some food: the boy had collapsed from hunger. Ever since then, this little Szymek has been a frequent visitor to his benefactors' home. He helps them clean up in the house and in return receives a dish of soup and a few zlotys a week. He takes great care of his appearance. Someone has given him an old suit, which hangs on him like a bag, but he is proud of having a complete suit of clothes because before he came to our building he was dressed in torn rags. He has quickly become a favorite with all the tenants. He takes down everyone's garbage and earns a few zlotys here and there. It turns out that he is much older than I thought at first. He does not look his eighteen years, he is so small and thin. He is a full orphan and homeless. When I spoke to him, I was surprised at his intelligence and his unbroken faith in the future.

Our courtyard at 41 Sienna Street is the scene of many happenings during the day, perhaps because more well-to-do people live here than anywhere else. During the morning, Professor Kellerman of the Leipzig Conservatory often comes here to play the violin. He is a little, gray-haired old man with fascinating long fingers. When he begins to play, windows open on all the floors. I often close my eyes and imagine that I am attending a concert of some great virtuoso, discreetly accompanied by a distant orchestra. But his playing is often interrupted by the noise of the pieces of hard bread and the coins thrown down to him.

We invited this professor to take a cup of tea with us. He came up, put his violin in a corner, and told us his story: he was brought to the ghetto in January of this year. Together with

Professor Kellerman playing his violin, possibly
with his wife, drawn by Mary Berg

his wife, he had traveled in a sealed car for ten days. Several
members of his group had died on the way, and the living
traveled on with the corpses. He had managed to send his two
sons to England before the war. "I don't complain," he said. "I
earn a living for myself and my wife. In the afternoon I even
give a few lessons for which I am well paid, and on the whole
people are extremely sympathetic to me. And to be frank," he
added in a tone of remorse, "we German Jews do not deserve
so much kindness. We have sinned very greatly toward the
eastern Jews..."

My mother asked him to give lessons to my younger sister,
who studied the violin before the war. He agreed, and now
comes twice a week. He gets five zlotys per hour.

On the street near our doorway a young woman often comes
to sing. She is a madwoman. The words of her plaintive song
reach me in the early morning: "A whistle of the locomotive,

farewell, my beloved, be happy..." The song ends with the train disappearing and the girl waiting for her lover.

This woman is the daughter of a rich and well-known Warsaw merchant. During the bombardment, her house was burned and her only brother perished in the flames. She jumped out of the third story into a net, and suffered a nervous shock as a result. Her mother was saved by a miracle. Now this girl sings on Sienna Street. All the inhabitants of the street know the strange words of her little song about the departing train and the return of the lover.

Today there are no more returns and there are no trains for the inhabitants of the Warsaw Ghetto, only a red-hot pavement and hordes of children who get entangled in one's feet and beg for a crust of bread.

True, not all the children beg. Many of them earn their living, often much more easily than their elders. Whole gangs of little children are organized, made up of boys and girls from five to ten years of age. The smallest and most emaciated of them wrap burlap bags around their bony little bodies. Then they slink across to the Aryan side through the streets that are fenced off only by barbed wire. The bigger children disentangle the wire and push the smaller ones through. The others watch for German guards or Polish policemen.

A few hours later they come back laden with potatoes and flour. Usually they go to the suburbs where food is cheaper than in the center of the city. Often peasants give them potatoes for nothing. Their terrible appearance arouses pity. In addition to bags of potatoes they often bring loaves of black country bread. With a happy smile on their little green faces, they slink back to the ghetto. On this side of the barbed wire, their older partners wait for them. Very often they stay there for hours, waiting until the Nazi guard is busy checking the passport of some foreign citizen or Polish Gentile visiting the ghetto. This gives them an opportunity to smuggle their foodstuffs. Sometimes the German sentry does not notice them,

A young boy is caught smuggling by a German guard

sometimes he does, but pretends that he does not. The latter
case is rarer, but there are such Germans, especially among
the older ones, who must have little children of their own at
home, and for that reason display a spark of pity for these
Jewish tots who look like little walking skeletons covered with
a velvety yellow skin. But most of the German guards fire in
cold blood at the running children, and the Jewish policemen
must then pick up the bleeding victims, fallen like wounded
birds, and throw them on passing rickshaws. Still, when the
children return safe and sound with their trophies to their
starving parents, there is boundless joy in the household. The
starchy potatoes and the black bread taste wonderful.
The next morning, the little foragers try once more to cross
the ghetto boundary at the corner of Sienna and Zelazna
Streets. Perhaps the same kindly guard will be there who let
them pass once before.

JUNE 17, 1941
Today I went to a gathering of the Bielsk people, to which I was invited by Vera Neuman. We have been acquainted for only a short time, but we are great friends. She is a tall blonde, a real German type, and a living refutation of the Nazi race theory. Vera is all alone here. Her mother died several years ago, and her father, a millionaire owner of several mills, is in Lwow, which is under Soviet occupation. At rare intervals, Vera receives letters from him through a well-paid smuggler, for there is no official communication between the Gouvernement General and the Soviet-occupied region. On such occasions the girl is crazy with joy. She comes to see me and laughs and cries. She suffers a great deal from her loneliness, and for that reason, attends the gatherings of the Bielsk refugees where she meets friends from her old home and recalls the carefree, luxurious style in which she once lived.

There are several such groups from various Polish cities— among them Lodz and Lublin—which are quite active. The larger groups have headquarters of their own, which are kept open all day, and some even have their own kitchens to serve meals to the homeless. There the refugees from the same city meet and organize relief for the newcomers. From time to time they arrange concerts; all the money they raise goes to the needy. These groups are often asked by the community to take care of their compatriots, whom they set up in the homes of refugees who arrived earlier. All the ghetto apartments are overcrowded, and on average one room is occupied by six to ten people. As a result, there is serious danger of epidemics, especially typhus. The chief carrier of this terrible disease is the clothes louse, and it is hard to avoid encountering this repulsive insect. It is enough to walk in the street and rub against someone in the crowd to become infested. Alarming news of typhus victims comes from everywhere.

CHAPTER V

RUSSIAN BOMBS

JUNE 26, 1941

I am writing this in the bomb shelter of our house. I am on night duty, as a member of the home air defense. The Russians are bombing more and more frequently. We are situated in a dangerous spot, close to the main railway station. It is now eleven o'clock. I am sitting near a small carbide lamp. This is the first time since the opening of hostilities between Russia and Germany that I have been able to write. The shock was tremendous. War between Germany and Russia! Who could have hoped it would come so soon!

On the historic day of June 22, at four in the afternoon, our theater group was giving its traditional Sunday performance in the Weisman hall. Misha had recited his number, and then I went on the stage and, I cannot say why, for the first time felt stage fright. Romek, who sat at the piano, noticed my distress and, in his characteristic tender way, whispered, "Don't be afraid, just remember the key!" His look encouraged me, and after the first measures, my stage fright vanished.

I sang my first song and had begun my second when, suddenly, a terrible explosion was heard, and the whole stage shook. I did not realize what had happened. Through the window I saw the ruined building across the street (which had been struck during the siege of Warsaw) burst into fragments. What could that be? I thought in a flash. Are we being bombarded again? By whom?

The spectators became restless, but Romek did not interrupt his playing and whispered to me, "Keep singing, it's nothing." I felt unsteady on my legs, and all sorts of ideas whirled in my head, but I went on singing. The explosions continued, but seemed to have moved further away. When I had finished my number, panic broke out in the hall and the audience began to rush for the exit. Harry tried to stop them, but in vain. In a few moments, the hall was empty. Someone brought the news that the Russians had bombed the station and that many houses on the right side of Sienna Street where we lived had been hit. I rushed to the exit, but Romek stopped me. Only after the explosions had ceased did we leave together. At the corner of Sienna and Sosnowa Streets, I saw that our house was undamaged, and breathed with relief. On the streets people tore from each other's hands the extra edition of the *Nowy Kurjer Warszawski*[1] with its enormous headlines in color: "War Against the Red Plague," and "The Germans Are Defending the World Against the Bolshevik Deluge." These headlines brought smiles to everyone's lips.

Warsaw was immediately declared to be in a state of siege. The curfew in the ghetto now began at seven instead of nine, and the death penalty was inflicted for violating the blackout. But all this is nothing new. The sirens howl quite often now. The dazzling light rockets thrown by the Soviet fliers over Warsaw are tremendously impressive. They help the Red Air Force to bomb accurately the military stores and airfields around Warsaw.

Today's German official communiqué in the *Nowy Kurjer Warszawski* says that the "Soviet bombardment of Warsaw last night did not cause any military damage, but the civilian population suffered a great deal. The Bolshevik fliers concentrated on the residential part of the city and also bombed a hospital." This newspaper appeals editorially to the Polish population to "take an active part in the holy war against the Red barbarians," and suggests the creation of a special Polish legion for the struggle against the Bolsheviks.

In the afternoon I received an illegal bulletin that reported the exact opposite. The Russian bombers had caused great damage to the main railway station and destroyed a long stretch of tracks. The Okecie airfield was destroyed too, and in a few munitions factories, a large number of Polish workers were killed.

The underground press now appears more frequently and performs an important function. The little sheets bring us a breath of hope and strengthen our morale.

I think there is an alarm now—yes, a long blast of the siren. I must run to awaken the commandant.

JULY 1, 1941

The Gentile janitors still remaining in the ghetto have been ordered to move out at once, and many Jews are anxious to get their jobs. My father tried to secure the position of janitor[2] in our house for Uncle Percy, who has nothing to live on except what we give him. But our reserves will not last long if we continue supporting so many relatives. It is not easy to obtain this job. The unanimous consent of the tenants is needed, and even after the applicant has obtained that, his appointment must be approved by the community administration.

Uncle Percy's chances of being appointed are slim, inasmuch as he is not a tenant in our house. For that reason, my father finally decided to put forward his own candidacy and take Percy as his assistant. This plan may work. There are four hundred tenants in our house, and the janitor can earn a fair income.

69

JULY 4, 1941

Examinations are approaching at the school of graphic arts. The school year has lasted only seven months; the Germans refused to extend it. The professors are satisfied with the progress made by the majority of the students. However, there is a great shortage of supplies; only two stores in the ghetto still sell small quantities of paper and paints at fantastic prices. A sheet of paper that cost twenty groszy before the war now costs four zlotys. India ink, brushes, and pens are not to be found. Nevertheless, we manage somehow to go on with our studies. A certain number of students have been forced to drop the course because they had to take jobs in order to live.

The most popular student is twenty-three-year-old Zdzs-law Szenberg, a scrawny young man who wears military boots and an elegantly tailored coat. He has a thin face and big ardent black eyes with strangely long lashes, quite odd for a man. His hands are blessed with a marvelous gift for drawing and painting. He has a predilection for designing and makes fun of the painters who, according to him, waste time and material on useless things. But this is only a pose with him. He, too, paints the "misery" figures of the ghetto, and land-scapes consisting of a rickety chestnut tree against a background of bombed-out houses.

Joziek Fogelnest and Kazik Kestenberg are interesting types, too. They are perfect foils for one another, and always sit together at one desk. They are the despair of the teachers, and every time one of them says a word, the whole classroom resounds with laughter. Kazik has a comical elongated face that reminds one of a pony and Joziek is a splendidly built fellow with innocent childlike eyes. His glasses have a way of sliding down to the tip of his nose. Both are of the same age—nineteen—and they are taking the courses only to avoid doing compulsory labor for the Germans. They have not the slightest idea of design, and passed the entrance examinations only through "pull." But they manage to cope with the problems our teachers give us by pretending that they are neo-impressionists and drawing complicated, incomprehensible, and often quite absurd compositions. When the teachers point out that their work does not solve the problem given, they accuse the teachers of conservatism and adherence to obsolete ideas and begin to explain the profound symbolism of their own compositions. The rest of the class almost bursts with laughter, and the teachers give up and often join in the fun.

Bolek Szpilberg is another curious personality. He comes to school in a different suit every day. He is the son of wealthy parents, and is quite talented. He seems older than his eighteen years, is of medium height and is very distinguished looking. Bolek was born in Palestine, although he is really a British subject, and as such, was obliged periodically to report to the Gestapo. But he procured an Italian birth certificate for a considerable sum of money, and registered with the Gestapo under his own name, but as an Italian citizen, and struts around the school without an armband.[3] Yet one day when the Germans came to inspect our school, he quickly donned an armband. His face was flushed and he trembled all over. I realized then what a coward he is.

Among our students there are also two German refugees, the brothers Liebermann. The younger of the two, aged sixteen, is tiny and unattractive, but a skillful draftsman. The older brother, who is twenty-three years old, shows particular talent in the field of decorative art and poster designs. They are the nephews of the famous German-Jewish painter, Professor Max Liebermann.

Among the girls, Inka Garfinkel is remarkably talented in interior decorating and fashion designing. She has original ideas, and her whole personality is distinctive. Tall, slender, with auburn hair, black eyes, and a pale complexion, she often looks like a model in a fashion magazine. I recently made a portrait of her in pastels, which our teacher liked very much. Inka is very decided in her ideas. Soon she will marry the student Jozef Swieca, an official serving with the ghetto police. The couple have known each other for a year and are so much in love that they are completely unaware of the world around them. Up until now their economic situation has thwarted their plans, but now Inka is earning a little and her fiancé gets a good salary, so they are preparing to get married.

Nina Wygodzka and Janette Natanson are an inseparable pair; they are pretty and smart-looking, but dreadfully affected. They have a great deal of success with the boys. One of their mannerisms is that they always speak French. I always answer them in English. They do not look Jewish and therefore often manage to get across to the other side, where they do important errands for which they are well rewarded. Although they are very young, they have had a great deal of experience. Both are only daughters and live with their mothers. Their fathers died several years ago. Nina is nineteen, of medium height, rather plump, and she wears her hair in braids around her head. Janette, too, is of medium height, has long curls and a pale face covered with tiny freckles. Her catlike green eyes are full of fire. These two turn the heads of all the boys at the school and are regarded as dangerous "vamps."

On the whole, the students get along well together and help one another in every way they can.

JULY 10, 1941
The Russian fliers frequently visit the environs of Warsaw, and the sound of bombs makes the air tremble. I often hear the drone of the Russian planes, which spare the ghetto. For that reason we no longer go to the cellar so often when we hear the alarm. The heat is terrible now, and I often sit on the balcony of our second-floor apartment. The tomatoes, peas, carrots, and radishes in the window boxes are thriving. Overhead the sunny blue sky is the only reminder of freedom. I come here very frequently with my friend Lutka Leder, who lives on the

sixth floor, and we discuss plans for our future. Lutka is here with her stepmother and younger sister. Her father is in Russian-occupied Poland, and, since the German invasion of Russia, she has not heard from him. Lutka is a middle-sized plumpish brunette, eighteen years of age. Vera Neuman and Mickie Rubin often come here, too.

We breathe the fresh air and for a while forget the sad world around us. But one glance at the yard, divided by a wall, suffices to dispel our sweet dreams. Our balcony faces the Aryan side of Zlota Street. From a window on the fifth floor come the sounds of piano playing, usually the same tune, Schumann's *Traumerei*.[4] I often think that some noble Christian soul is trying, with the help of this tender melody, to comfort the unfortunate inhabitants of the ghetto locked up behind gates, and that perhaps she is even expressing a sort of regret at the fact that stones are often thrown into the ghetto from the Aryan side. This melody of Schumann's transports each of us into a different world.

Lutka dreams of her beloved Kazik Briliant, who lives only one house away. She never stops thinking or speaking about him, but, unfortunately, he is completely indifferent to her. Mickie Rubin's thoughts are always of her native Leipzig where she spent the best years of her youth. She is very sentimental and remembers the most insignificant incidents of her life in the German city, from which she was deported to the ghetto. Despite the bitter injustice she suffered there and the injuries the Germans inflicted upon her, she cannot forget the country where she and her parents were born.

I am full of dire forebodings. During the last few nights, I have had terrible nightmares. I saw Warsaw drowning in blood; together with my sisters and my parents, I walked over prostrate corpses. I wanted to flee, but could not, and awoke in a cold sweat, terrified and exhausted. The golden sun and the blue sky only irritate my shaken nerves.

JULY 27, 1941

After a long struggle, my father has finally got the job of janitor with all the privileges this office entails. He has been "in office" for two weeks now, and, in addition to the regular Jewish armband, he now wears a yellow armband with the inscription "House Master." He has also received a passport from the community, which states that he is exempt from compulsory labor duties. Thus he can circulate freely in the streets without fear of manhunts. The janitors are exempt from various community taxes, receive extra food rations, two hundred zlotys a month as a salary, and free lodging. But their main income is derived from opening the door at night. In accordance with the curfew regulations, the door is closed at an early hour, and to have it opened the tenants pay twenty groszy or more. Some nights these fees total as much as twenty zlotys. In brief, a janitor's income under the present conditions is unusually good, so it is no wonder the job is hard to obtain.

Because my father is not strong enough to perform the heavy duties of a janitor, to wit, keeping the building clean, scrubbing the staircases, and removing the garbage, he has followed his original plan, and has taken my Uncle Percy as his assistant. To him he gives all his direct money receipts.

At first our neighbors were distrustful of their new janitor, who, only yesterday, was a tenant like themselves. They could not conceive that an art dealer and expert on classical painting could perform the duties of an ordinary janitor. But they soon grew accustomed to the idea that even a respectable citizen can become a janitor and still remain a respectable citizen. Now they show the greatest respect for both my father and uncle. Incidentally, they are not the only people in the ghetto who have fallen so low on the social scale. The janitor in the building next to ours is Engineer Plonskier, a close friend of our family's, and a great number of lawyers are now glad to work as janitors.

CHAPTER VI

TYPHUS

JULY 29, 1941

The typhus epidemic is raging. Yesterday the number of deaths from this disease exceeded two hundred. The doctors are simply throwing up their hands in despair. There are no medicines, and all the hospitals are overcrowded. New beds are constantly being added in the wards and corridors, but this does not solve the problem, and the number of victims is growing daily.

The hospital at the corner of Leszno and Rymarska Streets has put up a sign in the window of its office reading "No vacancies." The Berson Children's Hospital on Sienna Street is packed with children of various ages, all of them ill with typhus. The hospital at the corner of Leszno and Zelazna Streets has closed its doors; there is no room for even one more patient.

A few days ago, on Leszno Street, I saw a father carrying a fairly grown-up boy in his arms. Both father and son were dressed in rags. The young patient's face was burning red, and he was raving deliriously. As he approached the corner of Leszno and Zelazna Streets, the man stopped hesitatingly in front of the hospital gate. He remained standing there for a while, apparently wondering what to do. Finally, the unfortunate man laid his sick son down on the steps leading to the hospital office and withdrew several paces. The exhausted boy tossed in convulsions and groaned heavily. Suddenly, a nurse in a white apron came out and began to berate the grief-stricken father, who stood with lowered head, weeping bitterly. After a while I noticed that the sick boy had ceased tossing, as though he had fallen asleep. His eyes were closed and a look of serene contentment was spread over his face.

A few moments later the weeping father cast a glance at his son. He bent over his child and, sobbing brokenheartedly, stared at his face for a long time, as though trying to discover a trace of life in it. But all was over. Soon a little black cart, a free service to the community, appeared, and the still-warm body of the boy was added to several others that had been picked up in adjoining streets. For some time the father gazed at the cart as it moved away. Then he disappeared.

Setting sick people down in front of hospitals has become a daily occurrence. Mothers, unable to stand the sight of their children suffering without medical aid, hope that by this method they will succeed in getting the patients to a hospital.

The epidemic has assumed a particularly acute form in the regions of Gesia, Nalewki, Nowolipki and Nowolipie Streets. In the Little Ghetto, the situation is somewhat better, because it is inhabited by relatively well-to-do people who can afford private medical care.

Recently, antityphus serum has been imported from Lwow, which fell to the Germans a month ago. The Soviets, when they evacuated Lwow, left a large store of antityphus serum in tubes. Now this precious medicine is being smuggled into Warsaw. But only wealthy people can afford to buy it—the price runs as high as several thousand zlotys a tube.

Some inhabitants of the ghetto receive packages from Switzerland by mail containing various medicines, especially

Mary and her sister Anna in the Warsaw Ghetto

antityphus serum. The Swiss serum is superior to the Russian. A lively trade in medicines is being carried on in the ghetto. Heniek Grynberg, one of my acquaintances, is engaged in this business, and has told me some details about it.

Heniek is a tall blond, a real Nordic type, who has not one Jewish feature. Through an underground channel, he often crosses over to the other side where he easily passes as a Pole with the help of forged identification. He somehow manages to get permission to go to Lwow and there he buys a certain number of tubes of antityphus serum for which he has received advance paid orders from well-to-do Jews in the ghetto. This trip is not easy to make despite Heniek's Aryan appearance and forged document. Searches are constantly made on the trains, and the Germans not only confiscate smuggled articles but impose heavy penalties—which would be particularly severe if Heniek's Jewish identity were discovered. But Heniek is an experienced smuggler. During the three years of the war he has crossed several frontiers, engaged in various trades, hidden from the police of various countries, and managed to elude all sorts of dangers. He is one of the most successful people in this new business. This can be seen from his prosperous appearance and the elegant dresses worn by his wife and daughter. His sister, Eva Grynberg, is a member of our House Committee, and Rutka, his cousin, is a friend of my younger sister, Anna. Rutka spends entire days in our apartment, and my parents treat her almost as their third daughter.

JULY 31, 1941
Yesterday the last of our examinations took place. I passed everything, and immediately enrolled for the so-called advanced course, which will last another seven months.

I am now sitting at the window of the new apartment that has been given to us as the janitor's family, and am watching the street. The window faces the part of Sienna Street that is near Sosnowa and is always a scene of great animation. At the corner of the street there is a news-stand. It goes without saying that the newspapers sold there are smuggled, because officially only the *Gazeta Zydowska* can be sold in the ghetto. But the *Nowy Kurjer Warszawski*, *Das Reich*, the *Krakauer Zeitung* and even the *Voelkische Beobachter*[1] are obtainable. Sometimes the official Nazi newspapers contain interesting items concerning the various ghettos in Poland.

Near the news-stand there is a vendor of candy and cigarettes. He is an elderly man with the appearance of an intellectual. He is leaning against the wall, half slumbering. The candy he sells is made of molasses and saccharine in tiny ghetto factories. Sugar now costs thirty zlotys a pound. Some of the candies are wrapped in papers bearing the Star of David and the inscription "The Jewish Quarter." They cost from twenty to thirty groszy apiece. There is also candy which sells for a zloty for one piece.

Close by, an elderly woman at a little table sells armbands of various qualities, from fifty groszy to two zlotys each. The cheapest are made of paper with a printed Star of David; the most expensive are of linen with a hand-embroidered Star of David and rubber bands. These armbands are very much in demand in the ghetto because the Germans are very sensitive on this score, and when they notice a Jew wearing a crumpled or dirty armband, they beat him at once.

Sienna Street has several popular personalities. One of the favorites is Mrs. Bela Gelbard, a tall, plumpish, smart-looking woman with smooth black hair, lightly streaked with gray. She walks slowly, trying to adapt her pace to the tiny steps of her black pet dog. Every day at the same hour she walks this animal, sometimes surrounded by the students of our school, in whom she is particularly interested as she is a patroness of the arts. She carries on lively discussions with them and feels young among young people, although she is nearly fifty.

The house across from ours, Number 42, was burned during the siege. This morning a middle-aged woman sat down in front of the ruins. Her bare feet, which she stretched out in front of her, were covered with festering wounds, her face was swollen with scurvy, and her nostrils were unnaturally dilated, as though she were suffocating. She tried to raise her heavy body, but could not. People passed by her in a hurry without even looking back. Anyway, they could not have helped her. From a bundle beside her, she drew out a piece of bread and tried to bite into it, but her teeth stuck and her head sank heavily to the pavement. A little later she raised herself, bit off some bread and began to chew it. But her stomach refused to digest it, and she spat it up.

Then she tried to get up again with the help of her stick, and finally succeeded. She took a few steps, began to totter, leaned stubbornly upon her stick, and suddenly began to beat the wall with her head, crying, "People, have mercy on me, kill me!"

Then she fell heavily, with her arms outstretched, and I thought for a moment that her sufferings had come to an end. But a moment later she began to move, and in a hoarse voice, cried out incomprehensible words. I ran to the ambulance station and made such a fuss that finally someone was sent to take the poor creature away.

Such scenes occur relatively rarely on Sienna Street, but near Grzybowska, the streets are full of starving people who come to the community for help. There are a great number of almost naked children, whose parents have died, and who sit in rags on the streets. Their bodies are horribly emaciated, and one can see their bones through their parchment-like yellow skin. This is the first stage of scurvy; in the last stage of this terrible disease, the same little bodies are blown up and covered with festering wounds. Some of these children toss around and groan, as they have lost their toes. They no longer have a human appearance and are more like monkeys than children. They no longer beg for bread, but for death.

Where are you, foreign correspondents? Why don't you come here and describe the sensational scenes of the ghetto? No doubt you don't want to spoil your appetite. Or are you satisfied with what the Nazis tell you—that they locked up the Jews in the ghetto in order to protect the Aryan population from epidemics and dirt?

Some time ago I read in the Nazi-controlled *Nowy Kurjer Warszawski* just such reports on the ghetto by Spanish and Rumanian correspondents. And how surprised I was to see that an American correspondent, too—one who represented a large magazine—had let himself be deceived by the Nazi propaganda about the hygienic necessity for a ghetto in Warsaw! Is the whole world poisoned?[2] Is there no justice anywhere? Will no one hear our cries of despair?

Komitetowa Street, near Grzybowska, is a living graveyard of children devoured by scurvy. The inhabitants of this street live in long cellar-caves into which no ray of the sun ever reaches. Through the small dirty window panes one can see emaciated faces and disheveled heads. These are the older people, who have not even the strength to rise from their cots. With dying eyes they gaze at the thousands of shoes that pass by in the street. Sometimes a bony hand stretches out from one of these little windows, begging for a piece of bread.

The ghetto scenes on Grzybowska are no less sad. Hot iron or brick stoves are set up at every few steps. Large pots of water are boiling on them. Near by, at little tables or benches, there are thin slices of bread. Here, for forty groszy, one can get a glass of hot water with saccharine and a slice of bread. A huge crowd of people mills around amidst an incredible bustle. Here is a woman selling jelly made out of horse bones, ten groszy a portion, then a candy vendor, and a little further on a woman selling fish cakes made of the tiny fishes that are called "stinkies" in the ghetto. Such fish cakes cost thirty groszy, or, with a slice of bread, fifty groszy. There are many buyers of these, too.

Grzybowska is always filled with hordes of beggars, for here is the largest public kitchen maintained by the community. This street is also a terrible breeding ground for typhus. There are several typhus patients in every house. But those who can still walk hope that they will succeed in surviving all this horror. Everyone tries to forget the death and ruin that lurk everywhere. A favorite place for distraction in the heart of the ghetto is the Café Hirschfeld.

This establishment is situated at the corner of Sienna and Sosnowa Streets. Everything your heart desires can be had there—the most expensive liqueurs, cognac, pickled fish, canned food, duck, chicken, and goose. Here, the price of a dinner with drinks is from a hundred to two hundred zlotys. This café is the meeting place of the most important smugglers and their mistresses; here women sell themselves for a good meal. Sixteen-year-old girls come here with their lovers, the few scoundrels who work for the Gestapo. These girls do not think of what will happen to them later—they are too young for that. They come here to eat well. The next day such girls may be found shot to death together with their lovers. The organized youth of the ghetto deals ruthlessly with traitors.

A frequent habitué of this café is a Gestapo agent who goes by the name of Milek—no one knows his real name. He is a tall well-fed blond who wears officer's breeches and a long sports coat. He is a notorious Don Juan, and when he notices a girl she cannot escape him, because if she resists, she is threatened with the Gestapo, which usually means death. Milek always carries a gun, and boasts of having shot several underground workers who tried to do away with him.

Heniek Grynberg, too, is a frequent visitor at the Café Hirschfeld, which is a good place for business deals, for selling or buying a ten-carat diamond, a quantity of gold, a gram of platinum, or even forged identification papers. Heniek told me about the tragedies that sometimes take place in this café. The Germans often search it. They surround the establishment, go through the pockets of all the guests and carry away a handsome loot. Nevertheless, Hirschfeld's is always packed to the brim. Among the habitués there is Pola Fuchs, or, as she has been nicknamed, Polcia Mops. She is eighteen years of age, tall and blonde with magnificent legs.[3] A young *Volksdeutsche* from Silesia, Alfons P., has fallen in love with her. Pola is making the most of the affair, and perhaps she even likes him. P. is a handsome blond young man of medium height, whose parents are of German origin, but who considers himself a Pole. He is a friend of Heniek Grynberg's, and once even helped him out of a difficult situation.

Whenever Alfons P. visits the ghetto, he stays with his mistress at Grynberg's. Pola is always dressed elegantly and wears the most expensive French silks, which she gets as presents from her lover. I often see her walking on Sienna Street, and all the inhabitants of the quarter know her well.

Recently it has become harder for Poles to visit the ghetto, but, although he does not admit his German origin, P. has excellent connections in the Gestapo. Yet who knows the whole truth? Perhaps he is a Gestapo agent.

The leaders of the underground movement also meet at Hirschfeld's—the fact that the establishment is known to be the meeting place of the debauched elements in the ghetto makes it an excellent hiding place for the illegal fighters.

Despite the various prohibitions, many things are done in the ghetto, as they are on the Aryan side, which are forbidden under penalty of death. As a matter of fact, everything is forbidden. It is forbidden to print newspapers uncensored by the Nazis, to sing national songs, to attend religious services or schools, to enter public parks, to travel in trains, to own radios, phonograph records, telephones—in brief, it is forbidden to live! Yet we are living in spite of the Nazis, and hope somehow to survive this regime of slavery.

SEPTEMBER 10, 1941

Our theatrical group, LZA, often meets at our home. It seems to me that we cannot continue to exist much longer. A mood of terrible depression prevails everywhere. Edzia Piaskowska's mother is sick with typhus. They live on Karmelicka Street, where the epidemic is particularly severe. Edzia was compelled to leave her home, and now she is staying with us. Misza's father, too, is very ill. Mietek Fein has gone away somewhere to the provinces and we have not heard from him. Stefan Mandeltort's father died of typhus, and now Edek Wolkowicz has it.

Harry is very depressed. The doctors recently discovered that his tuberculosis had taken a turn for the worse. Bolek Gliksberg is preparing to flee from the ghetto. Dolek Amsterdam is wearing a mourning band for his father. Ola is very dejected; her material situation has deteriorated considerably. The moment she came in she asked me for some bread, saying that she had forgotten to eat before leaving home. It goes without saying that I offered her a little supper at once.

Unlike most of us, Tadek is in a cheerful mood, and it is no wonder. His father, a well-known Lodz lawyer, is the aide of the commandant of the so-called "Thirteen" who are fighting against speculation in the ghetto. He earns good money and I suspect that on the quiet he does business with the Nazis. Tadek is always well-fed and smartly dressed, and looks really well. He is in love with me; he told me so the other day quite openly. He often comes to see me, but makes a long face when he finds me in the company of Romek, whom he rightly considers a dangerous rival. Tadek and Romek are good friends, and usually get along well together, but the moment they are with me, their harmony breaks and they begin to quarrel.

Romek is embittered, because he must work hard to feed his family, and every day he gets home exhausted. Yet he visits me

Tadek Szajer wearing the cap of
an Ambulance Service worker, circa 1942

almost every evening. Tadek has no cares, he only studies, and in his free time, he bores me with his declarations of love. He does not interest me; quite the contrary! He irritates me with his natty appearance, elegant clothing, and the fact that he never walks on foot, but has himself driven around in a rickshaw. God knows that I do not envy him, but it makes me unhappy to think that Romek must work so hard. But he does not complain of his lot. When he comes to see me, he sits down in a deep armchair and remains silent for a long time, closing his eyes, as though he were dreaming. He is always depressed. When he leaves, he kisses me and tries to say a few hopeful words about the future. But a few days ago, he embraced me and said, speaking as an adult to a child, "Little girl, it is good that you don't understand too much. I am happy that you don't suffer as I do."

Tears choked me, because I do know and understand everything, but I am powerless and cannot help anyone.

Sometimes our group gathers at Romek's, although the way from my house to his is dangerous. German guards fire at passers-by without cause or warning. For that reason, Harry and Bolek, who live near us, came for me yesterday, and we went to Romek's together.

It was a hot day. We went out at about four in the afternoon. In the streets people were hurrying about with an extraordinary expression of fear in their faces. The tension could be felt at every step. When we reached the passage at the corner of Leszno and Zelazna Streets, we saw that the neighborhood was entirely empty. I asked Harry to take me back home, but it was too late, for at that very moment, we noticed a German guard at the passage aiming his rifle at us. Everything died in me, and I felt that my last moment had arrived. My legs began to crumple. The boys seized me under my arms and began boldly to cross the street. I felt a stinging sensation in my shoulders, as though a bullet had hit me. There was a petrified calm in the hot street. Suddenly, a dry crackle resounded and a bullet flew along the middle of the street; fortunately, we had passed the most dangerous section. Harry and Bolek were deathly pale. I myself was green when I entered Romek's house. I was deeply shaken and could not calm down.

A few minutes later, Romek's sister Marysia dashed into the room and, still panting, began to tell us about the shooting in the streets. Romek remained silent and I could read profound resignation in his eyes. Later he took me home. When we approached the passage at the corner of Leszno and Zelazna, we found an SS man, armed with a stick, who was hitting every passer-by on the head. All the pedestrians were compelled to run this gauntlet because there is no other way to get to the Little Ghetto from Leszno Street.

We somehow managed to hide among the crowd that pushed through the passage, and fortunately avoided the blows. All the men were forced to remove their hats when passing the gate in order to salute the Germans. As they did this, the SS man continued his work of hitting them on their bared heads, and many people came through to the other side with blood running down their faces.

When will this hell end?

SEPTEMBER 20, 1941

The Nazis are victorious. Kiev has fallen. Soon Himmler will be in Moscow. London is suffering severe bombardments. Will the Germans win this war? No, a thousand times no! Why do not the Allies bomb German cities? Why is Berlin still intact? Germany must be wiped off the face of the earth. Such a people should not be allowed to exist. Not only are the uniformed Nazis criminals, but all the Germans, the whole civilian population, which enjoys the fruits of the looting and murders committed by their husbands and fathers.

If only we had arms, if only we could defend ourselves, take revenge! But we are helpless; we can only bow our heads and pray to God.

Tomorrow night is Rosh Hashana, the Jewish New Year. We fear that the Nazis are preparing something horrible for this sacred day, for they do something particularly savage on every Jewish holiday. They have issued a special warning to the community that the Jews must not gather together for prayer, lest they be shot. Meanwhile, there is continuous talk about the plan for separating Sienna Street from the ghetto. The Germans are demanding seven pounds of gold as a ransom for this street. Valuables are being collected among the inhabitants of Sienna Street. Everyone has given his last ring or earring in order to prevent such a calamity.

CHAPTER VII

"VIOLENCE AGAINST
THY BROTHER"

SEPTEMBER 23, 1941

Alas, our apprehensions before the holidays were justified. Only yesterday, on the eve of Rosh Hashana, the Germans summoned the community representatives with Engineer Czerniakow at their head and demanded that they deliver at once five thousand men for the labor camps. The community refused to obey this order. The Germans then broke into the ghetto and organized a real pogrom. The manhunt went on throughout yesterday and this morning, and shooting could be heard from all sides.

I happened to be in the street when the hunt began. I managed to rush into a doorway which was jammed with people, and I waited there for two hours. At a quarter past eight, considering that it takes half an hour to walk from Leszno Street to Sienna Street, I decided to go home in order to arrive before nine, the curfew hour, after which it is forbidden to be in the streets.

At the corner of Leszno and Zelazna Streets, an enormous mass of people stood drawn up in military ranks in front of the labor office. Most of them were young men between eighteen and twenty-five. The Jewish police were forced to see to it that no one ran away. These young men stood with lowered heads, as though about to be slaughtered. And actually their prospects are not much better than slaughter. The thousands of men who have been sent to the labor camps thus far have vanished without leaving a trace.

Among these unfortunates I saw many familiar faces, and I was glad that Romek had not taken me home that night. Suddenly the door of a stationery store near which I stood—as if petrified, staring at the group of condemned men—opened, and I felt a hand on my shoulder. It was a Jewish policeman, who quickly dragged me inside.

A moment later, on the very spot where I had been standing, a man fell, struck by a bullet. A lamentation ran through the crowd like an electric current, and reached through the closed door of the stationery store. The fallen man groaned for a while, but was soon taken away in a hand truck. The janitor at once proceeded to scrub the still-warm blood from the pavement.

Trembling, I looked at my watch. The curfew hour, the hour of sure death on the ghetto streets, was approaching. Instinctively, I moved toward the exit. But the policeman would not let me go. When I told him how far I lived and that I did not care whether I was shot now or later, he promised to take me home.

I left the store with a few other people who wanted to get home. It was five minutes to nine. The policeman brought me to our doorway, and when I entered our apartment, it was thirty minutes past curfew time. My parents had almost given me up for dead and flooded me with a hail of questions. But I was in no condition to answer them, and fell at once on my bed. Even now, as I write these lines, I am still shaken by my experience and I see before me the thousands of young Jews standing like sheep before a slaughter house. So many sons, brothers, and husbands have been torn away from their loved ones, whom they may never see again, to whom they will not even be allowed to say farewell.

In a few months, the mothers, wives, and sisters of these men will receive official postcards informing them that number such-and-such has died. It is inconceivable that we have the strength to live through it. The Germans are surprised that the Jews in the ghetto do not commit mass suicide, as was the case in Austria after the *Anschluss*. We, too, are surprised that we have managed to endure all these torments. This is the miracle of the ghetto.

SEPTEMBER 25, 1941

Romek has a mild case of typhus. The spots are pale and his temperature is not very high. Rutka's condition is much more dangerous—she has the disease in its worst form. A few days ago she began to suffer from brain complications. She has lost her mind completely, and refuses to let the doctors come near her; they have little hope for her, in any case. My sister Anna is in a state of despair; she weeps night and day and prays constantly for unfortunate Rutka, her dearest friend.

Edzia Piaskowska's mother feels much better. A few days ago her sister and brother-in-law, Roman Kantor, the famous fencer, arrived from Lwow. Under the Russian occupation, he was a fencing instructor in that city and did very well. When the Germans entered Lwow, he had to flee.

Many refugees are now arriving from the regions formerly occupied by the Soviets. Wherever the Germans entered, they slaughtered the Jewish population en masse. In Bialystok they drove more than a thousand Jews into the great synagogue and then set it on fire from all sides.[1] In many smaller towns the rabbis and community leaders were taken to the cemetery and shot.

These refugees told us one very curious story. Shortly before the Nazi invasion of Russia, rumors suddenly began to circulate that the Jews in the Warsaw Ghetto were living as in a veritable paradise. Who was responsible for these rumors nobody knows. At any rate, as a result of them, many Jews did not flee with the Soviet armies and returned to Warsaw instead. Now they realize that the rumors were the work of Nazi agents who thus snared them into the death-trap.

The manhunts still go on. Shots are often heard, and it is dangerous to go out into the street. The only one of my acquaintances who still visits me, in spite of all this terror, is Tadek Szajer. I suspect that his father has procured some sort of document for him which exempts him from being taken to a labor camp.

Today Tadek dropped in, beaming with joy: he has a new little sister. He came to me directly from the hospital where he saw the newborn child of his father's second wife. She does not treat Tadek like a stepchild; on the contrary, they love each other very much. She is not much older than he is—he has just completed his twentieth year and she is less than thirty.

He told me enthusiastically how beautiful his new sister is. Her father has decided to name her Ilana. Tadek also told me about the great number of flowers the mother received in the hospital, and about the elaborate reception that is being planned immediately after her return home.

He talked and talked about the care with which the new mother is surrounded in the magnificent private hospital, about the two nurses attending her, etc. etc. But as I listened to him expatiating on the luxury of this private institution, I saw before me the homeless naked children lying hungry in the dusty streets, the children with swollen bellies and distorted bony little legs, and suddenly, as though awakening from a bad dream, I shouted out, "Stop! Shut up!" But then I at once realized that it is not Tadek's fault that his father is growing rich on unsavory business deals. I tried to overcome my aversion to the boy, but I could not, and I asked him to leave me on the pretext that I had a headache. He departed very sad, with his head hanging down.

For the time being, our theatrical groups have suspended performances. The most active members are ill or dispersed. Harry is confined to his bed; his consumption is getting worse and worse. Bolek has escaped to the Aryan side and we do not know yet what is happening to him, nor to Mietek Fein. Stefan is working at a newly opened branch of the Jewish post office.

Edek Wolkowicz has recovered and resumed his police duties. He does not take off his cap even for a moment, not out of pride, but because of his bald, emaciated head. Everyone who recovers from typhus shaves his head to prevent his hair from falling out. In the streets of the ghetto, one can see many women with shaven heads wrapped in kerchiefs in the form of turbans. Those who can afford it have wigs made, but these are expensive and difficult to obtain.

The epidemic is taking a terrible toll. Recently the mortality rate reached five hundred a day. The home of every person who falls ill with typhus is disinfected. The apartments or rooms of those who die of it are practically flooded with disinfectants. The health department of the community is doing everything in its power to fight the epidemic, but the shortage of medicines and hospital space remains the chief cause of the huge mortality rate, and the Nazis are making it increasingly difficult to organize medical help. There is a widespread belief that the Nazis deliberately contaminated the ghetto with typhus bacilli in order to test methods of bacteriological warfare, which they intend to apply against England and Russia. It is said that the community has irrefutable proof of this theory from world-famous bacteriologists, Jewish professors from France, Belgium, and Holland, who have been deported here by the Nazis. Thus it is no longer a question of inadequate sanitary measures, or the overcrowding in the ghetto. Tomorrow the Nazis may plant their bacilli in the cleanest section of the ghetto, where the sanitary conditions are exemplary.[2]

However, the bacilli do not recognize racial laws or the borders of the ghetto. A few fatal cases of typhus have been recorded on the Aryan side, and some Nazi guards have become infected. But even this fact is exploited by the Nazis for their anti-Jewish propaganda; they now say that the Jews spread infectious diseases.

SEPTEMBER 28, 1941
Today I was on duty at the exhibition of the work of our school. Most popular are the still lifes. The spectators feast their eyes on the apples, carrots, and other foodstuffs so realistically painted. Less successful are our drawings of beggars. They are no revelation to anyone. The exhibition is tremendously popular and many hundreds of people have visited it.

The first and second halls contain the graphic designs. At first there are compositions on various themes, cut in black paper on a white background, or in two or more colors. There are designs for powder compacts, book covers, newspaper illustrations, letterheads, and trademarks. Then comes the lettering section. Various alphabets are shown with stylized letters of all periods, ending with modern block letters. The Gothic and Hebrew letterings are particularly magnificent. They are carried out in black India ink on parchment, with illuminated initials.

The lettering exhibit is followed by posters for business enterprises with industrial and folklore themes for theaters, factories, cafés, and stores. All these have been executed with great precision, yet they are full of life and the arrangement of the colors is very artistic. Looking at these designs, I often find it hard to believe that they are the work of our hands under these terrible conditions.

Then comes the section of landscapes and portraits. Everyone notices the paintings of Zdzislaw Szenberg, which are distinguished by their original composition and brilliant perspective. The portraits are no less successful. I have been complimented for my portrait of Inka Garfinkel.

There is much praise for the graphic work of gifted young Manfred Rubin. The teachers predict that a great future is in store for him. He has many ideas and is particularly talented at illustration. He has received a few large orders from various ghetto firms.

A special corner is reserved for the textile designs. Thanks to their meticulous execution and the naturalness of their color, these projects look like real samples of materials. Against the background of these samples, fashion drawings have been lightly woven in. This produces an interesting effect. In this section, Inka Garfinkel's works stand out. She has drawn magnificent models of dresses with boldness and ease and also sketched some interesting accessories. I am convinced that if she survives the war, she will be one of the best fashion designers in the world.

There are also many visitors in the hall devoted to the exhibits of architectural designs. These projects are somewhat complicated for the average spectator. There are plans for modern residential blocks and drawings of postwar one-family houses surrounded by gardens, and these houses have many windows. They are almost like the glass houses of which the great Polish writer, Stefan Zeromski,[3] dreamed. The visitors at the exhibition look with pride at these housing projects for the Jewish population of the free Poland of the future, which will abolish the crowded houses of Krochmalna and Smocza Streets, where the darkest cellars of the ghetto are situated. But when will this come about, and who of us will live to see it?

In the section on machine designs, there are tables with blueprints of various machines, but only experts can understand these.

People seem to leave the exhibition full of impressions, and even on the street continue to discuss the various pictures and projects for a long time. Everyone simply refuses to believe that such works could be produced within the walls of the ghetto, especially under the present conditions of constant manhunts, hunger, epidemic, and terror. And yet it is a fact! Our youth has given tangible proof of its spiritual strength, power of resistance, courage, and faith in a new and more just world.

Many visitors had radiant faces, shining with pride when they left. Others were serious and absorbed. I also saw a few persons with tears in their eyes, one of whom was the gray-haired Professor Majer Balaban. He seemed deeply moved, as he stood in front of an original stylized Hebrew poster and read to himself in a low voice the beautiful text of Obadiah.[4] I had the impression that he was reading this text over and over again as though trying to memorize the timely words of the prophet:

> For thy violence against thy brother Jacob shame
> shall cover thee,
> And thou shalt be cut off for ever.
> In the day that thou stoodest on the other side,
> In the day that the strangers carried away captive
> his forces
> And foreigners entered into his gates,
> And cast lots upon Jerusalem,
> Even thou wast as one of them...
> Neither shouldest thou have stood in the crossway
> To cut off those of his that did escape;
> Neither shouldest thou have delivered up those of
> his
> That did remain in the day of distress.

Today during my hours of duty, I noticed several dozen people stopping to look at the same poster. The Hebrew letter *lamed* in the text it quotes is drawn in such a way as to suggest hands stretched out in prayer. These spectators must have known Hebrew, and I could read on their faces feelings of mingled satisfaction and fear before the audacity of the young artist.[5]

OCTOBER 1, 1941

The Nazis strictly follow the Jewish calendar. Yesterday before sunset, at the time of the Kol Nidre prayers which open the Day of Atonement services, big white placards were posted with the sad announcement that before October 5, the inhabitants of the right side of Sienna Street, of sections of Gesia and Muranowska Streets, and of a number of houses near the ghetto boundaries must leave their apartments.

Thus the ransom paid by the inhabitants of these streets was of no avail—what everyone feared has actually come to pass. At first there was a panic, but as soon as night came, the cellar of our house was filled with worshipers and the sounds of suppressed lamentations could be heard. Absorbed in their prayers, they forgot for a while what surrounded them. Outside a guard was posted in front of the doorway to warn them should a German beast come down the street.

As though to emphasize the sad mood of our people, it has been raining all day without interruption. My father stayed in the cellar the entire day and prayed to God while my mother looked for a new apartment. She has not found anything so far, but brought home a new piece of sad news. It seems that the Nazis are going to liquidate the so-called Little Ghetto and add only Chlodna Street and the further end of Zelazna to the Big Ghetto.

This rumor is confirmed by the fact that the Christian tenants of these two streets have received an order to move out before October 15. The inhabitants of Sienna Street are supposed to be given apartments on Chlodna. But this will be done later, and for the time being we must find some roof over our heads. Tomorrow morning all of us, including myself, will set out to look for an apartment.

OCTOBER 3, 1941

A large number of the tenants of our house have moved out, but we still are unable to find an apartment. Today, together with my Aunt Lucia, I went around all day in a rickshaw, but found nothing. The addresses I obtained happened to be in the remotest corners of the ghetto. At first we "drove" to Stawki Street,[6] where we were told three rooms were available, but they turned out to be three dirty holes in the wall and the kitchen had no running water. The region around there is completely deserted, and it is nothing but ruins and piles of ashes. The nearest means of communication, that is to say, the nearest "Kohn-Heller," is several blocks away. And the price asked for this apartment is two hundred zlotys a month. Then we went to Nalewki Street and saw a room with a kitchen on the fifth floor, half-ruined. At Smocza Street, we were shown a room where there still lay the body of a man who had died of typhus the night before. The landlady told us that the room would be free as soon as the corpse was removed.

We ran away quickly, and gave up any further search. At this moment, as I write these lines, my parents are out looking for a place to live. I have mobilized all my friends, boys and girls, to help us. It is lucky that they at least do not have to look for apartments.

OCTOBER 6, 1941

Yesterday we were in a state of utter despair. The cart with our furniture was ready, and we planned to occupy temporary quarters in the room of my schoolmate, Zosia Zakheim, at 24 Panska Street. Suddenly, Ola Szmuszkiewicz, my friend, came running to tell us that she had found two rooms for us in a large comfortable apartment on Leszno Street, where there is even a piano.

The emaciated horse with the heavily laden cart turned into Chlodna Street. We all had to help push it. We saw several other groups of people helping half-dead mares.

My father is remaining at Sienna Street for the time being, as the Germans ordered all Jewish janitors to remain at their posts until Gentile janitors replace them. Thus Father is alone

97

in the empty house. Today I brought him some food and spent a while there. Sienna Street has a frightening appearance. The whole neighborhood, which bustled with activity only a few days ago, is now deserted. A fence of barbed wire has been set up across the middle of the street. From time to time an armed Nazi guard or a Polish or Jewish policeman appears. The windows are closed everywhere and the openings pasted with paper. The Jewish sanitary squads completely disinfected all the houses before handing them over for the use of the Aryan Polish population.

On some balconies there are still boxes with half-faded plants. On Lutka Leder's balcony a few tomato plants remain. The little red balls shake in the wind. Apparently, before leaving, Lutka forgot to pick the precious fruit that she had nursed throughout the summer. She was very upset at having to leave because she thus became separated from her neighbor, Kazik Briliant, who has now moved to a quarter situated very far from hers, and thus all the hopes she had woven around him have been destroyed.

I wandered for a long time on the staircase of our house, and in my ears there still resounded the conversations and laughter that I used to hear through the open doors and the sounds of pianos and phonographs. So many pleasant memories are associated with the house on Sienna Street. Our youth committee did excellent work there, and our house committee, too, was a model for all other house committees. Our tenants got along well together. From there we also had a view of the other side, and thus maintained the illusion that we were at the very gates of freedom.

OCTOBER 10, 1941
Today the first snow has fallen. Strangely enough, every year since the outbreak of the war the first snow has fallen on my birthday. From the adjoining room comes the smell of freshly baked cookies. Miss Sala is bustling about in the kitchen,

preparing a meal for the guests I have invited. Her little hands are moving fast. I can see her putting tiny pieces of dough carefully on a pan. My God, how terribly thin she is! She has lost a great deal of weight since the last time I saw her.

Miss Sala was my governess for several years. She was brought to me when I was nine years old, after a number of nurses had resigned from the position because they could not endure my caprices. My mother often tells me what an unbearable child I was. I would not let anyone come near me and I was wild, untamed, unmanageable. But tiny Miss Sala found favor in my sight, not because I respected her, but because I pitied her. For the first few days I made her suffer, but then I suddenly changed my tactics. Miss Sala was happy with us, and began to love me and my sister as though we were her own children. She stayed with us until the outbreak of the war and became almost my second mother. When we fled from Lodz, my mother left many valuables with her so that she might sell them and use the money for her support. Some time later, she, too, fled to Warsaw together with her family and found us here. Her father and brother are violinists. Formerly they were members of a good café orchestra; now they play in the streets and give music lessons. One of her four sisters is a teacher of mathematics at an illegal private school. Her youngest sister died of typhus two months ago, and now her mother is in bed. Miss Sala is keeping alive with the last ounce of her strength. She often visits us, tries to make herself useful, and takes her meals with us.

I often watch her consume several bowls of soup and eat our leftovers voraciously, as though all the hunger of the ghetto were concentrated in her. I cannot understand where all this food disappears in her tiny thin body. After eating she timidly cuts off a few slices of bread and wraps them in a piece of paper, saying that she has eaten enough and she will finish her bread later. But I know that she keeps it for her sick starving mother.

Now she is in the kitchen, preparing cookies for my well-fed friends, while her family suffers so terribly from hunger.

It is really frivolous to celebrate birthdays when there is so much unhappiness and misery around us. Uncle Percy is gravely ill with typhus. His condition is almost hopeless, and my mother spends entire days with him. Several former inhabitants of Sienna Street have died of typhus after moving to their new quarters; from our house alone, six persons have died, among them Engineer Sapoczynski and the wife of the lawyer Zalszupin. Typhus spreads with frightening speed. Yesterday I discovered a louse on myself. If it was contaminated I shall show the first symptoms of the disease in two weeks.

It is under such circumstances that I am waiting for the friends I invited to my birthday party, of which they have been reminding me for the last several weeks, so that I had not the courage to deny them this pleasure.

My friends have just left. We spent a few pleasant hours together, transported into a completely different world. My guests were Bronka Kleiner, Irka Bialokorska, Ola Szmusz-kiewicz, Edzia, Vera Neuman, Lutka Leder, Romek, Tadek, Dolek, Edek, and even Harry left his bed to be at the party. We talked a great deal and discussed our plans for after the war. I had to read several passages from my diary, which everyone praised, and several of my friends brought me nicely bound little notebooks to continue my journal.

We drank cherry liqueur, which my mother had made in the first year of the war. We proposed several toasts and even sang the traditional birthday song, "A Hundred Years."[7] At the end, Romek played the piano while we danced. A few minutes before nine all the guests went home.

Tadek and Romek, who live near by, were the last to leave. I walked with them a little way. When we went out of my warm room into the snowstorm, an icy wind cut our faces, and the cold penetrated to the marrow of my bones, although I was wearing a fur coat. The only light came from the snow and the night signs of the stores. Instead of the former neon lights, the shop windows now have black paper shades that do not let through the slightest reflection. But despite the darkness, it is possible to read the inscriptions pasted in white paper strips on the black shades, and they help us to distinguish food stores from stationery stores.

Along the walls sat huddled human figures like discarded bundles of rags. At one point I stumbled over a human body; in the darkness I did not notice that I had walked on a corpse. It was a half-naked corpse, covered only with a few fluttering newspapers that the wind tried in vain to tear away from the stones put on them to hold them down. The long milk-white legs were rigid and straight.

Back from this ghastly trip, I found my mother had returned from Uncle Percy's. Today the doctor gave him the last decisive injections; if they do not help him, he is lost. Rutka feels much better, but she still will not let anyone come near her except my sister Anna, who does not leave her bedside for a minute.

OCTOBER 29, 1941
Today I went with Romek to the opening of a play at the Femina Theater. It was a musical comedy dealing with present-day life in the ghetto, entitled *Love Looks for an Apartment*. A young couple is shown looking for a place to live. After long search and much traveling about in "Kohn-Hellers," they succeed in finding a tiny room in the home of a wily landlady who has divided a large room into two parts in order to be able to rent it to two couples. She manages to find a second couple for the other half of the room, and then the excitement begins.

It so happens that neither of the two couples is well adjusted; as a result, two illicit love affairs develop, at first secretly, but, because of the overcrowded living conditions of the people involved, they soon become known. The two husbands switch rooms, and for a while everyone is happy, but then the husbands begin to quarrel with their former wives.

At night, when the two men come home exhausted from looking for jobs, they find their wives flirting with the president of the House Committee, who sings a funny little song about the various taxes he has to collect for the community.

The end of the two love affairs is a sad one: all four young people are evicted for non-payment of rent. The play concludes with a mass scene in a trolley car in which the travelers tell facetious stories about life in the ghetto, especially the various committees and commissions, whose number is constantly growing.

The audience laughed heartily and spent a few pleasant hours in the comfortable theater, completely forgetting the dangers that lurk outside. The author of the play is Jurandot,[8] and the principal parts are acted by Stefania Grodzienska, Aleksander Minowicz, Rigelski, Noemi Wentland. Liebermann painted the settings.

At the theater I met many acquaintances, among them Ola Szmuszkiewicz, my schoolmate whom I had not seen for a year. She was with the policeman Max Bekerman. His father, who died of typhus two months ago, occupied a high post in the Jewish ghetto police. During the First World War he was one of the founders of the Polish Legion, and a close friend of Marshal Jozef Pilsudski.[9] The funeral rites of police commandant Bekerman were celebrated with great solemnity. All the community officials, the whole Jewish police force, and thousands of civilians accompanied him to his last resting place.

I also met Edzia with her friend Zelig Silberman, who was one of the most successful smugglers of Sienna Street before it was separated from the ghetto. He has made a fortune in this business and wants to marry Edzia, but her parents are opposed to the match because she is much younger than him. Edzia is only seventeen and Zelig is thirty years old. However, this difference in age does not prevent them from loving each other.

There are many such couples in the ghetto, of quite young girls and older men. One seldom meets a woman or a man alone. Men and women are attracted to each other even more than in normal times, as though thirsty for protection and tenderness. To have a close friend helps you to conquer your dejection. None wants to be alone. Yet morality in the ghetto is just as strong as in pre-war times.

The number of marriages has dropped recently as compared with the first months of the war. The chief cause of this is the shortage of apartments, which is a serious problem in the ghetto. A special office of the community has been created to cope with this situation, but it can do almost nothing. Its task is to find suitable subtenants for owners of vacant rooms and to see to it that young couples enjoy some degree of privacy. But today everyone's nerves are jumpy and the subtenants generally do not get along with their landlords. Very often they are unable to pay rent, and the landlords have nothing to live on. Moreover, the community collects various taxes. Few people today are earning their living by doing normal work. Real money can be made only in dishonest deals, but not many people engage in them; most Jews choose to go hungry rather than become tools in the hands of the Nazis.

But sometimes people are compelled to accept this role. If a person is caught committing a minor violation of the laws, such as wearing the armband in a manner slightly different from that prescribed, he is arrested and tortured. Such a person is often anxious to commit suicide, but has no easy way of doing it. The Germans find their victims among these tortured people whose spirit and body are broken, and confront them with the choice of life or death. Such people lose all power of resistance; they agree to anything, and thus automatically become tools of the Gestapo. Their chief function is informing. The Nazis want to know who owns jewelry or foreign currency. An informer can never get out of the Nazis' clutches; he must "accomplish" something to pay for the favor of being allowed to live and receive food. And the Nazis keep threatening him with the renewal of the same tortures.

There are a number of such Gestapo agents in the ghetto, but they are not really dangerous, for they are more or less known and, whenever they can, they even warn the prospective victims of the Gestapo against projected house searches. However, there are a few underworld characters who are really dangerous, because they take their services for the Gestapo seriously, just as they used to commit crimes in dead earnest.[10]

Even these sad conditions give rise to various bits of gossip and jokes among us, and serve as material for songs and skits that are sung and played in cafés and theaters.

Every day at the Art Café on Leszno Street one can hear songs and satires on the police, the ambulance service, the rickshaws, and even the Gestapo, in a veiled fashion. The typhus epidemic itself is the subject of jokes. It is laughter through tears, but it is laughter. This is our only weapon in the ghetto—our people laugh at death and at the Nazi decrees. Humor is the only thing the Nazis cannot understand.

These programs are tremendously successful. I used to be indignant at the jokes, which took as their butt the most tragic events in ghetto life, but I have gradually come to realize that there is no other remedy for our ills. Marionettes have been made to represent our community leaders and the presidents of the various welfare institutions. One of the most abundant sources of the new humor is the conversations heard in the "Kohn-Heller" trolleys.

As for the owners of these trolley cars, everyone is now talking about the child to whom Madame Kohn gave birth a week ago. Mr. Kohn informed the population of this event by means of gigantic placards which were posted not only in the trolley cars, but also on the walls of the principal streets. This placard announced that the circumcision rites would take place in a large hall, that a solemn reception and dinner would be given to important guests, and that the occasion would be used to collect money for relief.

I read this placard with a feeling of disgust, and I saw many people spit as they finished perusing this tactless declaration of the allegedly charitable purpose of a lavish party organized in the midst of starvation.

Fantastic stories circulate about the luxurious lives of Messrs. Kohn and Heller. Every day they give receptions while in front of their door people die of hunger. These two gentlemen have other sources of income in addition to their trolley cars. They play an important role in the so-called *Transferstelle*.[11] This institution, supported by the Germans, is concerned with the exchange of various types of merchandise between the ghetto and the Aryan part of Warsaw. Everything that enters the ghetto legally is controlled by this office, which takes a handsome commission on every transaction. Kohn and Heller have great influence at the *Transferstelle* and they are often bribed by businessmen on both sides of the wall. Thus they act as intermediaries between the Germans and the owners of the various loads of foodstuffs and industrial goods that pass from the ghetto to the Aryan part of Warsaw, and vice versa. The starving people of the ghetto must all pay higher prices for bread and potatoes in order to fill Mr. Kohn's and Mr. Heller's pockets.

NOVEMBER 15, 1941

Two new classes for younger students have been opened at our school. Our present quarters are much smaller than our old ones on Sienna Street. Often we are unable to hear our teachers because of the noise from the adjoining rooms, which are separated from ours by the thinnest of partitions. Of the former one hundred students in our class, only about twenty-five remain. Many are unable to pay the tuition fees and a great number have perished of typhus.

Here we have no central heating, such as we had on Sienna Street. Our hands freeze and it is impossible to hold a pencil. We sit in our coats and woolen gloves. The little iron stove in the middle of the classroom is insufficient to heat it. The enormous Venetian windows are covered with ice on both sides. The stove is heated with the wood of the benches that once stood in the corridors.

Recently a great number of "educational circles" have been formed at the various schools for the purpose of studying subjects that are officially forbidden. These circles were formed spontaneously out of our deep need.

At the meetings of these circles Polish is chiefly spoken, but in many cases, Yiddish or Hebrew is used as a matter of principle. The interest in Hebrew has increased tremendously, because the youth are pinning their hopes to a great extent on Palestine. In some circles, the language used is English or French, usually the former. Many of my friends are taking special courses in English. English literature is read very widely.

The conspiratory character of these circles brings them close to the underground political movement. Often our meetings are held in the same rooms and basements where the cells of the political parties meet.

The number of underground bulletins is growing daily. No one in particular circulates them; they simply travel from hand to hand, and who received them first remains a mystery.

CHAPTER VIII

HORROR STALKS
THE STREETS

NOVEMBER 22, 1941

Today the annual winter-relief collections began. The president of the community, Engineer Czerniakow, together with all the members of the council, stood in the street with collection boxes and stuck paper flowers in the lapels of the givers.

The community announced a contest for a poster in connection with this relief campaign. Dr. Poznanski, the educational director of the community, came to our class to explain the conditions of the contest. The last day for submitting designs is December 24.

Today on my way home from school, I dropped in to see Rutka, who is now finally out of danger. I found her lying on a field cot. She looked like a child, with her pale face, her silvery blonde hair clipped short, and her dull eyes. When she saw me, her white lips smiled, and she tried to raise her head. Then she began to whisper. Her weak body trembled and her head shook nervously as she made an effort to speak.

At first I had the impression that she had lost her mind. She spoke in short incoherent sentences. But after overcoming the initial difficulties, she began to sound more sensible. "Now I'm well again; at last I've gotten over it. Why do you look at me like that? Have I changed so much? Tell me the truth!"

My eyes were filled with tears and I was unable to utter a word. Rutka looked like a corpse. That is what typhus does to you. I tried to persuade her that she looked well and that in a few days no trace of her illness would remain. However, I sounded unconvincing and was feeling more and more embarrassed, when suddenly the doorbell rang and Romek came in. The subject of our conversation changed at once. Romek was left practically unscarred by his attack of typhus, which he had in an exceptionally mild form. He is in very good shape now.

I have a feeling that Rutka will never completely recover. Will she ever be able to walk? For the time being she cannot even sit up.

Uncle Percy, too, has recovered. He was saved by the powerful injections our energetic doctor gave him. Today he came with his wife, Lucia, to visit us for the first time since his illness. He barely moved and leaned on Lucia all the time. He looks like the ruins of his former self. No more than twenty-seven years old, he used to be strong and handsome, and now he is hunched over and all skin and bones. At every step in the ghetto one encounters such human wrecks, and these are the lucky ones who succeeded in escaping the Angel of Death.

Outside, a blizzard is raging and the frost paints designs on the window-panes. During these terribly cold days, one name is on everyone's lips: Kramsztyk, the man who presides over the distribution of fuel. Alas, the amount of coal and wood the Germans have assigned to the ghetto is so small that it is barely sufficient to heat the official buildings, such as the community administration, the post office, the hospitals, and the schools, so that almost nothing is left for the population at large. On the black market, coal fetches fantastic prices and often cannot be obtained at all.

In the streets, frozen human corpses are an increasingly frequent sight. On Leszno Street in front of the court building, many mothers often sit with children wrapped in rags from which protrude red frost-bitten little feet. Sometimes a mother cuddles a child frozen to death, and tries to warm the inanimate little body. Sometimes a child huddles against his mother, thinking that she is asleep and trying to awaken her, while, in fact, she is dead. The number of these homeless mothers and children is growing from day to day. After they have given up their last breath they often remain lying on the street for long hours, for no one bothers about them.

The little coaches of Pinkiert's funeral establishment are constantly busy. When a beggar sees a usable piece of clothing on a dead body, he removes it, covers the nude corpse with an old newspaper, and puts a couple of bricks or stones on the paper to prevent it from being blown away by the wind. On

Chlodna Street Bridge in the Warsaw Ghetto, 1942. The Wattenberg family lived in one of the apartment buildings near the bridge before being sent to Pawiak prison

Komitetowa and Grzybowska Streets fewer beggars are seen this year than last; they have simply died off.

Hunger is assuming more and more terrible forms. The prices of foodstuffs are going up. A pound of black bread now costs four zlotys, of white bread, six zlotys. Butter is forty zlotys a pound and sugar, from seven to eight zlotys a pound.

It is not easy to walk in the street with a parcel in one's hand. When a hungry person sees someone with a parcel that looks like food, he follows him and, at an opportune moment, snatches it away, opens it quickly, and proceeds to satisfy his hunger. If the parcel does not contain food, he throws it away. No, these are not thieves; they are just people crazed by hunger.

The Jewish police cannot cope with them. And, indeed, who would have the heart to prosecute such unfortunates?

DECEMBER 1, 1941

The Germans have assigned a large load of potatoes to the ghetto. At first, people were surprised at such sudden generosity. But their surprise did not last long. It turned out that this load was originally destined for the Nazi soldiers on the Russian front but had frozen en route. Then the Germans opened their Nazi hearts and sent the frozen potatoes to the Jews in the ghetto.

Now long lines are forming in front of the various food stores. People are trying to get a few frozen potatoes, for, although they cannot be cooked as such, they make excellent pancakes. Everywhere you go, the smell of fried potato pancakes assails your nostrils. For fat we use black hemp oil, the cheapest there is. Even it costs eight zlotys a pound.

Miss Sala beamed with joy when my mother gave her some of these potatoes. Laden with a few bags of the damp rotting things, she ran home to her family to quiet their hunger. Her mother died a few weeks ago, and her father is in bed with typhus.

The epidemic is still raging unabated. Several people are buried in one grave. Because of the shortage of medical personnel, a medical course has been opened at Number 3 Leszno Street to train a large number of nurses and supplement the knowledge of the former medical students.

The hygienic conditions are constantly deteriorating. Most of the sewage pipes are frozen, and in many houses the toilets cannot be used. Human excrement is often thrown out into the street together with the garbage. The carts that used regularly to remove the garbage from the courtyards now come rarely or not at all. For the time being all this filth is disinfected by the cold. But what will happen when the first spring breeze begins to blow? There is serious apprehension that a cholera epidemic will break out to fill our cup of misfortune to the brim.

DECEMBER 9, 1941

America's entry into the war has inspired the hundreds of thousands of dejected Jews in the ghetto with a new breath of hope. The Nazi guards at the gates have long faces. Some are considerably less insolent, but on others the effect has been exactly opposite and they are more unbearable than ever. Most people believe that the war will not last long now and that the Allies' victory is certain.

Reports have reached us from the Lodz Ghetto that the Germans have confiscated all furs, warm underwear, and woolen clothes, even talliths. It is expected that the turn of the Warsaw Ghetto will soon come.

DECEMBER 11, 1941

Today I learned many interesting details about a quite separate little world in the ghetto. These are the converts, who are perhaps the most tragic figures among us. I had seen them on several occasions, but until now I had no close contact with them. Recently I came to know them through Julia Tarnowska, a student in one of the lower grades of our school.

Julia is the daughter of the writer, Marceli Tarnowski. She is an eccentric and likes to attract attention. The very first day she came to school I had a clash with her on the subject of her Jewish origin.

Julia, like her parents, is a convert. She learned of her Jewish origin only when her family received the order to move out of their apartment on the Aryan side and take up quarters in the ghetto. This incident shook her deeply, and she has not yet resigned herself to her fate. She is constantly indignant and angry, and I have a feeling that she is more resentful against the Jews than the Nazis. She considers her lot the result of a fatal mistake, for which I and others like me are responsible.

Around her neck she wears a large silver cross, and she tries to persuade everyone that she is a faithful Christian who has nothing in common with Judaism. Once, as I listened to her talk, I remarked heatedly that Christ, too, was a Jew but was never ashamed of his origin, and then I returned to my desk. The whole classroom was silent, and Julia did not dare answer me. Apparently, she felt that I was right and that all the other students agreed with me.

The next day she approached me as though nothing had happened, and from then on she has been speaking in a quite different tone. She no longer discusses these questions, and the cross has disappeared from her neck. Perhaps she now wears it lower down, or she may even have removed it altogether.

Because of this incident with Julia Tarnowska I became interested in the Jewish Christians of the ghetto. Their numbers now reached several thousands, and the Nazis have brought them together from several countries. The majority are converts of the Hitler period, that is to say, those who went over to Christianity during the very recent years, hoping to escape the fate of the persecuted Jews. But there are also converts who left the Jewish faith decades ago, and whose children were brought up as pious Christians. These children were accustomed to go to church every Sunday, and their souls were even poisoned with anti-Semitism taught them by their own parents, who thus tried to eradicate every trace of their Jewish origin.

These Christian-born children of Jewish parents are now living through a double tragedy as compared with Jewish children. They feel entirely lost, and there have even been cases of suicide among them, while there have been no such cases among the Jewish youth.

However, there are also Christians of distant Jewish origin who have been brought back to Judaism by the Nazis' ferocious persecutions of the Jews. A number of Christians of the third generation who did not have to go to the ghetto spontaneously went to the Gestapo and demanded to be sent there. These returned Christians wear the armband with pride, as a kind of new crown of thorns and martyrdom.

In the present ghetto there are three churches: the one on the square before the Iron Gate, which was partly demolished by bombs, another on Leszno Street, near Karmelicka, and a third on Zelazna Street. Only the Leszno Street church is open, and regular services are held there, and the priests, too, are of Jewish origin.

The converts have their own kitchens, the most important of which is near the half-demolished church by the Iron Gate. It seems that the converts are favored by the Nazis because the meals are much better and cheaper there than in other ghetto kitchens. This is supposed to serve as a lure for the missionary work the converts are carrying on.

Julia once invited me to her home, where I met her father, a thin middle-aged man of medium height. He stoops somewhat, and his forehead is covered with deep wrinkles. She has confided to me that he is working night and day at a book on the ghetto.

THE DIARY OF MARY BERG

DECEMBER 14, 1941
Today I attended a concert by Vera Gran. She is extremely
successful. She sings classical songs and modern songs by the
young composer Kuba Kohn, a product of the ghetto. His
music expresses all the sadness and resistance of the ghetto. It
has a new and original note that could only have been born in
this atmosphere of suffering, torture, and dogged endurance.

DECEMBER 17, 1941
Today we received a communication from the housing office
concerning the janitorial job my father is supposed to take
over at 10 Chlodna Street. He must go there at once, but we
shall be allowed to move in only after the street is walled up.

The same order has been sent to all the Jewish janitors who
were assigned to houses on Chlodna Street, which is now
joined to the ghetto. They must clean and put in order the
houses left by the Gentile tenants and prepare them for their
future Jewish occupants.

Romek, who is employed as an overseer at the construction
of the ghetto walls, is now working on Chlodna Street and
often takes over food for my father. Romek works hard. His
face is dark brown as though sunburned, but I know it has
been tanned by the frosty wind. He now remains out in the
cold for twelve hours a day, and his fingers are frost-bitten.
Yesterday he came to see me and, as usual, sat down at the
piano. He placed his long narrow hands on the keyboard, but
his fingers, which once could conjure up marvelous sounds,
now lay motionless and silent. I saw that he was struggling; his
face was distorted in a painful grimace, but his swollen rigid
hands would not obey him. He sat thus for a while, quite
silent, then lifted his fingers off the keyboard, turned to me
and asked, in a voice choked with tears, "Do you think I'll ever
be able to play again?"

I was silent. I looked at his hands, and could not believe
they were the same hands that not so long ago had moved

nimbly over the piano. Romek was terribly dejected, and I felt that he was trying to control himself so as not to burst into bitter weeping. All his hopes are gone, for instead of playing the piano, he must incessantly walk up and down the ghetto boundaries and see to it that the walls are solid, that no loose bricks are left through which food could be smuggled in at night.

At the same time as the wall is going up on Chlodna Street, a bridge is being built to connect the sidewalks, for the street itself is destined as a traffic corridor for the Aryan part of the town. All the building materials for this must be supplied by the Jewish community.

DECEMBER 24, 1941

Today everyone on the Aryan side is wearing his Sunday best. I even fancy that I can smell the odor of good food. It is Christmas Eve. Only half a year ago there were rumors that by Christmas the war would be over and that on November 11— Armistice Day—the Allied troops would march into Warsaw. True, there are foreign troops in Warsaw; whole battalions of them are marching in the streets in green uniforms, but they are enemy troops who terrorize the population.

The Nazis have just ordered that before January 1, 1942— what a New Year's gift!—the ghetto inhabitants must surrender all their furs, fur coats, collars, muffs, and even odd pieces of fur. Several collection centers have been organized by the community for this purpose. The order was signed by Commissioner Auerswald.

So far no one has been in a hurry to carry it out. Everywhere one hears mysterious whispering. People are discussing whether it is better to sell their furs or hide them. Many Poles are using this opportunity to sneak into the ghetto to buy up expensive astrakhans, silver foxes, and mink at ridiculously low prices. People prefer to sell their furs for a song rather than surrender them to the Germans. But some have made up their minds to hide them, and try to find various caches. The penalty for concealing the smallest piece of fur is death. But the death penalty threatens us on so many counts that this new one simply brings smiles to our lips.[1]

Today was the last day for submitting designs for winter-relief posters at our school. The jury will be composed of our teachers and directors Poznanski and Jaszunski, and will be presided over by Engineer Czerniakow. The results will be announced at the beginning of January.

DECEMBER 26, 1941
We have received permission to move to Chlodna Street, and today I went to visit our new house. It is an old two-story building which was once the home of a Polish magnate of the seventeenth century. The winding, narrow staircase, the Gothic turrets and bas-reliefs on the façade bring to mind a medieval castle. It looks very romantic. In the courtyard is a

Tadek Szajer (middle, in his Ambulance Service uniform)
with friends in the ghetto

smaller building that was added later, and in it is the Warszawianka bakery, which has now been taken over by Jewish bakers. The wall is built at the corner of this house. Thus we shall live at the very frontier of the ghetto. The red bricks are growing higher and higher, as well as the bridge at the corner of Chlodna and Zelazna Streets.[2] Everywhere we are walled up, locked in.

DECEMBER 28, 1941

Today we had a party, organized for the young designers. The students decorated the hall magnificently, and there was entertainment. On a small stage built at one end artists appeared. I took part in the program and sang a few songs in English. We danced to the tunes of an orchestra. It was warm, for the little iron stove was full of crackling wood from the school benches. There was even a buffet which served cookies and drinks. But the price of a cookie was three zlotys and of a small glass of liqueur, five zlotys.

The teachers danced with their pupils, and the general mood was cheerful, but I could not stop thinking of Romek, standing outside in the cold overseeing the construction of the ghetto walls.

I went home before eight o'clock. The sharp wind penetrated my bones. I am writing these words by the light of a carbide lamp. Its bluish flame does not flicker—it is as if it were petrified.

When I came home I found a sealed envelope which Tadek Szajer had left for me. It contained his photograph in his ambulance-man uniform. He now works as a volunteer for the ambulance service in order to appease his sense of guilt,[3] for he feels partly responsible for his father's unsavory deals.

On the back of the photograph is an inscription which shows how his conscience is plaguing him: "Some day, years hence, when I am far from you, you will perhaps recall the ambulance service, 13 Leszno Street... and Tadek who loves you very, very much." Near the inscription is the red trademark of Photo-Baum-Forbert, which has always been one of the largest photographic firms in Warsaw and is now the best in the ghetto. Mr. Baum, who is well known for his films, *The Polish Woods* and *Lamed Vuv*, is somewhere in Soviet Russia, and the business is now being managed by the two brothers Forbert.

There are several other photographers in the ghetto, for instance, Photo-Doris, but all the artistic world has its pictures taken at Baum-Forbert's. Even high Nazi army men and officials are among their customers.

CHAPTER IX

ANOTHER YEAR

DECEMBER 31, 1941

The last day of the old year... Let the days run as fast as possible; maybe we shall survive the war in spite of everything, and escape alive out of the ghetto walls. The café strategists say that the Allied offensive will start in the spring of 1942. Meanwhile, the Russians are fleeing and surrendering city after city. The only good news comes from Africa, but that is so far away.

Today, our theater group is giving a performance at Weisman's hall. The tickets were sold out two days ago. All the receipts will go to Korczak's children's home.

JANUARY 1, 1942

I feel completely empty, as though I were suspended over an abyss. Last night was a mixture of entertainment and nightmare. After the performance, my friends of the LZA suggested that we spend New Year's Eve at my home. My parents had gone to sleep in their new apartment on Chlodna Street, so we could spend the night here undisturbed. My guests were Harry with his beloved Anka Laskowska, Dolek with Stefa

Musskat, Bronek, Romek, and a few other couples. Instead of champagne, we had lemonade, and instead of cake, sandwiches of little pickled fishes, the so-called "stinkies." On my table the little carbide lamp was lit. The humming of its flame was drowned in the conversation, but the gas it emanated smelled all the stronger in the stuffy air of the room.

The hours flew fast, but about midnight I noticed that the little flame of the lamp had begun to grow alarmingly small, and I had forgotten to buy additional carbide for this New Year's Eve. Harry comforted me by saying it was fitting to meet the New Year in darkness.

At the same moment Dolek looked at his watch and cried, "Midnight is approaching." For a while there was complete silence. Romek went to the piano as the slow ringing of the clock striking twelve came from the nearby church tower.

Before the clock (which we accompanied in chorus) had ceased ringing, the narrow flame of my lamp began to grow longer and narrower, then it went out with a crackle. At that moment the clock struck for the twelfth time. The room was dark. I pulled up the black paper shade and some light came in. Outside a light snow was falling and the moon floated slowly across the cloudy sky.

In the semidarkness I saw Romek place his fingers on the keyboard. With a great effort he began to play Chopin's Funeral March. No one said a word. Anka huddled close to Harry, Dolek to Stefa, Tadek to Bronek—all of them were together; only I was alone. Sad ideas flashed through my mind. Was not all this symbolic? Was there not something terrible in store for me, something that would separate me from my friends?

Suddenly someone cried, "Romek, how about a different number? He has never been able to play the Funeral March, and now of all nights the Muse is helping him."

Romek did not answer. He tried a few other notes, but nothing came. At last, he rose from the piano and sat down by my side. "You know," he whispered, "I have a strange premonition on this New Year's Day, mark my words."

I do not know what he meant, but even in the semidarkness I could read utter despair in his eyes.

A little later we all began to talk. Harry said that our theater group no longer had any reason for existence because most of our members were gone, and that we would have to find new people, which was not easy. No one contradicted him. Apparently, we all felt the same. All of us were overwhelmed by the same apathy, the feeling that this was the end.

At six in the morning my guests began to leave. Romek was the last to go. At seven o'clock he had to be at his ghetto wall.

JANUARY 16, 1942

Today was the last day for surrendering our furs. The Nazis had granted two extensions of the term because they realized that no one was in a hurry to part with them. After the second extension, they began to make house searches accompanied by terrorism.

For three days there have been long lines in front of the community's collection centers, and the population has at last begun to carry out the Nazis' order. But the Nazis will not get much warmth out of our furs. Whatever could not be hidden or sold has been cut and ruined. The furs are full of holes, and the astrakhan or fox collars have their hair cut or shaven. In return for the furs, the owners receive a yellow slip for which they must pay a special tax of two zlotys.

It is said that the Nazis intend to use the furs for padding the boots of their soldiers who are freezing on the Russian front. But they did not succeed in taking much of their loot away from Warsaw, because the largest warehouses, which were outside the confines of the ghetto, were set on fire by agents of the underground.

Various fur substitutes are already on sale to replace the cut-off collars and linings.

We are now living on Chlodna Street. As the janitor's family we occupy two dark little rooms. There is no toilet. We do our cooking on a small iron stove. The walls are covered with ice, and when the stove warms up the ice begins to melt.

Chlodna Street, with its complicated geography, is a peculiar sight. The human traffic here is extraordinary too. A mass of people can be seen coming from the corner of Zelazna Street. They go to the wooden bridge, which is two stories high and connects the sidewalks on either side of the street. They fill the whole bridge, from which the entire length of the street can be seen. Walls extend along both sidewalks, and between the two walls, as though through a corridor, moves the Aryan population and the trolley cars. In the middle of the street between the two walls is St. Baromeus' Church, surrounded by ancient spreading linden trees.

Close to us is the ghetto's "Capitol." At 20 Chlodna Street are the residences of President Czerniakow, Colonel Szerynski, the chief of the Jewish police and the high officials of the various Jewish institutions. The photographic firm Baum-Forbert is at the same address, and a large portrait of Czerniakow has been hanging in front of the house for several days.

The President of the Provisions Office, Gepner, and Police Commissioners Leikin and Czerwinski also live on Chlodna Street. Commissioner Leikin occupies an apartment in our house. Marysia Eisenstadt, the "nightingale of the ghetto," and Hirschfield, the owner of the most popular Jewish café, have also moved to Chlodna Street.

The well-to-do, who could afford to bribe the officials of the housing office, got the best apartments on this street with its many large modern houses. Chlodna Street is generally considered the aristocratic street of the ghetto, just as Sienna Street was at the beginning.

The janitor at 8 Chlodna Street is Engineer Plonskier, formerly our neighbor on Sienna Street. Many doctors live in our street, and there is a doctor's or dentist's sign on almost every door.

At six in the morning, the janitors must remove the snow from the sidewalk, and Commissioner Leikin is teaching the former lawyers and professors their new trade. Often he takes a shovel or broom in his hands and gives a lesson to the helpless intellectuals whose fingers are not used to these new tools.

My father works hard and we help him, washing the staircase and sweeping the courtyard. There are only a small number of tenants in our house, and the income for opening the door after curfew amounts to no more than a few zlotys a night—only a fraction of what we got on Sienna Street. But he has another source of income. In our inner courtyard stands the Warszawianka bakery. Every night, a cart brings a dozen bags of contraband flour there, and each time my father opens the gate for such a transport he receives a certain sum of money, and in the morning he gets two small fresh loaves as an additional reward.

This is an accepted custom in all the courtyards where bakeries are situated, and many janitors even get a fixed percentage according to the number of bags they smuggle in. But my father has not yet advanced that far in his new profession.

FEBRUARY 5, 1942

Today was the solemn distribution of prizes among the participants in the contest for a winter-relief poster. I won the first prize—two hundred zlotys. President Czerniakow and Engineer Jaszunski, educational director of the community schools, personally handed the envelopes of money to the winners and made short speeches to each one.

The posters that won prizes are all in several colors and to print them these days would be very expensive. For the time being they will be hung in the meeting hall of the community, and smaller posters reproduced in two colors will be used for winter relief.

THE DIARY OF MARY BERG

FEBRUARY 20, 1942

The cold spells are increasingly severe. More and more frozen bodies can be seen in the streets. They lay near the doorways with their knees hunched up, petrified in the midst of their struggle against death. This is a hair-raising sight, but the passers-by are used to it.

A pound of potatoes now costs two zlotys. Only a few people in the ghetto are still eating normally: the managers of public kitchens, the very wealthy, and the food smugglers.

Thousands of ghetto workers depend upon the smugglers, and their situation literally changes from day to day. If during the preceding night a few large transports of food and raw materials have managed to reach the ghetto, the various underground workers are busy, but if a so-called "slaughter" has taken place, that is, if the Gestapo has intercepted a few loads of grain, leather, or other material, the workshops are empty and the workers go hungry.

There are hundreds of secret hand mills in which the smuggled grain is milled. The chaff, too, is sold as a special kind of flour which is used for black cakes. They taste like hay.

The secret hand mills are hidden in basements, attics, and in specially built underground cellars. They function for twenty-four hours a day, but the eight-hour day is strictly observed. The underground trade union sees to this, and there are three regular shifts. The work, which consists in constantly turning the handle of the mill by hand, is hard but well paid. A worker of average skill earns twenty to thirty zlotys a day, and the night shift receives a bonus of fifty per cent.

Various kinds of cereal, too, are made with these hand mills. Recently, Tadek Szajer, without his father's knowledge, took a job in such a cereal factory. His conscience drives him to do various useful jobs, because, as he told me, he does not wish to live on his father's unsavory business. Today he came to see me directly from his work, and showed me his

Searching for food in the courtyard of 41 Sienna Street,
drawn by Mary Berg

fingers covered with calluses from constantly turning the
handle of the hand mill.

I have a feeling that he is doing this only to impress me,
because thus far he has not given up his father's comfortable
apartment and abundant meals.[1]

There are also little factories for canning fish in the ghetto;
the fish used are the so-called "stinkies." Recently the smugglers managed to bring in a huge load of dried flounder. When
ground, these flounder taste like good herring, which is unobtainable in Poland at present. Various spreads are made of
these fish to be used with bread instead of fats.

Some of the shops manufacture horse sausage—real fat
salami. But this is an expensive product which only very few
can afford.

Numerous shops make various kinds of candy. Jewish
chemists in the ghetto have invented new sugar substitutes

and artificial syrups that give these sweets a strange taste. Where do the chemists get this stuff from? Often I think that they must know the secret of manna. Perhaps in ancient days, too, Jewish chemists invented various syrups and spices to season the grass which the Jews ate in the desert. There are no proper laboratories in the ghetto, and the chemists perform all these miracles in holes and dark cellars.

There are also secret tanneries, for the manufacture of leather is strictly controlled by the Nazis. Leather is subject to a quota, and the amount of raw hides assigned to the ghetto is so small that it is insufficient to fill even a fraction of our needs. Leather shoes are terribly expensive, but nevertheless there is a shoe fashion in the ghetto and those who can afford it wear officers' high boots. This fashion prevails for both men and women. The price of such a pair of boots is about fifteen hundred zlotys.

There are many new dyeing shops. Because of the shortage of raw materials, old clothes are cleaned and dyed. In this respect, too, our chemists are producing miracles. It is said that the dyes are made of bricks from the ghetto walls. The wiseacres say that gradually all the walls will be dismantled by the chemists. Tailors are very busy remodeling the dyed materials.

The doctors and drugstores do the biggest business of all in the ghetto. The doctors work in the hospitals, and they also have large private practices. But they are helpless when it comes to writing prescriptions. They know that the most indispensable pharmaceutical items are not to be found in the ghetto drugstores, for the Nazis allow only ridiculously small quantities of medicine to pass into the ghetto. The drugstores are controlled by the community and the pharmacists are officials employed by it.[2] This control was indispensable, because quite often poor people were unable to pay for their prescriptions. In this field again our chemists are doing marvelous work.

Thus we are independent of the outside world, so to speak. Not only have we ceased to receive from the outside a number of items that were never before manufactured in the ghetto, but we even export certain products such as cigarettes, saccharine, wine and liquors, shoes, watches, and even jewelry. All these commodities must pass through the *Transferstelle* and the high customs duties are pocketed by the Gestapo officials. Officially, the Jewish workers are producing for the German administration that supplies them with raw materials, but in fact, the German officials play the part of well-paid intermediaries between the ghetto and the merchants on the Aryan side.

FEBRUARY 22, 1942

Today we had an impassioned debate on poetry at our school. During the intermission, Rachel Perelman, one of the students, drew a copy of an underground paper out of her pocket. The paper had reprinted a fragment of Julian Tuwim's poem, "Polish Flowers," which the great Polish poet had written somewhere in exile.

"Where is Tuwim now?" someone asked.

"In England or America," answered Rachel.

All of us crowded around the small page of the newspaper, and read the stanzas by the poet whom we had always worshiped. The fact that the poem came from the free world increased our excitement, and we expected that this poet, who is a Jew, would send us a message of comfort.

We were disappointed. The poem was full of love for Poland, the masterful verses contained profound symbols, but there was not a word of the encouragement all of us thirsted for.

The discussion on this poem was quite heated. Some of us criticized the great poet for not being here with us; others said that it was fortunate that he had escaped, and that being abroad he might succeed in arousing the world to the knowledge of our bitter fate.

"But does he know of everything that is going on in the ghetto?" one student asked.

I tried to defend Tuwim, who comes from the same city as I. I remembered him coming to my father's store to buy pictures. "Perhaps he does suffer in his exile, perhaps his heart is full of longing for his native land," I said.

But my arguments had little effect. Julian Tuwim's young worshipers expected more vigorous poetry from their favorite poet in these stormy times. Nevertheless everyone pressed the little sheet of paper as though it were a sacred relic, and some even copied the verses. I too wrote them down:

> How did you smell, lilacs of Warsaw,
> When dressing the shambles in brilliance,
> Came, insolent and warlike,
> The first spring of our new slavery?[3]

FEBRUARY 24, 1942

Yesterday Eva Pikman came to see me with her friend Bola Rapoport. They asked me to give them the words of a few English songs that I had sung on the stage. Bola wants to be a café singer and she needs to build up a repertoire. I promised to make up a program for her. She is a charming girl of nineteen, a typical southern beauty. After we had talked a while, I discovered that her father is an American citizen, and that at present he is interned in the Laufen camp in Germany. She said that women would soon be interned, too. I must persuade my mother to report again to the Gestapo that she is an enemy alien. Perhaps we will then be interned with her, as her family. There is a rumor that civilian and military prisoners will soon be exchanged.

Recently a sensational report shook the ghetto. Colonel Szerynski was arrested on the Aryan side while trying to smuggle some furs for sale. He is in prison at present, and nobody knows what will happen to him.

FEBRUARY 27, 1942

Romek is now working on the construction of a new prison on Gesia Street—the Jewish quarter is being enriched with another public building. I wonder what kind of criminals will be placed there. Will it be the beggars who snatch parcels in the streets to still their hunger, or the starving, groaning unfortunates who lie near the walls, or perhaps those who cross the ghetto boundaries looking for employment? The Germans impose the death penalty on people who leave the ghetto, and several people have recently been shot for this crime. But no one cares—it is better to die of a bullet than of hunger.

In the provinces, closed quarters for Jews are being created everywhere, even in the villages. Nevertheless, many Jews are leaving Warsaw and moving to small towns, particularly around Lublin, where food is cheapest. At the same time, large transports of Jews are being brought to Poland from Germany, Austria, and Czechoslovakia. They are settled in those ghettos where they will most surely die of hunger and cold. Recently a large number of foreign Jews were brought to Lodz. The President of the Lodz Council of Elders, an eighty-year-old man, Rumkowski, unlike our inflexible President Czerniakowski, is easily led by the Nazis and treats the inhabitants of the ghetto as his subjects.

Rumkowski was recently in Warsaw. I saw him on Leszno Street walking with some high community official. He is gray, but well-preserved, and has a springy gait. On his sleeve he had a yellow armband with the inscription, in German: "President of the Jewish Community of Lodz." All the reports that we receive from my native city come as postal forms, beginning with the words: "President Rumkowski informs you that such and such a family is alive and in good health." Any other correspondence is forbidden.

Shootings have now become very frequent at the ghetto exits. Usually they are perpetrated by some guard who wants to amuse himself. Every day, morning and afternoon, when I go to school, I am not sure whether I will return alive. I have to go past two of the most dangerous German sentry posts: at the corner of Zelazna and Chlodna Streets near the bridge, and at the corner of Krochmalna and Grzybowska Streets. At the latter place there is usually a guard who has been nicknamed "Frankenstein," because of his notorious cruelty. Apparently this soldier cannot go to sleep unless he has a few victims to his credit; he is a real sadist. When I see him from a distance I shudder. He looks like an ape: small and stocky, with a swarthy grimacing face. This morning, on my way to school, as I was approaching the corner of Krochmalna and Grzybowska Streets,[4] I saw his familiar figure, torturing some rickshaw driver whose vehicle had passed an inch closer to the exit than the regulations permitted. The unfortunate man lay on the curb in a puddle of blood. A yellowish liquid dripped from his mouth to the pavement. Soon I realized that he was dead, another victim of the German sadist. The blood was so horribly red the sight of it completely shattered me.

A man is stopped by a Nazi gendarme in the ghetto,
drawn by Mary Berg

CHAPTER X

SPRING IS CRUEL

MARCH 30, 1942

It is getting warmer and warmer. Yesterday, after the long months of terrible cold, spring finally came. Since our court-yard is not covered with asphalt, my parents dug it up for a little garden. The seeds we bought at the Toporol have already been planted. The little green radish leaves were the first to appear in the black ground. We have also planted onions, car-rots, turnips, and other things. We even have some flowers. And at the beginning of April we shall plant tomatoes and sunflowers.

A few days ago a transport of Jews from Danzig arrived in Warsaw. I saw them as they were led into the ghetto. There were only women and children among them. The deportees carried elegant luggage and were dressed far better than our own ghetto people. All the men of this transport were sent to the disciplinary labor camp at Treblinka, the worst in the ter-ritory of the Gouvernement General. The German author-ities had promised all these wives and mothers that their men would return after a few months of labor in the camp. Various unverified rumors circulate about Treblinka. It is said that the workers live in barracks surrounded by four barbed wire fences and an electrically charged cable. Doctor Miechowski, a brother of my mother's friend, was offered the post of chief physician at Treblinka, and he accepted because of his desperate economic situation. The community at once paid his family the sum of 5,000 zlotys. It must be very hard work if so much money is paid for it.[1]

Rutka now visits us quite frequently. She looks much better and is improving every day. But her beautiful, silvery blonde hair has been shaved off. She wears a wig made of her own braids, which is an excellent imitation of her natural coiffure. Rutka is always cheerful. Her eyes shine with enthusiasm when she tells about the studies she has resumed after her long illness. She attends a secret private school, whose chief teacher and organizer is Professor Taubenszlak. Rutka, who is very gifted, likes her studies. She is an inseparable friend of my sister Ann, and they take English lessons together.

Through Rutka I receive letters from Tadek Szajer every day. He is now working very hard. I told him that I did not wish to see him any more, for his conversation makes me nervous. He asked to be allowed at least to correspond with me. Since he lives near Rutka, he gives her his letters. They are written on gray letter paper, and every word suggests a gray sadness. He writes that he longs for me and thinks of me all day long, that he is working hard and that his empty evenings are so hopeless... that he is lonely and waits only for the moment when he will see me again. He describes all his worries and troubles; his whole life is on these gray sheets of paper.

Romek is working as usual. He now looks much better, and has gained some self-assurance, perhaps because his wages have been raised—he now earns as much as thirty zlotys a day, sometimes more, and two loaves of bread in addition. He has a better job, but a more dangerous one. He directs a large group of workers, and is much more responsible than before for the fulfillment of particular tasks. He tells me that, at every step, the Nazi guards threaten to shoot him for no reason at all. Recently a guard shot a worker before his eyes because a few ounces of butter were found in his pocket. Romek has iron nerves. Work under such conditions is horrible, he is in constant danger of death, yet he looks much better. Perhaps it is because the weather has suddenly become so mild, as though we were not in March, but in May. And his hands, which were swollen in the winter, now show only a few scars from his frostbite.

Recently Harry and Anka paid me a visit. As usual, they cuddle against each other, full of their love. I noted that they wore rings on their fingers. "So you got married without telling me?" I asked. "No, these are just our engagement rings," Harry said, with a shining face. "The rabbi refuses to marry us because Anka is not of age and we must have permission from her parents... but her parents are opposed," he concluded, with a note of disappointment. "But that doesn't matter," said Anka, laughing. "We're married anyway. We don't need witnesses. No rabbi will ever be able to express in any document a union as strong as that which joins us now and forever."

I envy them. Perhaps it is better thus. They do not think so much of the general situation of the ghetto. They do not get as upset as the rest of us, and they pay more attention to their own inner lives. Perhaps that is the way it should be?

The political news is better. Since their defeat at Leningrad, the Germans seem to be much more on the defensive than before. But the end is not yet in sight and the way to victory is hard.

APRIL 14, 1942
This morning at six o'clock Bola Rapoport, together with her mother and two sisters, was interned in the Pawiak prison. A German car stopped at the addresses of the American citizens still remaining in the ghetto and collected all the women. Only Mr. Rakow, an American citizen, was left at his home,

together with his wife and two children, because he is gravely ill. I thought that my mother would be taken at any moment, but somehow no one came for her. This is natural enough; how could she be found now that she has moved out of Sienna Street without reporting her new address? She must go to the Gestapo; this might save all of us, or perhaps we shall all be interned together.

APRIL 15, 1942

Today we received a mysterious letter from Uncle Percy, who left a week ago for Zaklikow-Lubelski. He says that he has arrived, but that his trip was long and dangerous, and that he left Lublin just in time. What he means is perhaps explained by the news which Mrs. Minc, a tenant in our house, told us tonight after supper. A close relative of hers recently arrived in the ghetto, and related to her the details of the terrible massacre of Lublin,[2] during which he lost his wife and two children. Here is his story: "The Germans ordered all the Jews to leave their homes and gather on the square. The majority did not obey this order, and began to hide in cellars and attics. Some barricaded their apartments. Then strong formations of Elite Guards began to fire at the windows, and anyone who left his house was shot on the spot. Little children were finished off with revolvers; some people were tortured until they lost consciousness. About half of the ghetto population was murdered, and a considerable number were deported to an unknown destination. About two thousand Jewish people remained of the original forty thousand. These two thousand were taken to the Majdanek camp near Lublin. Even today the streets of the Lublin Ghetto are drenched in blood and the victims have not yet been picked up. The houses are full of corpses."

Her relative, an eyewitness of this massacre, managed to escape because he hid in a house which the Nazis overlooked. All night long he made his way through barbed-wire entanglements, and, by the greatest good luck, managed to get out.

All this sounds horrible, and I simply cannot believe it. To kill so many people in such a cruel way. Perhaps that was why Percy was forced to interrupt his trip. How he must have suffered, seeing this tragedy! By what miracle was he saved?

Recently wild rumors have begun to circulate in the ghetto. It is said that all the Jews will be settled in Arabia or somewhere near there. I wonder what it all means? Governor Frank has recently been rather mild in his decrees. Curfew is later, and the Germans seem to be planning the creation of regular workshops in Warsaw, which would insure steady jobs for the Jews. But this seems to contradict the talk of mass deportation.

The *Warschauer Zeitung*, the official German-language newspaper in Warsaw, writes that the Jews have at last become a useful element, and the production of the ghetto is advantageous for the German army. For a long time now we have not heard slogans such as "The Jews must disappear from Europe," which all the German press screamed last year. Now everything is quiet. Is this the lull before the storm? What is the significance of the pogrom in Lublin?

APRIL 17, 1942
I am almost hysterical. A little before six o'clock today the police captain, Hertz, rushed excitedly into our apartment and said, "Please be prepared for anything; at eight o'clock there is going to be a pogrom." Then he tore out without further explanations. The whole ghetto was seized with panic. People hastily closed their stores. There was a rumor that a special *Vernichtungskommando* (destructive squad), the same which had perpetrated the Lublin pogrom, had arrived in Warsaw to organize a massacre here. It was also said that Ukrainians and Lithuanians would now take over the guarding of the ghetto because the Germans were to go to the Russian front.

In the provisions office, all the employees were sent home at six, and were told to go to their houses as fast as possible. My mother hurriedly packed some food in a basket, and went with father to look for a safe refuge in a cellar. I was terrified and could not control my trembling. Every minute was like a century. The hours went by—seven, eight, nine... Now it is eleven o'clock, and a dead silence prevails in the city.

A few minutes ago someone knocked at the house door. We were sure it was the Germans. My father opened the door—it was a messenger from Jewish police headquarters coming to ask Police Captain Hertz to report immediately at Ogrodowa Street. Something really serious must have happened if he has been summoned so late at night.

The hours drag by slowly. Not a sound comes from the street. We are all dressed, ready to rush to our hideout at a moment's notice. It is horrible to live under this constant tension.

APRIL 28, 1942

The number seven seems to have a mysterious influence in my life. Something sudden, unexpected, always takes place on the dates which contain this number, especially when I forget that there is a seven in the date. Since the seventeenth of this month the ghetto has been living in constant terror. On the night between the seventeenth and the eighteenth, fifty-two persons were killed, mostly bakers and smugglers. All the bakers are terrified. Epstein and Wagner, who own the bakery in our house, no longer sleep at home. The Germans come to various houses with a prepared list of names and addresses. If they do not find the persons they are looking for, they take another member of the same family instead. They lead him a few steps in front of the house, politely let him precede them, and then shoot him in the back. The next morning these people are found lying dead in the streets. If a janitor fails to open the door for the Germans as quickly as they want him to, he is shot on the spot. If a member of the janitor's family opens the door, the same fate befalls him, and later the janitor is summoned to be killed, too.

Yesterday I went to see Eva Pikman. Bronka, Irka, and Rena were sitting there with gloomy faces. Zycho Rozensztajn, the son of Eva's landlord, was also there. Zycho is a policeman. He told us macabre stories—several nights in succession he was forced to attend executions, for the Germans demand that Jewish policemen help them to perpetrate their crimes. Usually a patrol of two or three German officers come to Jewish police headquarters with a list of names and demand that one high-ranking and one ordinary Jewish policeman be added to their ranks. Then they order the Jewish policemen to lead them to the addresses indicated.

Zycho sat deep in a chair; the rest of us sat on a cot. He was pale and shaken; several sleepless nights had left their mark on him. "If my turn comes again to attend such executions," he said, "I won't go, even if I am killed for it. Last night after one o'clock, when they had finished off all their victims, they ordered me to walk ahead of them. I was surprised that they did not leave me, and I thought that now my last moment had come. I began to walk away. I felt my legs buckling under me. Why don't they shoot? I thought. Suddenly I heard them laugh loudly. Their voices sounded sinister in the dark empty street. When I was beyond the range of their guns I began to run... to run like the wind, as though they were after me. I returned home almost unconscious. My mother asked me what had happened, but I did not have the heart to tell her for what purpose I had gone out on patrol at night, between ten and two o'clock."

Eva had tears in her eyes. Irka kept repeating, "No, it's impossible, impossible." Rena sat in silence for a while, then she whispered, "I want to *live* so much." Eva said, "You'll see, Mary, you'll be interned just like Bola and you'll survive, but all the rest of us are doomed." As a matter of fact, a number of us have received letters from Bola Rapoport. She is interned at Liebenau on Lake Constance, and is in good health. We are glad that at least one of us has been saved. How I envy her! How I want to get out of this hell... I have no strength left.

It seems that the Germans can be bribed to intern families. Naturally, one must have some scrap of paper stating that at least one member of the family is a foreign citizen. My mother is lucky in this respect, for she is a full-fledged American citizen, but the status of my father, my sister, and myself is dubious. My mother has made inquiries in various quarters. It appears that there is a certain Ehrlich, a Gestapo man, who takes care of these matters. We shall have to go to see him. Perhaps we, too, can be interned. It seems that only a few American citizens remained in the ghetto after the first internments, probably only those who are in hiding like my mother.[3]

Last night sixty more persons were executed. They were members of the underground, most of them well-to-do people who financed the secret bulletins. Many printers who were suspected of helping to publish the underground papers were also killed. Once again in the morning there were corpses in the streets. One of the victims was the wealthy baker Blajman, the chief backer of an underground newspaper. His brothers, too, were sentenced to die but they managed to escape and are now in hiding.

In our garden everything is green. The young onions are shooting up. We have eaten our first radishes. The tomato plants spread proudly in the sun. The weather is magnificent. The greens and the sun remind us of the beauty of nature that we are forbidden to enjoy. A little garden like ours is therefore very dear to us. The spring this year is extraordinary. A little lilac bush under our window is in full bloom.

MAY 4, 1942

On the Aryan side the population celebrated May 1 and May 3 by a complete boycott of the Nazis. Throughout those days the people tried to avoid taking trolley cars or buying newspapers, for the money goes straight to the Germans. Someone put a wreath of flowers on the tomb of the Unknown Soldier. The people deliberately stayed at home, so that a dead silence prevailed in the city. In the ghetto, too, the mood was somehow different. Although many Poles, poisoned by anti-Semitism, deny that their brothers of the Jewish faith are their co-citizens, the Jews, despite the in-human treatment to which they are subjected, show their patriotism in every possible way. Recently there has been much talk of the partisan groups fighting in the woods of the Lublin region. There are many Jews among them, who fight like all the others for a common goal. And yet the Polish anti-Semites say, "It's a good thing, let the Jews sit behind their walls. At last Poland will be Jewless."

One of our frequent visitors is Mr. Przygoda, assistant to Administrator Chaskelberg. "As soon as something begins to stir," he always says, "I'll jump across the walls. And such rage has piled up in me that I'll soon be killing Germans by the dozen." I know that he belongs to one of the underground parties. Jurek Leder, a good friend of mine, who now works with the Jewish police, is an ardent Polish patriot. "If only I could get out of here and join the partisans!" he says. "Then I would at last be able to fight for Poland. I love my native land, and even if a hundred anti-Semites tried to convince me that I'm not a Pole, I'd get the better of them—if not by words then by the fist." Leder's father is a Polish army captain now interned in Russia.

There are many such Jews who would gladly sacrifice their lives for Poland and who, at present, are working in the underground. There are many Jews who grit their teeth and keep silent, and blush with shame and humiliation when, as sometimes happens, a Pole throws a stone from the other side of the walls into the ghetto. Recently, on Chlodna Street, Poles passing by in trucks hurled stones at showcases and windows of private apartments, emitting wild cries of triumph as they rode by.

Some Jews are ashamed to admit that Poland is their father-land, although they love it, because they remember how often their Polish co-citizens have said to them, "Go back to Palestine, Jew," or how, at the University, the Jewish students were assigned to the "ghetto benches," and were often attacked by Gentile students for no other crime than their Jewish faith. It is a fact that many Gentiles in Warsaw have been infected by Hitler's propaganda. Naturally, there are people who see the error of such ways, but they are afraid to say anything because they would at once be accused of having a Jewish grandfather or grandmother or even of having been bribed by the Jews. Only a few, and these are members of the working-class parties, speak up openly, and these, for the most part, are fighting in the partisan units. If all the Aryan Poles got together and tried to help the Jews in the ghetto, they could do a great deal for us. For instance, they could procure Aryan certificates for many Jews, give them shelter in their homes, facilitate their escape over the walls, and so on and so forth. But of course it is easier to throw stones into the ghetto.

MAY 6, 1942
Despite the prevailing terrorism, the community has opened a number of elementary public schools for children of seven. The teaching is done in Yiddish.[4] The community also supplies textbooks, which are very hard to get now. This program includes supervised play after classes. It is pleasant to see a group of children holding hands and proudly taking a walk with their teacher.

Yesterday, Professor Greifenberg took all the students in his class at our school to the little park opposite the community building. This park is on the site of a bombed house, where the Toporol gardeners have planted grass and flowers. Today it is green there. Jewish workmen have constructed swings, benches, etc. The pupils of our school went to paint a fresco of animal cartoons on one of the walls of the ruined house. All this is done to give the ghetto children a feeling of freedom. The park was inaugurated today, and President

Czerniakow and other high community officials attended the ceremony. Long tables were set up on the grass, and on them lay little bags of molasses candy manufactured in the ghetto. Every child was given a little present and a bag of candy. Their cries of joy and the gay songs sung by the chorus resounded in the air. The smiling rosy faces of the children were perhaps the best reward of those who had created this little refuge of freedom for the little prisoners of the ghetto.

MAY 7, 1942

Abie, my mother's brother, who works on the police force, recently had an adventure which almost cost him his life. A few days ago, he was assigned to a night patrol on Krochmalna Street, where most of the smuggling is done now. His task was to watch a section of the street and see to it that no smugglers went by there. But what could he do when he saw several Jewish smugglers trying to throw a few bags of flour or other foodstuffs across the wall? These few bags meant that the ghetto would have more food and that the price of bread would drop; Abie himself is not well off, and a loaf of bread or a pound of flour would be quite useful to him. The smugglers readily pay the Jewish policemen a few zlotys or give them some foodstuffs if they "close their eyes" or warn them of the approach of Nazi guards. Abie was just thinking of what he would eat the next day when one of the smugglers offered him some money. Everything would have gone smoothly, if suddenly a patrol of two German guards had not appeared. In the darkness they did not realize exactly what was happening, but they must have sensed that smugglers were active there and they opened fire. The smugglers were killed, and Abie ran for his life. The Germans noticed his police cap and band and began to pursue him. He managed to enter a passage that led to the uneven side of Chlodna Street where, at Number 17, is a Jewish police station. He had hardly had time to warn the night shift that if the Germans came they should be told that no patrol had been sent to his section of Krochmalna Street that night, when his pursuers came in. No one betrayed Abie's secret, and the Germans left without having learned anything. Abie has not yet recovered from the shock of his experience.

It seems that at last the knell is sounding for the Jewish traitors in the ghetto. Last night the notorious Milek and his companion Anders were executed by the underground, one of them at his home, and the other in the street. Jurek Jawerbaum, a close friend of Milek's, is imprisoned in the Pawiak.

It is beginning to be hot, and often, instead of going to school, I take a blanket and a pillow and go to our roof to sunbathe. This practice is widespread in the ghetto, and the houses with flat roofs have been transformed into city beaches.

At 20 Chlodna Street, the charge for entering the terrace-like roof is one zloty fifty groszy. There are folding chairs, cool drinks, and a bird's-eye view of Warsaw. On our own roof I am always alone. It is pleasant to lie there in the sun, where I can see the quarter beyond the wall. The white spires of a church are very near me. They are surrounded by linden branches and the perfume of these lovely trees reaches as far as my roof. Further on there are private houses now used as German barracks. The air is pure here, and I think of the wide world, of distant lands, of freedom.

CHAPTER XI

THE GERMANS
TAKE PICTURES

MAY 8, 1942

The Germans have decided to make a film of life in the ghetto. Early this morning, they set up a powerful camera in front of 20 Chlodna Street and took pictures of the street. Later they entered one of the most elegant apartments and ordered the table to be set in the parlor. From a nearby restaurant they confiscated the most exquisite plates with meat dishes, cakes, and fruit—probably the only fruit available in the ghetto. They seized the best-dressed passers-by, men and women, and ordered them to sit around the table, eat, drink, and talk, and then made their extraordinary reel. Will they show it in Berlin to prove that the ghetto population has everything in abundance and even has foods unobtainable in Germany?

When I arrived in school I found all the teachers and pupils standing at the windows. There was an unusual commotion in the community building across the street. Here, too, pictures were being taken. Powerful spotlights were set up at different parts of the building, and long wires and electric cables lay on the ground. Cameras on rails were traveling in all directions with their operators, surrounded by a crowd of community officials and visitors who happened to be in the building. I saw a German arranging a group of several persons, with President Czerniakow and the highest community officials in the center. Later, for some reason, all the people were herded into a hall and ordered to kneel. Of course, the corpses in the streets will not be photographed, nor the little children waiting in an agony of hunger.

The Germans must surely be making some unusual propaganda effort.[1] Recently the tone of their war communiqués seems to have changed; they speak of "temporary withdrawals" from several Russian localities. Those who can read between the lines of their news releases are elated.

The nights in the ghetto are hot and humid. In our own garden there is a smell of lilacs, and after sunset all our tenants sit in the courtyard. Everyone brings his own chair, but my favorite perch is a wooden frame used for beating rugs. Sometimes I sing at night and, strangely, none of the tenants object, apparently because they like to forget their worries.

Captain Hertz, who often sits with us in the courtyard, is very pessimistic and, in addition, always tells macabre jokes. For instance, today he told us about a policeman who was shot over a matter of strawberries. This policeman was sitting on a cart laden with hay that was entering the ghetto. The German guard asked the policeman whether the cart contained anything else. The policeman pretended that he did not understand. The guard ordered the driver to stop, and lifted up the hay. He found strawberries hidden underneath. The driver and the policeman were shot on the spot.

Hertz says that "soon everything will be over and all of us will be killed." But most people think that a pogrom like the one in Lublin cannot happen in Warsaw, because there are too many people here. According to official figures, there are 450,000 inhabitants in the ghetto, but actually there are many more, because this number does not include the unregistered fugitives from provincial towns and the loads of Jews from Germany, Czechoslovakia, and Austria. It is estimated that the total is really more than 500,000. To exterminate such a number of people seems impossible, inconceivable. Yet if the present nightly murders continue, it is quite possible that half the ghetto population will be dead before the war is over.

Recently I have not been seeing my friends as often as before, except for Eva Pikman, who lives around the corner. It is now very dangerous to take long walks in the ghetto. Life, however, follows its regular course. The stores are open, although there are very few foods to be had. The theaters are open as usual, and there are some good plays. The community imposes new taxes and tributes every day.

MAY 17, 1942

A few days ago a handful of people from the Lodz Ghetto succeeded in reaching Warsaw through the intermediary of Kohn-Heller. They had to pay 20,000 zlotys per person. Yesterday at about four o'clock, I was standing alone in the dark kitchen of our apartment, washing dishes. Suddenly someone stuck his head through the window and asked whether this was the janitor's lodge. Then he cried out in a changed voice, "Mary!" When I opened the door to my mysterious visitor, it turned out to be Heniek Zylber. He was almost unrecognizable. His greenish pale face showed that he had suffered from hunger for many months. He looked more like a skeleton than a man and his elegant suit seemed incongruous. I was surprised that he had been able to get out of Lodz. From the beginning of the war, I have always met Heniek under extraordinary circumstances. This is what he told me of the tragic fate of my native city.

Lodz is devastated by tuberculosis, and because of the total lack of medicine, few people will be able to survive much longer. There is no food, and a pound of potato peelings costs eight marks. The bread ration is only about three ounces a day per person, just enough to arouse one's appetite. There is no black market, and no food is cooked privately. In every block, a common cauldron of soup is prepared once a day, and this soup is little more than water. Some families have small vegetable gardens in their yards, but the yield is practically zero, because no one has the strength to cultivate them. The people in the streets look like shadows. There is universal labor service. In the workshops set up by the Germans, 150,000 people are employed, who are underfed and who work under unimaginably bad conditions. The Germans demand a definite amount of production, which must be ready on time, otherwise severe penalties are imposed. People often die of sheer exhaustion. There is no one to remove the corpses from private homes. Recently, for some small misdemeanor, Heniek was sentenced, with another comrade, to remove a corpse from an apartment. The body was in a state of decay. "I don't know where we found the strength to carry it out and place it in the cart," he told me. "I recall that we dragged the cart for several hours before reaching our destination. After this expedition I had to stay in bed for a week.

"All your schoolmates," he concluded, "are working hard. At the beginning of 1940, the high school was still functioning, but now it has been closed by order of the German authorities, who pretended there was an epidemic."

Rumkowski, the President of the Lodz Community, behaves like a dictator. It is said that he is a madman. This old man recently married his eighteen-year-old secretary. He walks about town with a riding crop and, when addressing people, assumes the tone of the Nazis. Sometimes he even strikes them. Consumption is making terrible ravages, and there is not a person in the ghetto who is not infected. And the Germans continually bring in new transports of Jews from Germany.

Heniek said that when he drove out of the ghetto into the Aryan quarter in a truck, and saw streets full of people walking normally and stores open for business, he felt as if he were in paradise. He noticed a basket of radishes in front of a stand. He asked the driver to stop, and he and his companions threw themselves on the vendor, and bought all his radishes.

Since his arrival here, he has not been able to gather enough strength to go out until today. "I am learning to walk like a little child," he said. "Moreover, I am on a diet, because my stomach is not accustomed to normal food. I have not touched meat for a year and a half and I don't remember what it tastes like. Everything still seems unreal to me. Some friends in Lodz asked me to visit their relatives who live at 10 Chlodna Street, and I was looking for their janitor when I found you."

For a long time I wondered whether it was the real Heniek sitting before me, or only his ghost. I had long since forgotten about him, and when I ceased receiving letters from him I decided that he had died. Every time during this war that I have met Heniek, it has been before some great change in my life, or an important departure. Can it be that I am about to depart from here? But that is absurd; no one can leave the ghetto.

MAY 27, 1942
May is unusually hot this year. I am still sunbathing on the roof, and am quite tanned now. When I look in the mirror I try to persuade myself that I have just returned from the seaside.

In our garden the little green tomatoes have appeared. They will ripen quickly in the hot sun. We have had three crops of radishes. Perhaps the young onions are the most tasty. And our flowers smell so intoxicating, and their colors are so charming. Szymek no longer comes to do the work... he will never come any more. A few days ago, after having finished work here, he fell down in the street from weakness. Abie found him lying on the sidewalk somewhere near Nowolipie Street. The boy had a high fever. It turned out that he had been sick for two days, but never said anything because he feared to lose his job. My mother, however, had noticed that his face was flushed and that he moved with difficulty, so she sent him home earlier than usual. Abie took him in a rickshaw to the refugee home in which he lived. There he died a few hours later. The cause of his death was scarlet fever. And Szymek wanted so much to live.

JUNE 3, 1942

One hundred and ten persons have just been shot in the Gesia Street prison, among them ten policemen. The Germans did this to intimidate the smugglers. But only a few of the executed people were smugglers. The others had been arrested for crossing over to the Aryan side, or for nonpayment of taxes, or for begging in the street. All efforts to save them or pardon them proved of no avail. The Nazis have posted huge red placards with the names of their latest victims.

The execution took place at six in the morning in the prison yard. The Polish police were ordered to do the shooting, but refused. They were, however, compelled to attend the execution, which was also witnessed by Szerynski, chief of the Jewish police, a few Jewish police captains, and the high community officials headed by President Czerniakow. One of the eyewitnesses told me that several Polish policemen wept, and that some of them averted their eyes during the execution. One of the community officials fainted. The Jewish policemen were completely shattered.

The victims went to their death in complete calm. Some even refused to be blindfolded. Among the victims there were several women, two of them pregnant. After this crime had been perpetrated in front of witnesses, Pinkiert's funeral carts took the bodies to the Jewish cemetery. There is general mourning in the ghetto.[2]

JUNE 9, 1942

Today we learned that the Swiss Commission, which takes care of American citizens in German-occupied countries, has permitted an American woman to take her child and husband to an internment camp. She recently left the ghetto for Berlin under German escort. My mother is in despair, because she failed to register in April when women began to be interned.[3] She wrote to the Commission some time ago, but we are still awaiting their answer. My mother also wrote to the representative of the American colony on the Aryan side, Mrs. Lawrence,[4] asking her for information about the exchange of prisoners. Mrs. Lawrence answered that the list of prisoners to be exchanged was closed, but advised my mother to report as soon as possible to Nikolaus, Commissioner for Foreign Affairs in the Gouvernement General. However, it is not easy to get to see this dignitary.

JUNE 15, 1942

After many attempts, my mother quite accidentally found a way to Nikolaus' office. A few days ago she met a friend who told her that she knew a Jew working under Orf, Nikolaus' deputy. His name is Z., and it turns out that we knew him in Lodz. My mother saw Z., who promised to help her. He told my mother how he fell into the clutches of the Gestapo. He was arrested while trying to cross the German border with a forged passport, and after long and refined tortures, was compelled to work for the Gestapo. He is now employed as a Polish-German interpreter at the Gestapo headquarters on Aleja Szucha. He comes from a well-known Lodz family, and it seems that despite his position, he has remained a decent man. He is doing everything he can for us. He has registered my mother with the Gestapo, and promises to keep us posted on the course of events.

There are three families in the ghetto whose situation is like our own: American women whose husbands and children were born in Poland. My mother informed these women of the exchange that is about to take place and sent them to Z. They, too, have been registered.

JUNE 30, 1942

There is a real pilgrimage to our house now; an endless line of persons keeps coming to my mother to give her the addresses of their relatives and friends in America so that she can ask them for help. The exchange is supposed to take place on July 6. Everyone wants the same thing: they must send us affidavits, they must help us get out... and don't forget to tell them what we are going through here... and please let this be the first thing you do when you get to America, don't delay one minute, so that we may live to see the moment of our liberation... All of them pour their troubles out to my mother—they have nothing left to sell, nothing to live on, and in another few months they will perish.

It is horrible to have to listen to all this, especially since we have troubles of our own. My mother is terribly upset because Nikolaus registered only her and my sister Ann. He says that only children under sixteen are allowed to stay with their mothers, and Ann is fifteen. So it looks as if father and I will have to remain here. But although we have little hope, our friends say that all this will be smoothed out and that the whole family will go. I wish I could believe them.

Today when I was at Eva's, we wrote a joint letter to Bola, and at the end I said that I hoped to see her soon. I do not know why I wrote this, for I do not believe it in the least. Eva and Irka keep repeating that I shall soon leave them, and they insist so much that in the end I shall believe it too.

When Zycho Rozensztajn entered the room I told him, "You know, I'm going to America." "Really?" he said with a sneer. "And I to Africa!" "Going to America"—these words sound fantastic.

JULY 5, 1942

Fewer and fewer students come to our school, for now they are afraid to walk in the streets. The Nazi guard Frankenstein is raging through the ghetto, one day he kills ten persons, another day five... everyone expects to be his next victim. A few days ago I, too, ceased completely attending school. The heat is terrible. In the morning I go to have my teeth attended to by my cousin, Dr. Felicia Markusfeld. Her husband is a doctor who works at the Leszno Street hospital. They live on the even side of Sienna Street, but now there is access to it from Zelazna Street. The distance from Chlodna Street to Sienna Street takes half an hour of quick walking. I must cross Zelazna Street near the barbed-wire entanglement, where guards are posted at every few steps. I think all the time that one of them will fire at me, that the next one will be Frankenstein. I try to keep close to the doorways so that I can rush in if there is any shooting.

The manhunts in the ghetto continue. There are also rumors of the imminent deportation of the whole ghetto. I do not know where the monstrous report comes from that the Warsaw Jews have only forty days left to live. Everyone is repeating this rumor. No doubt the Germans have spread it

One of many workshops in the ghetto, where jobs were hotly fought over, as it was said workers would not be deported

themselves in order to create a panic. Many Jews are register-
ing at the so-called "shops," which are now mostly on Leszno
Street. These are workrooms which chiefly produce German
military uniforms. It is said that people employed in these
workshops will not be deported.

There are also rumors that soon the Cracow Ghetto will be
liquidated, although for the time being there is no official confirmation of this.[5] Many Jews who concealed their origin and
remained on the Aryan side are being denounced and transported to the ghetto. They are shot the moment they get off
the trucks that bring them.

Despite all this, the concerts of the Jewish police at the
Femina go on as usual. They are extremely popular. The
orchestra includes more than a dozen of the best musicians in
the ghetto.

JULY 14, 1942
Today I went to school, and met Bolek Szpilberg, whom I had
not seen for a long time. He told me that he had had to register
as a British subject, and that he now feared he would be
interned without his parents.

After school I stopped at my dentist's. Sitting there in the
chair, I heard pigeons cooing. This noise came from the Aryan
side, because the windows face the uneven side of Sienna
Street. My cousin Felicia, who was standing next to me with
her instruments, said, "You know, Mary, I don't like the
cooing of pigeons. For me, they are always a bad omen." I do
not know why, but in my ears, too, this sound evokes something unpleasant, hostile.

JULY 15, 1942
Today while returning from school I met the janitor's wife
from Number 16. She rushed up to me in great excitement and
told me in one breath that a policeman had just come from
headquarters and brought an order from the Gestapo that all

foreign citizens should report to the Pawiak prison on July 17, early in the morning. I rushed home, and my mother, who was just eating dinner, dropped her spoon upon hearing the news, and I thought she would faint. But she soon rose from the table and went to see Z. to learn the meaning of this sudden order. She came back without any concrete information. It seems that everything will be decided tomorrow. Later, Captain Hertz came with the same news. "Now," he said, "you'll see that I was right. We are all doomed. The foreign citizens are being removed because the Germans do not want them to witness what they are preparing for us."

JULY 16, 1942
After dinner, mother went to the Gestapo with Z., to Orf's office. He declared that my mother was entitled to take all her family with her. I still cannot believe in my good fortune. It seems inconceivable that I am really to leave this hell. And it is horrible to think of all my friends and relatives who must stay here after I go.

I spent all day buying various trifles which are necessary for our trip. My mother was told that we would stay in the Pawiak for only three days and then be sent for exchange to America. All my friends came to say goodbye to me. All of them envied me and were in despair over their own fate. Bronka Kleiner wept. She gave me her picture and wrote on it, "Don't forget me on your way to Paradise." I gave her all my posters, blueprints, instruments, colors, and paper.

Rutka came to see me in the afternoon, and we all went to Forbert to have a picture taken together for a souvenir. The photographer took a good picture: Anna, Rutka, Bronka and myself. They promised to have it ready tomorrow afternoon, and it will be delivered to the Pawiak. I also had time to stop at the school, and asked Councelor Poznanski to give me a graduation certificate for the third course. The Councelor was unable to do this, because President Czerniakow's signature is necessary and he is very busy today. He promised to send my certificate to the Pawiak within twenty-four hours.

Romek came to see me at eight o'clock (curfew does not begin until ten). He refused to believe that I was about to go to America. He looked at me strangely, as though he were sure he would never see me again. We walked along Chlodna Street. Today I boldly removed my armband. After all, officially I am now an American citizen. Romek pressed my arm and kept repeating, "I know you're not going, it's only a joke, isn't it? You won't leave me alone, you won't go." The inhabitants of the street looked at me with curiosity, "That's the girl who is going to America." In this street everyone knows everyone else. Every few minutes, people approached me and asked me to note the addresses of their American relatives, and to tell them to do everything possible for their unfortunate kin.

It is now close to midnight. Mother is packing. There is a terrible disorder in our apartment. It was crowded with people until ten o'clock, all of whom came here for the same purpose—to give us the addresses of American relatives and ask for help. There were many wives with children, whose husbands and fathers had gone to the World's Fair in 1939 and had remained in the United States. They brought us dozens of photographs. It was a horrible farewell. All over the house people were sobbing and there was no end to the heartfelt wishes and tearful embraces.

I am saying farewell to the ghetto. It is dark and quiet everywhere, but it seems to me that, from somewhere in the distance, there is a sound of sobbing. I see Romek's face before me just as it was when he said goodbye to me. I told him to go, that it would be better for both of us... but he refused, and when, finally, the lateness of the hour forced him to leave, he refused to shake hands with me. "I know," he said, "that if I shake hands with you I will say 'see you again,' and I don't want to say that because I know we'll never see each other again." I was amazed. "So you don't want to say goodbye to me, Romek," I reproached him. "Will you let me go without a word of farewell after two years of friendship?"

Dusk was falling. The sky was still red from the setting sun. We stood near a wall, together perhaps for the last time. I saw his eyes begin to shine, as though a lamp had been lighted in them. It looked as though he were bending to kiss me, but at the last moment he straightened. "No," he said, "we won't part. I want to see you, I want to have you here with me, I must have you here. You will stay. No one will take you away from me." I took him by the hand. "What kind of nonsense are you talking?" I said. "Aren't you glad that I can go? Can't you understand that I may be able to save others too, perhaps you yourself?"

I felt that if I stayed another minute I would burst into tears. I turned my face away and held out my hand. It remained suspended in the air. Romek, too, turned his face away and said in a tone of resignation, "Goodbye." I remained standing in the same spot, unable to move. I hoped that he would look back, but he plunged into the dusk and disappeared.

CHAPTER XII

THE PRIVILEGED GO
TO PRISON

JULY 19, 1942

This is only the third day of our internment in the Pawiak prison, but I can hardly believe that we have not been here much longer, for so many things have happened during this short time. We are now adjusted to the new conditions and we feel as if we belonged to the same family as the people who share this room.

My last night on Chlodna Street is still vivid in my memory. We made our last preparations with taut nerves. I was in a state of utter confusion and had to repack my suitcase several times. Over and over I asked myself the same question, "Have I the right to save myself and leave my closest friends to their bitter fate?" Each of us was allowed to take only one suitcase, and I had to be careful in choosing among my belongings. However, I took my notebooks, my photographs, my drawings, and my armband.

Uncle Abie stayed with us for the night. He is going to take our furniture and the other things we left. My father took his tallith and phylacteries and the little volume of the Psalms from which he had not parted in all his wanderings during the entire war. We went to sleep at two in the morning, but I had no sooner fallen asleep than I was awakened by the noise of frequent shots accompanied by police whistles sounding near by. I ran to the window. My parents had preceded me there. We could not see anything unusual on our street, but the firing continued. The sky was red, and for a moment I thought that a building was burning, but it was the sunrise, as red as the blood that has been shed in the streets of Warsaw for the past three years.

At seven in the morning, two Jewish policemen came to escort us to the Pawiak. They told us that the cause of the shooting was an attack by an armed group of people belonging to the underground movement on a workroom manufacturing uniforms for the German army. I wondered whether Romek had taken part in this attack, for I knew that recently he had been very active in the underground movement, although he never told me any details about it.

We left our house with tears in our eyes. My parents went first, and beside them were the two policemen and Uncle Abie. My sister Ann and I followed. Miss Sala, Bronka, Rutka, and Vera, who had come at daybreak to spend the last few hours with us, accompanied us. Groups of people from all the neighboring houses on Chlodna Street came out and watched the procession with sad eyes.

This July 17, 1942, was a sunny Friday. The sky was of a pure blue color, completely cleansed of the early morning redness, just as the ghetto pavement was washed of the blood that had been shed during the night. It seemed to me that never before had there been such a clear beautiful day in the ghetto.

We were led to the yard of the police station on Ogrodowa Street, where we found about seven hundred citizens of various neutral European and American countries. A police commissioner quickly checked our papers. Then a group of policemen drew up in two ranks, formed a closed circle around us, and ordered us to walk.

I recognized one of the policemen—he was Jozef Swieca, my friend Inka's fiancé. He came over to me to wish me a pleasant journey. "Inka was sorry she couldn't come," he said, "and asked me to give you her regards. I hope we'll see each other again," he added automatically, as though he believed what he said.

When we came out into the street, hundreds of people stood waiting on both sides of the pavement. Suddenly I heard several voices crying together, "Mary! Mary!" I saw Eva, Rena, Bronka, and Vera Neuman, trying to make their way to me through the crowd. Vera and Rena succeeded in getting through, and Rena handed me a bag of candy and a letter. "Don't forget us!" she called after me. Eva, Rena, and Bronka waved to me with one hand, and with the other wiped their eyes. Miss Sala followed us with lowered head, sobbing loudly.

The mob on the sidewalks grew constantly. Everyone wanted to have a look at the lucky seven hundred foreign citizens. At the corner of Zelazna and Leszno Streets, the police were compelled to make use of their sticks to disperse the crowds that barred the passage. From all sides came remarks. "It's a bad sign if they're being taken away," said one. "True, we can't expect that anything good will come of it for us," said another, and a third added, "Now they'll finish us off."

Literally all the able-bodied inhabitants of the ghetto were up that morning. Beginning at the corner of Smocza Street, that is to say, in the most crowded part of the ghetto, access to the street was completely closed. At last our procession reached Dzielna Street and stopped in front of the Pawiak gate opposite the church. The German officers who were waiting for us there ordered the Jewish policemen to leave. Uncle Abie, who had been helping us to carry our luggage, quickly gave it to us, and murmured to my mother, "How can you leave me?"

I burst into tears. Uncle Abie's words were spoken in a tone that shook me completely. But we could do nothing. My mother embraced him for the last time, and I, too, hugged him warmly.

The Germans called out the names in alphabetical order and ordered each internee to pick up his own suitcase. All of us said goodbye to our friends among the Jewish policemen and to our close relatives, who were the only persons allowed to accompany us to the Pawiak. Finally, the prison gates opened and we found ourselves behind the bars. The Germans kept counting us. I do not know whether they did it out of fear that someone was missing or that someone had sneaked into this paradise behind iron bars. We were led through various winding corridors until we reached the large prison yard. In a corner, I noticed prisoners at work.

A table and chairs were set up in the courtyard, and the German officers sat down and spread out their lists. Then Assistant Commissioner Orf ordered the American and British citizens to form one group and the neutrals another. Now the real registration began. Each name was read several times, and the person named had to appear before the table and answer questions. When my turn came, I was seized by the fear that my father and I would not be recognized as entitled to be exchanged. I approached the table with shaking knees. The Germans asked us why only my mother's and sister's names had been reported. My mother explained that at first Commissioner Nikolaus had refused to register my father and me, but that later the order had been changed. Without saying a word, the German officer put our names down in the files.

After the registration, a woman approached the Germans and asked what she should do about her sick child who was in a ghetto hospital. "My little boy is dangerously ill and has a high fever," she explained. The German officers answered, "He must be brought here at once!" This answer filled us with amazement. Several of us expressed the opinion that some drastic action against the inhabitants of the ghetto was surely imminent.[1]

We were led again through complicated corridors. Finally, the group of Americans and British were brought to a one-story building formerly inhabited by prison employees. We were placed in several rooms, ten persons per room, women and men separately. The other foreign citizens of neutral, occupied, and South American countries were locked up in prison cells, the men in the central building and the women in the special women's wing, the so-called "Serbia." There are rumors that these foreign citizens will be transported to the Aryan side and released. They were not allowed to take any luggage.

The room in which I am staying now is on the second floor. It is four to five square yards in size. Straw mattresses have been placed on the floor along two walls—six on each side. There is no other furniture. We are supposed to remain here for only a few days. At least, that is what we were told, but nobody believes it. I know that my friend Bola spent two whole weeks in the Pawiak before being taken to the Liebenau camp.

There are thirteen women and one eight-year-old girl in our room. My mother, my sister, and myself occupy two mattresses pushed together to form one large bed. Two of the women are British, the rest American. The whole apartment consists of four rooms, a kitchen and a bathroom. Two of these rooms are occupied by men. The woman attendant who guards us has a little room of her own. We are prisoners, but have the right to move freely from one room to another.

The first night of our imprisonment, we recalled the history of this prison and the heroic exploit of Jozef Pilsudski, who saved ten prisoners who had been condemned to death here by Czarist judges. This incident served as a subject for one of the best Polish moving pictures, *The Ten Prisoners of the Pawiak*.[2]

JULY 20, 1942

Today we were summoned for a new registration that took place in the little prison yard. It turns out that most of us are citizens of various South American republics—there are only twenty-one United States citizens. The others, in order of their numerical importance, are citizens of Paraguay, Costa Rica, Nicaragua, Ecuador, Haiti, Bolivia, and Mexico.[3]

Thus it is clear that many Jews could be saved from the ghetto with the help of South American passports. The Germans recognize the validity of such passports, although their possessors can speak neither Spanish or Portuguese. It seems that the Germans need human material for exchange against the Germans interned in the American republics. How can the world be informed that human lives can be saved with these little slips of paper?

During the late afternoon there was terrible agitation among the internees. Letters arrived from outside with frightening news. The ghetto is in a state of panic. The population expects a mass deportation of three hundred thousand people. President Czerniakow and all the community leaders have tried to calm the people by declaring that the Germans have officially denied these rumors. But the panic increased when it became known that the *Transferstelle* had received several freight cars used for transporting animals, cars which some time ago had been crowded with Jews transported from the ghetto to various labor camps.

In the eyes of the ghetto inhabitants, deportation is worse than death, for it means death after the most horrible tortures and humiliations, and it means death without burial. The thousands of Jews who were sent away with the first transports vanished without a trace.

The news of the imminent deportation has particularly shaken a young woman in our room who left her parents and three younger sisters in the ghetto. She is lying on her mattress, muttering unintelligible words.

The "information service" of the Pawiak works well; the guards let themselves be bribed without difficulty, they take out and bring in letters, and give us detailed information about what is happening in the ghetto.

Opposite our building is the prison laundry, where many women prisoners are employed. Near by is a kitchen in which potatoes are peeled, and beets, turnips, and carrots washed. I can observe all this from our windows, some of which face the prison yard. The women prisoners sit on little stools, and work without enthusiasm. There are women of various ages and appearance. Some of them have intelligent faces, but they look dejected, and there is not the slightest smile on their lips. Sometimes one of the prisoners quickly bites off a piece of carrot, and looks around with a frightened expression to see whether the guard has noticed her. I also observe the prisoners when they take their regular walk in the yard, with their hands behind their backs.

From the other window, which faces Dzielna Street, I see the policeman on guard walking back and forth. There are no passers-by because Pawia and Dzielna Streets, which run parallel on both sides of the prison buildings, are closed to traffic.

Close to our window we sometimes see a Jewish policeman walking out of Numbers 27–31 Dzielna Street, which is Dr. Janusz Korczak's children's home.[4] I can see many little beds through the windows of this house. During moments of quiet I hear the sweet voices of the children who live there, quite unaware of what is happening around them.

An hour ago, a guard ordered all the British nationals to come to the yard with their luggage. We do not know whether they are really going to be sent away. Meanwhile, our room is less crowded. On one side, the mattresses are occupied by the W. family—the mother, a daughter, Rosa, and a daughter-in-law, Esther. The two opposite corners are occupied by Mrs. H., Mrs. R., and ourselves. On the remaining mattresses

Jews smuggling a sack of food into
the Warsaw Ghetto

are Mrs. G., her little daughter Alusia, and a young girl, Guta E. Each of us is busy with something different, but all of us are constantly thinking of our relatives and friends in the ghetto, whom we are unable to save from the mortal danger hanging over them, only a few steps from our prison.

JULY 21, 1942
Today sixty hostages were brought to the prison, among them prominent members of the Council of Elders and well-known physicians and engineers. The most prominent of these hostages are Engineer Jaszunski, the educational director of the community, Abraham Gepner, chairman of the Provisions Office, S. Winter, and Dr. Kohn.

The ghetto is still in a state of panic. The great disaster is expected at any moment. Nazi guards run through the streets shooting people for no reason at all. The hunger is increasingly terrible—food has simply vanished. A pound of bread now costs twelve zlotys. All of us in the Pawiak are living in the same state of panic, and we, too, are literally starving. Our reserves are exhausted. The food we get here consists of a little boiled water with a piece of potato or beet in it. These soups are given out twice a day, for lunch and dinner. In the morning we receive a slice of black bread, and water, which is called "coffee." But this is nothing when compared with the hell outside the Pawiak gates.

JULY 22, 1942

Today the ghetto had a bloody Wednesday. The misfortune everyone expected has struck. The deportations and street pogroms have begun. At daybreak, patrols of Lithuanians and Ukrainians led by Elite Guards surrounded the ghetto, and armed guards were stationed every ten yards. Anyone approaching the gates or showing himself at a window was shot on the spot. The Lithuanians and Ukrainians displayed great zeal in their murderous work. They are tall young beasts of seventeen to twenty who were especially trained for their job by German instructors.

For a long time there has been talk in the ghetto of the impending replacement of the German guards, mostly old soldiers, by young Ukrainians and Lithuanians. Now these rumors, which were generally disbelieved, have been confirmed.

Last night the German authorities informed the Jewish community that all the inhabitants of the ghetto would be transported to the east. Only forty pounds of luggage are allowed per person; all remaining possessions will be confiscated. Everyone must bring provisions for three days. The deportation was supposed to begin this morning at eleven o'clock. The order exempts only those Jews who are employed in German factories and workshops in the ghetto, as well as the officials of the various ghetto institutions. This includes the Jewish police force, the community officials, the employees of the ambulance service, the hospital staffs, the undertakers, and all possessors of registration cards issued by the Labor Office who have not yet been assigned jobs. The families of these chosen people are also exempt from deportation.

The Jewish police is charged with the sad task of preserving order during the deportation and of employing force against those who refuse to give themselves up.

The concentration point of this mass migration is situated at the Umschlagplatz on Stawki Street. The Germans demand 3,000 persons a day for deportation. The panic in the ghetto is indescribable. People with bundles in their hands run from one street to another, and do not know what to do. Many are trying at the last moment to obtain jobs in the German factories of Toebens and Schultz, which are situated in the ghetto. I was told that some people are paying bribes of as much as a thousand zlotys for such a job. The Jews themselves are trying to organize large workshops to make goods for the Germans, in order to give employment to people threatened with deportation.

Today the Jewish police gathered up all the beggars from the streets and emptied the refugee camps. These unfortunates were locked up in freight cars without food or water. The transports are being sent in the direction of Brzesc, but will they ever reach there? It is doubtful that all these starving people will arrive at their destination alive; they will perish in their sealed cars. A hundred persons are crowded into each car. The Polish prison guard who whispered all these details to us had tears in his eyes. He lives near Stawki Street, and he witnessed horrible scenes of people being driven into cars with whips, just as though they were cattle.

Today we received a package of food from Uncle Abie, in which he enclosed a note. Fortunately for us, he is on the police force, otherwise he would not have been admitted to Dzielna Street. His short note expressed despair. He cannot accept the idea that, as a policeman, he will have to help in the deportation, and is thinking of resigning from his job. But, on the other hand, his job protects him from deportation. He wants to know what we think about it.

From our window I can see that something unusual is going on in Korczak's children's home. Every now and then someone walks in and, a few minutes later, comes out leading a child. These must be the parents or families of the children, who in this tragic moment want to be with their loved ones. The children look clean, and are dressed neatly though poorly. When I bend out of the window I can see the corner of Smocza Street. There is terrible confusion there; people are running back and forth as though possessed. Some carry bundles, others wring their hands.

Dzielna Street must have been opened for traffic, because suddenly many passers-by have appeared there, and until now it was empty. Often I can see whole families, parents with their children, the mothers holding babies in their arms, and the bigger children following them. There must be many Jews who are reporting voluntarily for deportation—those who have no other way out, no possibility of hiding. The Germans give them a kilogram of bread per person, and promise them better working conditions. But these desperate volunteers do not fill the quota of 3,000 people a day. The police must supply the rest by means of force. They drag their victims out of their homes or seize them in the streets.

CHAPTER XIII

THE CHILDREN
GO FOR A WALK

JULY 24, 1942

President Adam Czerniakow has committed suicide. He did it last night, on July 23. He could not bear his terrible burden. According to the rumors that have reached us here, he took his tragic step when the Germans demanded that the contingents of deportees be increased. He saw no other way out than to leave this horrible world. His closest collaborators, who saw him shortly before his death, say that he displayed great courage and energy until the last moment.

The community has elected a new president to replace Czerniakow. He is old Lichtenbaum, whose son, Engineer Lichtenbaum, is the director of the Construction Office of the community.

A new group of hostages from among the members of the Council of Elders were brought to the Pawiak today.

Szerynski is again at the head of the ghetto police, although last February the Germans had arrested him.

A considerable number of Jews succeeded in getting across to the Aryan side, despite the reinforced guard. It is said that an armed unit of the Jewish underground liquidated a German sentry post near one of the gates, thus enabling a large group of Jews to escape.

AUGUST, 1942

Behind the Pawiak gate, we are experiencing all the terror that is abroad in the ghetto. For the last few nights we have been unable to sleep. The noise of the shooting, the cries of despair, are driving us crazy. I have to summon all my strength to write these notes. I have lost count of the days, and I do not know what day it is. But what does it matter? We are here as on a little island amidst an ocean of blood. The whole ghetto is drowning in blood. We literally see fresh human blood, we can smell it. Does the outside world know anything about it? Why does no one come to our aid? I cannot go on living; my strength is exhausted. How long are we going to be kept here to witness all this?

A few days ago, a group of neutrals was taken out of the Pawiak. Apparently the Germans were unable to use them for exchange. I saw from my window several trucks filled with people, and I tried to distinguish familiar faces among them. Some time later, the prison guard came panting to us, and told us that the Jewish citizens of neutral European countries had just been taken to the Umschlagplatz to be deported. So our turn may come soon, too. I hope it will be very soon. This waiting is worse than death.

The Germans have blockaded entire streets in the ghetto. Since the 10,000 people a day they are now demanding have failed to report, the Nazis are using force. Every day they besiege another street, closing all the exits. They enter the apartments, and check the labor cards. Those who do not possess the necessary documents or who, according to the Germans' estimate, are unqualified for work, are taken away at once. Those who try to resist are shot on the spot.

Just now, while I am writing this, such a blockade is taking place on Nowolipie Street, only two blocks from our prison. It has been going on for two days now. The street is completely closed; only the Jewish policemen are allowed to use it.

The wives and children of the men employed in the German factories in the ghetto are officially exempt from deportation, but this exemption is effective only on paper. In actual fact, a husband returning home from work often finds that his whole family has been taken away. He runs in despair to Stawki Street to find his kin, but instead of being able to rescue them, he himself is often pushed into one of the cattle cars.

The German factories in the ghetto now work twelve hours a day, with only one hour's rest. The workers receive a quart of watery soup and a quarter of a pound of bread a day. But despite their hunger and slavery, these workers are among the luckiest in the ghetto, for their jobs protect them from deportation.

Dr. Janusz Korczak's children's home is empty now. A few days ago we all stood at the window and watched the Germans surround the houses. Rows of children, holding each other by their little hands, began to walk out of the doorway. There were tiny tots of two or three years among them, while the oldest ones were perhaps thirteen. Each child carried a little bundle in his hand. All of them wore white aprons. They walked in ranks of two, calm, and even smiling. They had not the slightest foreboding of their fate. At the end of the procession marched Dr. Korczak, who saw to it that the children did not walk on the sidewalk. Now and then, with fatherly solicitude, he stroked a child on the head or arm, and straightened out the ranks. He wore high boots, with his trousers stuck in them, an alpaca coat, and a navy-blue cap, the so-called Maciejowka cap. He walked with a firm step, and was accompanied by one of the doctors of the children's home, who wore his white smock. This sad procession vanished at the corner of Dzielna and Smocza Streets.[1] They went in the direction of Gesia Street, to the cemetery. At the cemetery all the children were shot.

One of numerous starving children treated in the
Berson and Bauman Jewish Children's Hospital on Sliska Street

We were also told by our informants that Dr. Korczak was forced to witness the executions, and that he himself was shot afterward.

Thus died one of the purest and noblest men who ever lived. He was the pride of the ghetto. His children's home gave us courage, and all of us gladly gave part of our own scanty means to support the model home organized by this great idealist. He devoted all his life, all his creative work as an educator and writer, to the poor children of Warsaw. Even at the last moment, he refused to be separated from them.

The house is empty now, except for the guards who are still cleaning up the rooms of the murdered children.

Yesterday I saw a detachment of Ukrainians and "Shaulists" (Lithuanians) fully armed, with helmets on their heads, running along Dzielna Street. It had been quiet when, all of a sudden, I heard the clatter of boots. The men ran with fixed bayonets, as though to a front-line attack. Those at the end of the detachment held small hatchets in their hands, such as are used to break down the doors of barricaded apartments. These beasts often use hatchets against human beings too. The Lithuanians are the worst of all.

During the last two weeks, more than 100,000 people have been deported from the ghetto. The number of those murdered is also very large. Everyone who can is trying to get a job in the German factories of Toebens, Schultz, and Hallmann. Fantastic sums are paid for a labor card.

Our family of internees in the Pawiak now numbers sixty-four persons. United in our common unknown fate, we are trying to organize our gray, unhappy lives as best we can. We have elected a representative, Mr. S., who from time to time discusses our affairs with Commissioner Nikolaus. This gentleman is a citizen of Costa Rica. He speaks excellent German and knows how to handle the Commissioner. Twice a week we are allowed to use the prison telephone to communicate with Gestapo headquarters at Aleja Szucha.

Nemetz, Nikolaus' deputy, an officer of the Elite Guards, often visits us. Usually we can see him arriving from our windows and then we hurriedly put our things in order. Mr. S. quickly notes down our requests, and when Nemetz arrives, he is ready with a list.

Nemetz tries to play the role of a gentleman, just like all the other German officials who deal with us. He always promises to grant our requests, which are usually very modest—for instance, we ask to have the straw in our mattresses changed, or our rooms disinfected, or to be given soap or better food. But Nemetz never keeps his promises. He is polite; apparently there has been an order from above to behave courteously to American citizens. When he leaves, he shakes hands with Mr. S., smiles at everyone, and promises to visit us again in a few days.

Thus weeks go by. We are allowed to go out in the prison yard only once a day. We walk for an hour between the laundry and our building, and during that time we are guarded by two Ukrainians. One is posted near the gate which separates our building from the "Serbia," or women's prison; the other often accompanies us and listens to our conversations.

The Ukrainian guards are often relieved. They, too, must have been given orders to be polite toward us. There is a marked difference in their behavior toward us and toward the other prisoners, whom they often abuse with the coarsest words and beat till they bleed. These beasts actually smile at us.

The daily walk begins at five in the afternoon. At six, one of the Ukrainians declares in his comical German-Ukrainian jargon: *"Spazier skinchini!"* (Walk finished.) Then we return to our mattresses.

Last night was horrible. It was stuffier than ever. We lay naked on our straw bags. The atmosphere was so thick that it could almost be cut with a knife. Through the window a patch of blue sky and a few stars could be seen. Not the slightest noise came from the street. None of us could sleep.

At about eleven o'clock, we suddenly heard the heavy screech of a lock opening, and two persons left by one of the prison gates. The heavy steps of soldierly boots could be clearly distinguished from the small steps of a woman. The steps came gradually closer to our windows. Then we heard a woman's tearful voice and several words pronounced in a German-Yiddish accent: *"Lieber Herr... Lieber Herr..."* But suddenly these words were drowned by the sound of revolver shots. The first shot resounded high in the air near our window, the second was lower, and the third level with the pavement, as though the soldier were firing at the unfortunate woman as she lay on the ground. Then we heard muffled noises, which might have been kicks, and then, finally, there was silence.

Esther W., who lay near the window, peered cautiously out into the street. The victim lay on the sidewalk. The German soldier walked quickly to the Polish policeman on guard opposite the gate, spoke to him, and then left. The Polish policeman began to walk back and forth, in measured steps, under our window. Apparently to give himself courage, he began to whistle a tune, the same one over and over. In the empty street, it had a strangely sad sound.

About a quarter of an hour later there came a cart from Pinkiert's funeral establishment. We heard the dull noise made by the body thrown into the box. Then the wheels of the cart rolled over the stony pavement. The Polish policeman continued whistling the same sad tune for a long time. This was the only sound in the dark August night. No one in our room said a word.

The shootings and the cries coming from the streets are slowly driving us mad. The nights are horrible. Last night nearly forty persons were shot under our windows. All of them were men. The slaughter lasted for two hours or more. The murderers finished off their victims with kicks and with blows with the butts of their guns. Pinkiert's cart made several trips. In the morning we could see the janitor of the house opposite the prison scrubbing the sidewalk and spraying it with water from a rubber hose. The bloodstains were stubborn, and despite the long scrubbing the sidewalk still has a yellowish color.

The pogroms are continuing; streets are still being blockaded. The Nazi sadists are not yet sated.

The slaughter in the Pawiak yard is continuing too. As soon as night falls, the executions begin. The former commandant of the prison is on furlough, and his deputy, Bürckel, is one of the worst of the Nazi beasts. All the prisoners know this sadist well. He sometimes visits us too, walking with slow steps from room to room and smiling all the time. He does not speak much, but he pierces every one of us with his eyes.

One day he came to our room while Mrs. W. was lying unconscious from an attack of nerves. He began to speak to her, and when she remained silent, he began to shout. The woman still did not answer. Then he calmed down and, turning to us, began to make philosophical speeches about the Jewish problem and the political situation. "Germany is so small," he said, drawing the outlines of his fatherland on the wall with his finger, "and America is so big!"—this time his finger made a wide circle in the air. "But the Germans will conquer America too, we will be there before you, before you have been exchanged."

Not one of us answered him. He accompanied every word he said by a blow of his riding crop on his high shining boots. From time to time he slashed the air with the whip, and I had the feeling that he longed to hit someone. But he controlled himself, and just went on slashing the air, no doubt to make us feel his power.

This morning, before his visit, we saw him through our windows chasing a cat in the garden of the former children's home. He ran like a madman among the bushes, looking for the little cat, which had suddenly vanished. He drew out his revolver and began to shoot wildly.

Dzielna Street is no longer empty. Large groups of workers, led by their overseers to the various labor camps, constantly march by. Korczak's children's home has been transformed into a storehouse for various merchandise and furniture. Also shoes and clothing are being brought here— apparently the possessions of the murdered.

The Germans systematically empty the apartments from which they have dragged the Jews. A large number of people are employed in sorting the loot. Yesterday we saw several dozen women scrubbing the rooms of the children's home. On the third floor front, in one of the middle rooms, they set up an office for the German who supervises the sorting. I saw furniture being placed there; a vase of flowers was put on the desk.

I almost had hysterics when, among the women who were scrubbing the floors and windows, I suddenly recognized

Edzia, and a while later, saw Zelig Zylberberg talking to her. They noticed me, too, and as soon as their German overseer left the room they began to talk to me, and told me that they had been married for two weeks, and that the wedding had been attended by many of their friends. This took place at the very time when their street, Nizka Street, was being blockaded by the Nazis. "We had a hard time getting a rabbi," Edzia shouted to me. Zelig is working as an overseer, and this protects them both from deportation.

I was able to converse with her through my window for a few hours, with interruptions. She told me that on the very first day of the deportations, Edek Wolkowicz was shot dead at the Umschlagplatz because he refused to enter a cattle car. Ola Szmuszkiewicz was deported with her mother. The Germans separated the able-bodied men and women from the older people and children, who were sent in sealed cars in an unknown direction. Ola was found able to work, but she

Jews from the Warsaw Ghetto wait to board a deportation
train in Umschlagplatz

refused to separate from her mother, and ran to the sealed car to join her. Marysia Eisenstadt was shot when she tried to join her parents in a cattle car. The "nightingale of the ghetto" is now silent forever.

Romek is alive and in good health. He is still working as an overseer on the construction of the ghetto walls. He is a neighbor of Zelig's and Edzia's on Nizka Street. Zelig promised me that he would soon bring me a letter from him. This is not easy, because no one is allowed to move freely in the streets, and the workers employed in a given quarter must live in the same quarter. At 7:30 a.m. the whole group marches out together from an assembly point, and at 7:00 p.m. they return to the same place. It is very difficult to meet anyone who lives in a different quarter. But Zelig has more freedom, because he is an overseer. However, he goes out as little as possible, because of the constant shootings.

I have recognized other acquaintances among the workers employed across the street. Edzia Piaskowska's brother oversees a large group of workers at the children's home. Zelig is an overseer in the building adjoining ours, at Number 24 Dzielna Street. On the ground floor of Numbers 27–31 Dzielna Street, pharmaceutical items are now being sorted. We can see the employees arranging bottles, jars, boxes, and various glass vases—all these come from the looted drug-stores of the ghetto. In one of the ground-floor windows I saw one of my former teachers at the school of graphic design. He often looks up at me and smiles bitterly. What is he thinking? His pupil is behind bars, and he himself works under the Nazi whip.

Some of our internees receive packages from the ghetto, which their family or friends bring to the prison gates. The largest number of packages come to Guta E. Her mother sends them to her through a policeman they know. Every package contains a long letter from a close friend of hers, a certain Mr. Z., who is a community official. He informs us of all the happenings in the ghetto. Thus, through him and others, we have fairly detailed reports. Not a day passes without several letters coming to our group.

SEPTEMBER 19, 1942

My mother lies on her mattress all day long; she is so starved that she cannot move. Ann is like a shadow, and my father is terribly thin, just skin and bones. I seem to bear the hunger better than the others. I just grit my teeth when the gnawing feeling in my stomach begins. At night I begin to wait for the next morning, when we are given our four ounces of bread and the bitter water that is called coffee. Then I wait for lunch at noon, when we are brought our first soup, a dish of hot water with a few grains of kasha. Then again I wait impatiently for the evening, when we get our second dish of hot water with a potato or a beet. The days are endless, and the nights even more so, and full of nightmares. The shootings continue, hundreds of people are perishing daily. The ghetto is drenched in blood. People are constantly marching along Dzielna Street toward the Umschlagplatz on Stawki Street. No job or occupation is a complete protection any longer. Recently even the families of those employed have been deported, mostly the women and children.

A few weeks ago the Nazis began to round up the wives and children of the men working at Toebens and Schultz. Those who are not working are ruthlessly dragged away. Parents now take their children with them to their work, or hide them in some hole.

Food is now cheaper in the ghetto. Recently a pound of bread cost forty zlotys, but now it is only twenty zlotys. There are fewer mouths to feed.

SEPTEMBER 20, 1942

There have been fewer shootings today. Resistance is subsiding. Starving, exhausted people are still streaming to the Umschlagplatz.

Today Engineer Lichtenbaum and his friend First, a high community official, came in a car to visit their interned friends in the Pawiak. They had received special permission to visit us, and from them we learned a number of details about the campaign of extermination.

The moment the mass pogrom in Warsaw began to subside, the Germans started a slaughter in the little towns around the capital. Yesterday they finished their "campaign" in Otwock, whence no one was even deported. Some of the Jews ran away to the surrounding woods, where they are still hiding. At night they come to nearby villages for food.

Engineer Lichtenbaum asked Mrs. W. whether she had been told by any of the prison officials what the Nazis were planning to do in the Warsaw Ghetto. How absurd for him, a high community official, to ask us what is going to happen to the survivors in the ghetto! Is there still any doubt after what has happened before our very eyes? But everyone asks everyone else, hoping to hear a hopeful word.

According to Lichtenbaum and First, more than 200,000 Jews have been deported, and more than 10,000 have been killed. Thus nearly 200,000 people still remain.

The underground movement has become more active than ever. Death sentences were carried out not only against the Nazis, Ukrainians, and Lithuanians who murdered the population during the bloody days, but also against the few Jews who allowed themselves to be used as Nazi tools during the massacre. Colonel Szerynski and several community officials are now on the black list. They know it, and dare not appear on the streets without armed bodyguards.

The Germans for their part are liquidating all the collaborators whom they can no longer use. They shoot them without ceremony, and their bodies are often found on the streets. Recently, the Gestapo agents Erlich and Markowicz, and the founders of the ghetto trolleys, Kohn and Heller, ended their fantastic careers in this manner.

The massacres have aroused the underground leaders to greater resistance. The illegal papers are multiplying and some of them reach us even here in the Pawiak. They are full of good reports from the battle fronts. The Allies are victorious in Egypt, and the Russians are pushing the enemy back at Moscow. The sheets explain the meaning of the deportations and tell of the fate of the deported Jews. The population is summoned to resist with weapons in their hands, and warned against defeatist moods, and against the idea that we are completely helpless before the Nazis. "Let us die like men and not like sheep," ends one proclamation in a paper called *To Arms!*

The situation improved somewhat in the last days of August, and some began to take an optimistic view of the future. But this was only the lull before the storm. On September 3 and 4, the Germans began to blockade the workshops organized by the community. Elite Guards, accompanied by Lithuanians and Ukrainians, entered the shops, and took several dozen people out of each, alleging that they needed skilled workers. These workers, numbering more than a thousand, were led away to Stawki Street and deported to the Treblinka camp.

Now it is generally known that most of the deportees are sent to Treblinka, where they are killed with the help of machines with which the Germans are experimenting for war purposes. But no one knows any details.

On September 5, the German factories of Toebens and Hallman were blockaded, and a considerable number of workers were deported.

On Sunday, September 6, the Jewish police force received an order to prepare for another campaign. This followed an announcement published by the community in the name of the Resettlement Commission, according to which all the remaining inhabitants of the "Big Ghetto" (within the limits of Smocza, Gesia, Zamenhof, and Szczesliwa Streets, and Parisowski Square) were to report on September 5 for registration. The text, printed in German and Polish, contained a warning that everyone must bring food for two days and that the apartments must not be left locked. "Those who fail to report on time will be shot," the order concluded.

The area defined in the order was surrounded with barbed wire and thick rope. It actually formed an enlarged Umschlagplatz. The registration began at eleven in the morning and continued for a whole week, until Saturday, September 12.

The purpose of this registration was to hunt out those who were hiding, and the wives, children, and parents of the Jews still employed in the ghetto factories. A large number of people barricaded themselves in their apartments, choosing to die at home rather than in the camps.

Whole units of Elite Guards and Lithuanians visited the apartments in the area subject to registration, and shot everyone they found. Several Jews walled themselves into cellars, after having stored food and water there. Long tunnels have been built under the ghetto streets. There is now a real underground ghetto. Many people hid in bombed-out houses, hoping that it would not occur to the Germans to search the ruins. The shooting went on for a whole week. During that time more than 50,000 men, women, and children were taken to Treblinka.

The Jewish police now occupy an entire block on Ostrowska and Wolynska Streets. All the Jewish policemen and their families were ordered to leave their former apartments in the various quarters of the ghetto, and to occupy the emptied and looted apartments of the deported. Apparently the Germans want to have the Jewish police concentrated in one spot. There are rumors that the Jewish police force will soon be greatly reduced.

For several days we have had no news from Uncle Abie, although he now lives quite close to us; it is only a few steps from the Pawiak to Wolynska Street, and Edzia is no longer working at the former children's home. I wonder what has happened to them.

CHAPTER XIV

THE END OF THE JEWISH POLICE

SEPTEMBER 22, 1942
Yesterday was the Day of Atonement, and on this sacred day the Nazis, as is their custom, chose to blockade Ostrowska and Wolynska Streets. Out of the 2,500 policemen, they singled out 380 for continued service, and more than 2,000 others were deported, together with their families.

We thought it significant that on this day, Warsaw was bombed by Soviet planes, which came in greater force than ever before.

A temporary synagogue was organized in the room occupied by the men. We had sentries, who were relieved every quarter of an hour, to warn us if the Nazis came to visit us, too. But no one came. The women prayed together with the men. Madame Sh., the wife of the Grand Rabbi of Warsaw, stood near the improvised altar, and prayed in heartfelt tones. Now and then she wrung her hands, and I saw her eyes fill with tears. Then, suddenly, she began to sob loudly, and all those present wept with her.

On a little table covered with a white cloth stood two candles on a tin dish turned upside down. Only a few of the men wore talliths, but the rest, too, prayed with all their hearts. At first one could hear the words pronounced by the cantor, but soon everything was drowned in one lament and in sobbing. We went to our rooms at eight o'clock when the guard came to lock us up for the night.

Amidst our prayers, I suddenly heard the noise of shooting and continuous desperate cries. It was eleven o'clock, and the Nazis had just begun their blockade of the block occupied by the policemen and their families. I thought of Uncle Abie and his wife. Suddenly, someone noticed flames bursting forth from the church opposite our windows. After a while, a few cars with firemen came to the spot, and the fire was put out.

By nightfall we saw fires in several places in the city, and then suddenly the factory sirens began to roar, announcing an imminent air raid. Soon there came the noise of gunfire and bomb explosions. We had not heard detonations of such force for a long time. The thick darkness over the city was split by rockets. Hundreds of bombs exploded in the air. My mother, Ann, and I huddled together and shook along with the whole prison building. It seemed to us that the fliers were aiming at the prison, and we clearly heard bombs falling in the adjoining streets: Nowolipie, Nowolipkie, Nalewki, Gesia. One bomb fell in the prison yard, only a short distance from our building, and its explosions shook the walls so strongly that, for a moment we thought they were going to collapse.

I thought that it would be horrible to be killed here by a bomb of Hitler's enemies, but at the same time, I could not repress my satisfaction at seeing the Nazis bombarded on the very day they had organized a manhunt against the Jews.

The bombardment lasted throughout the night. New planes constantly arrived with new loads of bombs. The all clear was not sounded until five in the morning.

The *Nowy Kurjer Warszawski* today printed only a few lines about this air raid. According to this Nazi newspaper, no military objectives were hit. But we have learned that actually many military installations were completely demolished. In the ghetto, the court building on Leszno Street and the hospital were hit, and a number of houses around the Pawiak were demolished, but most of the bombs fell on the airfields around Warsaw and on the main railroad station.

SEPTEMBER 29, 1942

The area of the ghetto has been considerably reduced. Its boundary now runs along Smocza, Gesia, Franciszkanska, Bonifraterska, Muranowska, Pokorna, Stawki, Dzika and Szczesliwa Street, and Parysowski Square. All the community institutions and remaining workshops were ordered to transfer to the new area. This order of the German authorities bears the date of September 27. The walls surrounding the new quarter will be nine feet high. The Jewish police must maintain order during the transfer. The factories which cannot be moved will be surrounded by special walls, and the workers will have to live in adjoining buildings. The work will be supervised by the *Werkschutz*, consisting of former members of the Jewish police.

A number of factories with their Jewish workers have remained outside the reduced ghetto, on Leszno, Karmelicka, Nowolipki, Smocza, Nowolipie, and Zelazna Streets—these are the factories of Toebens, Schultz, Roerich, Hoffman, Schiling, and Hallman. Toebens also has factories left on Ciepla, Twarda, Prosta, and Ceglana Streets. Certain firms have resorted to branding their workers with seals in order to make them more easily recognizable during the blockades, thus protecting them from deportation. The workers are "stamped" on various parts of their bodies, so that the Nazi manhunters will make no error.

For being stamped, the workers must pay a tax of three zlotys a day, which is deducted from their wages. They also pay two zlotys a day for the food they receive at the factories. Each worker must now wear a number and the badge of his factory. It is said that all these factories now employ nearly 30,000 Jewish slave laborers. The community employs nearly 3,000 people.

Every day the Nazis come to the community with new demands. They ask for all kinds of articles, for instance, coffee, chocolate, and other nonexistent delicacies.

OCTOBER 1, 1942

The ghetto is now nothing but a huge labor camp. During the day the streets are almost empty. There is traffic only at six in the morning when people go to their work. Through the windows we can see men and women leaving their houses and hastening to the various points of assembly, from which they march in military formation to the factories. They are drawn up in rows of four and are accompanied by members of the *Werkschutz* and German patrols. After eight in the morning it is rare to see a man on the streets of the ghetto. From twelve to one there is an intermission for lunch. A large caldron is brought to the factory yard, and the workers stand in line with bowls in their hands to receive their thin soup.

After seven at night the streets are once again filled with workers hastening home to their apartments. Later, no one dares go out, because German patrols are lurking everywhere.

Such is life in the ghetto now. Our people are living in the very shadow of death, but each one thinks that, in spite of everything, he may manage to endure all this and survive. Without this hope, which stems from some miraculous source, the surviving Jews in the ghetto would commit mass suicide.

Bombings by Soviet planes have been taking place every night. The explosions shake the walls of the Pawiak. We are now so accustomed to these bombings that we wait for them eagerly: they are like a greeting from the free world. The planes come every night at about the same time, around eleven o'clock, and the all clear is not sounded until two in the morning.

But what is most horrible is the constant whistling and shooting by the Elite Guard, which lasts all night—for the manhunt in the ghetto is still going on.

OCTOBER 2, 1942

Today I saw my friend Edzia through the window. Apparently she is again working at the former children's home. During the lunch hour, when the Polish policeman and the German guards patrolling the Pawiak turned into Wiezienna Street, her husband Zelig tossed a letter from Romek to me. I unfolded the note with trembling hands. It was the first news I had had of him in four months.

He wrote that he did not know I was still in Warsaw, but thought I had been deported long ago. His mother and sister are alive and are working in one of the workshops. He is no longer living with his family, but is staying with a cousin and a young girl. At first, this arrangement made me indignant, but later in the letter he explained the reason for such a strange partnership of two young men and a girl. Thousands in the ghetto are living like this; husbands have been separated from their wives and children, children from their parents, and everyone is sleeping wherever he can find a place. People who formerly were complete strangers to each other are now living together like close relatives. Husbands whose families have been deported try to escape their loneliness and ask the first woman they meet to stay with them. A woman makes life somewhat easier for a man, and two people together feel more secure amidst the terror. Thus individuals get together quite by accident and comfort each other. Romek also wrote that on Sundays, when he does not work, he meets Tadek Szajer and other friends. Hardly any of our common acquaintances have remained in the ghetto. Dolek Amsterdam is living somewhere on the Aryan side; he fled with his uncle, who was one of the leaders of the so-called "Thirteen." Rutka is alive. "I will try to write you again whenever possible," Romek concluded his letter. "You can answer through the same channel. Ever yours, Romek."

OCTOBER 4, 1942
Today Uncle Abie unexpectedly appeared in front of our windows. We had not heard from him since the deportation of the Jewish police force, and thought he was no longer in the ghetto, so we were overjoyed when we saw him. But he no longer wore his police uniform, and he looked terrible. He told us that during the blockade he had succeeded in running away to another part of the ghetto with his wife, Lucia. He is now working in a factory which is situated outside the new boundaries. He rolled up his sleeve and showed us a large blue stamp on his thin arm. Thus he is one of the lucky ones, the stamped slaves. "I am trying to be transferred to work in the house opposite the prison, so that I will be able to see you," he said. "Zelig is helping me, and I was told that my transfer will come through tomorrow."

OCTOBER 5, 1942
This morning we were up at seven, watching the street, and we were delighted when we saw Uncle Abie among a group of people who had come to work in the former children's home. We saw the supervisor counting the workers at the entrance. Zelig waved to us and pointed to Uncle Abie, who apparently did not dare turn around to greet us. Later we saw him through the windows of the home, and he beamed with happiness when he looked at us.

Among the workers, I also saw the former chairman of our Youth Club on Sienna Street, Manfred Rubin. Zelig did everything he could to gather all our surviving friends into the group he supervises. When Manfred Rubin saw me behind the bars of the Pawiak he stared at me, apparently unable to believe his eyes. Later he managed to tell me that his parents and Mickie had been deported, and that he is alone. Edzia told me today that Stefa Muszkat has also been deported.

Today a large group of Jews caught on the Aryan side were brought to the Pawiak. We saw them when we were taken to the baths for our weekly disinfecting treatment. In the baths, too, we were separated from the other women prisoners, but at the entrance and exit, and while dressing, we could speak to them quite freely. The attendant, whom we bribed long ago, pretends she does not see anything.

On our way out of the baths we met a woman, Mrs. P., and her little daughter leaving the special disinfecting chamber for those who have skin diseases. The little girl, who was about five years of age, ran around in the prison yard unconcerned and smiling, attracting everyone's attention by her pretty little face, which reminded one of Shirley Temple. Many of us commented on this resemblance. Her mother turned out to be an acquaintance of one of the interned women, Tusia W. We learned that the mother and daughter had been hiding on the Aryan side under an assumed name until a Polish neighbor denounced them. Now her fate and that of her little daughter is sealed. The little girl has memorized her new name and when someone calls her by it, she replies at once.

We met another mother and child in a similar situation. The women wept bitterly as they told us their stories, while their children calmly played at their feet.

In the yard where we take our daily walks, there are piles of turnips and beets prepared for the coming months. Our menu is now slightly different; the soups are made of turnips. Whenever the Ukrainian guard seems inattentive for a moment, we rush over to the pile of vegetables and snatch one of the big yellow turnips. They taste good raw, and fill your stomach for a whole day. Often we also manage to steal a few beets. If the Ukrainian goes behind the gate for a minute, the whole group of prisoners rushes toward the vegetables like a pack of hungry wolves. Sometimes there are a few carrots that fell out of the pot in which they were being cleaned. Carrots are a delicacy, and only on Sundays and other holidays do we find a piece of one in our soup.

During our walks around the little garden in the prison yard we talk about our uncertain future. Today, as we stood in the shade of the three large trees of the Pawiak, Felicia K., the daughter of the Grand Rabbi's wife, Madame Sh., told us that should we be sent to the Umschlagplatz, we would do better to take poison. She assured us that she would soon get some special pills for that purpose. I shuddered when I heard these words, and, strangely enough, at that moment my will to live was stronger than ever.

The commissioner who sometimes visits us said today that on the twenty-third of this month we would be taken to the internment camp for Americans in Germany. The women, he said, will be sent to Liebenau near Lake Constance, and the men to Laufen. I do not know how much truth there is in this statement. When our representative, Mr. S., asked the commissioner where the English and neutral citizens were interned, he answered that they were in a camp near Sosnowiec. This is a lie, because we know there are no camps around Sosnowiec, and we also know that these people have been deported to a death camp together with other inhabitants of the ghetto. Mr. S. asked his question only to see how the Nazi would react.[1]

Every day dozens of carts with furniture and other objects are brought to the warehouses for looted Jewish possessions, set up in the houses on Dzielna Street opposite the prison. Some of the internees have recognized their furniture on these carts. It is also horrible to see that the drivers of these carts are often close acquaintances—a doctor, an engineer, a former wealthy merchant, or a lawyer. The Nazis single out intellectuals for the heaviest physical work.

On one of these carts I noticed our great pianist, Wladyslaw Spielman. His appearance made me shudder. He was thin and exhausted, his suit hung like a bag. His sleeves were full of patches and his collar was torn. Slung over his arm was a bag with some bread. His eyes were hollowed out and he hardly seemed to breathe.

The carts go by in a long row in front of our windows. Two men accompany the driver to help him unload. When Spielman's turn came I could see him gasp each time he had to lift a piece of heavy furniture. He and his two assistants struggled for a long time with a grand piano which kept dropping back into the cart, its strings twanging. Suddenly a German who had been watching ran out of the doorway and began to berate him. Spielman tried to justify himself, and pointed to the piano's heavy legs, but all he got for an answer was a slap in his face.

At one point the pianist turned toward us; apparently he had felt our gaze. He smiled bitterly, and lowered his head. He recognized his acquaintances, former enthusiastic listeners at his concerts. Bewildered and ashamed, he turned away and resumed his work. Half an hour later the cart was empty. Wladyslaw Spielman climbed back onto the seat and wiped the sweat off his forehead with his hand. He pulled at the reins and the horses ambled off.

OCTOBER 8, 1942
Through Zelig we have received a letter from Rutka in which she tells us how she was saved from deportation by a near miracle. "We were standing in a long line," she writes, "all of us workers from Aschman's factory where my father is one of the chief overseers. Brandt (the Nazi who is directing the deportations in Warsaw) stood near by and indicated which persons were destined for Treblinka. At a certain moment he pointed to my mother and ordered her to leave the line. I ran to her and said that I would go with her. Brandt looked at me and all of a sudden began to smile. I thought he would have me shot on the spot but, to my surprise, he ordered my mother and me to return to the line of people who were supposed to continue working in the factory. At first I thought he was

joking, but he meant it. I was so shaken by this experience that I fell sick and spent two weeks in bed. I got up a few days ago, but still feel pains in all my joints. I have not seen any of our friends, most of them have been killed or deported. We work hard all day long; when we come home we sleep like the dead, and at six in the morning we are barely able to get up again. Several men have asked me to stay with them. This must not surprise you; all the girls are doing this. Very few women are left in the ghetto, and young girls, especially, receive daily proposals to live with men who have jobs and rooms near the factories. But for the time being I can still support myself. In a few days I will try to accompany Abie to Dzielna Street to see you."

OCTOBER 10, 1942
Today is my birthday. I spent all day on my mattress. Everyone came to congratulate me, but I did not answer. That night my sister managed to snatch three turnips, and we had a real feast to celebrate the occasion.

OCTOBER 12, 1942
All the American women from the Aryan side have been taken to the Pawiak. Perhaps this shows that we will soon be exchanged. They were put in the "Serbia," together with a transport of American women from Lwow. Because of the lack of space, some of them were put in the prison church, and some mothers and children were placed in two little rooms on the ground floor of our building.

We met them at the bath; the church is not far from there. Some of these women are Jewish, and they told us that an unpleasant anti-Semitic mood prevails, even among the internees. The Jewish women are constantly made to feel that they are outsiders. Only the nuns who are in this group protect them and condemn the anti-Semitic remarks of certain women. The nuns take care of the children without discriminating between the Jews and the Gentiles. They display true sisterly love and Christian charity; everyone respects them.

OCTOBER 17, 1942

Today we received a package from our Gentile friend, Zofia K. A few days ago my mother wrote to her, asking her for some food, and she answered at once. In this ocean of misery in which we are living, it is a comfort to find a warm-hearted person. Zofia K. and her husband have shown us much kindness throughout the war, and we owe them a great deal. Mr. K. even risked his life to bring us from Lodz to Warsaw. For some time he kept my sister and me in his house, thus exposing himself to the gravest danger. Mrs. K. writes that she will try to help Uncle Abie, and that she will send us more food as soon as possible.

The Soviet bombings are more and more frequent. It is impossible to sleep at night because of the explosions. Moreover, we have a terrible plague of insects. After the months we have been living here, the straw in our mattresses has been rubbed to dust, and turned into a hard mass. The paper on the walls is in tatters and there are whole nests of bedbugs behind it. Our bodies are covered with red spots. The fleas are even worse. No disinfectants seem to help.

We have three new internees, the wife of the American citizen, Adam L., who until now has been somewhere near Warsaw, and two women from the ghetto, the mother of Guta E. and Lily, the wife of the internee Leon M., a citizen of Haiti. They lived through the horror of the recent "campaigns" and it has left an indelible mark on their souls.

Mrs. Lily M. has moved into our room. She is twenty-two years old. She left her parents and a brother in the ghetto. A few nights ago, during a particularly intense air raid, all of us jumped from our beds; only Lily remained lying where she was. Someone tried to make her get up, but she turned to the wall and said, "I don't care. No air raid can frighten me. I even hope I'm hit by one of the bombs. Life has no value for me, anyway."

The rest of us are trying to maintain our morale, and each evening we gather in one of the rooms and discuss various subjects. We also feast on the stolen turnips, while everyone tells of his experiences.

Usually we sit in the room occupied by Guta E., her mother, and Marysia Sh., a Bolivian national. Her husband is in Bolivia now. She likes to show us pictures of that exotic South American country. Marysia is a comical person, small, plump, and blonde. She does not complain of being hungry; on the contrary, she is glad she is losing weight.

The W. family—the mother, her three daughters, Noemi, Tusia, and Dita (who is here with her three-year-old daughter Krysia)—are the most entertaining of all. The youngest of them is Noemi, a beautiful delicate blonde. She quickly won everyone's affection. Her older sister, Tusia, has a great sense of humor. Noemi and Tusia spent three months in the Pawiak in 1940 for failing to wear armbands. Our prison attendant knows them well, and they have no difficulty in bribing her. The attendants are still our main means of communication with the ghetto as well as with the Aryan side. After duty they return home to the Aryan side, and must pass the ghetto. They take our letters and bring us letters from friends and relatives.

Noemi is a born actress and recites extremely well. She studied for a year in Zelwerowicz's Dramatic School and acted in several plays at the Femina Theater in the ghetto. Today she recited Tuwim's brilliant poem, "Pif-paf." When she finished we all had tears in our eyes. This poem is as timely as though it had been written today. Noemi was so exhausted by her efforts that she sank on her mattress after she finished. Marysia ran over to her and gave her a piece of turnip.

Among the new prisoners in the Pawiak there is a certain Mr. D., a Swiss citizen, who was arrested on the Aryan side. D. is a good friend of Guta E. He told us that Jews are being

deported all over Poland, and that they are offering particularly stubborn resistance in the Lublin region. They prefer to
die where they are rather than to be sent to the death camps.
The young people are running away to the woods and joining
the guerillas.

OCTOBER 20, 1942

The Jewish police commissioner, Leikin, and Mr. First of the
community's building department, have been killed by
underground agents.

Many prisoners from the Pawiak are sent to the camp at
Oswiecim, from which no one returns. Everyone now knows
that this is a death camp like Treblinka, with the sole difference that its victims are chiefly Poles.[2]

On the Aryan side, too, the tension is increasing. Thousands of Poles are being sent to do slave labor in Prussia or
Central Germany. Labor service is now obligatory for all
Poles, and a system of labor cards has been introduced. Mass
arrests take place under any pretext, or without any pretext at
all. Mostly it is the intellectuals who are arrested. Yesterday in
the prison laundry I saw the well-known Polish playwright,
Mina Swierszczewska, among the prisoners.

Today we had a visit from Commissioner Nikolaus, who for
the "n"th time solemnly told us that on October 23, that is to say,
next Friday, "at exactly ten in the morning," all the American
citizens would be sent away. Although we do not believe him, all
of us are terribly upset. The citizens of South American countries do not know what to think; some of them are pessimistic and
say that they will probably be sent to Treblinka. I do not even
want to think of this. We have been with them so many months,
united in a common fate, and now we must separate.

OCTOBER 22, 1942

Is this really our last night in the Pawiak? Is it possible that
tomorrow we shall leave? Before nightfall, we arranged a

farewell dinner in the men internees' room. We ate turnips, and our representative, Mr. S., made a speech to the twenty-one American citizens. On the table we placed two little American flags that I had kept in my suitcase, as a relic, since the beginning of the war. The mood was one of elation. Noemi W. wore a silk wrapper that looked like an elegant evening gown. She recited and sang songs. I, too, sang several English songs. The attendants watched us and I had the feeling that they envied us.

OCTOBER 23, 1942

We are terribly dejected and disappointed. At ten in the morning, all the American citizens, Jews and Gentiles, numbering about one hundred and fifty persons, stood in the prison yard, ready to leave. Suddenly Bürckel and the commandant of the Pawiak appeared, and in angry voices ordered all the interned men to draw up before the gate within two minutes. This produced a terrible panic, because the South American citizens had not expected to be sent away. They rushed madly for their suitcases, and, without even closing them, tumbled toward the gate so as not to be late. A little later Commissioner Nikolaus arrived, and said that there was no room for the women in the train and that they would leave tomorrow. The men were then taken away in trucks. The women barely had time to say goodbye to their husbands. I just managed to kiss my father, and we did not exchange a word. My mother was in a state of utter bewilderment. We returned to our room, and I fell on my mattress with my hat and coat on.

An hour later, all the South American citizens came back. It turned out that the order applied only to United States' citizens. But Bürckel had deliberately mixed everything up in order to create panic and disappointment.

We are glad that father has gone. He has no American papers; he is really a Polish citizen, and here he was in constant danger of being deported to Treblinka. In the camp he will at least be under the supervision of the Swiss Exchange Commission. Mr. Sh. and Mr. G. are in a situation similar to my father's—they are husbands of American women. My father must be in the train by now. Shall we ever see him again?

OCTOBER 30, 1942
By order of Commissioner Nikolaus, the prison physician has examined us all. Those of us who are ill were supposed to be released and sent to the Aryan side. This physician is a Pole of German origin and he uses German methods. In his eyes, everyone was healthy. However, he released Mrs. Sh., who has a complicated eye disease, her daughter, Mrs. K., and her three grandsons, a pregnant woman in her seventh month, Mrs. Dita W., whose daughter Krysia has a skin disease, and Mrs. S., our representative's wife, who has an inflammation of the joints. All the released women received permission to live on the Aryan side.

CHAPTER XV

BLOODY DAYS AGAIN

NOVEMBER 15, 1942

The ghetto is again passing through bloody days. From the ninth to the twelfth there was another manhunt. This time the Germans demanded a large number of workers from the tailors' and shoemakers' shops. We had hoped that the Nazis would leave the remaining survivors in the ghetto alone—since their number is now officially only 40,000. During the first day of the new massacre, I saw through the window several older Jewish policemen pass by in rickshaws. Among them I recognized Commissioner Hertz. When he saw me he first smiled lightly, then saluted and went on, with lowered head.

The leaders of this new deportation campaign are Brandt and his aide, Orf, who formerly supervised the registration of the foreign citizens in the ghetto. For a short time Orf also supervised us at the Pawiak. This tall, handsome, blond man was always polite, always smiling, and the general opinion was that he was an exception among the Germans, incapable of harming a human being.

Now it turns out that Herr Orf, who for the moment is on furlough in Germany, was the chief murderer, and that he is responsible for the worst cruelties. Once, it is told, he was seen speaking smilingly to one Jew while at the same time he drew out his revolver and fired a bullet into the head of another Jew who stood near by. Then he turned and fired at the Jew with whom he had been talking so politely. One day we saw him under our windows discussing something with a group of women, in a very chivalrous manner. This was at the very height of the deportation campaign. Our attendant told us that he got his furlough as a reward for his great services during the deportation campaign, and that he is going to spend two weeks in Germany where his wife has just given birth to a child. Thus this murderer will caress his newborn baby with bloody hands.

Today Jewish policemen brought several cows to the Pawiak.[1] Apparently they were requisitioned from Jewish dairies. They are perhaps the last cows in the ghetto. The Storm Troop leaders and Nazi officials of the Pawiak will have better meals now.

Commissioner Nikolaus keeps making new promises about our departure. The date set is now December 16, but no one takes him seriously.

It is getting colder and colder, a frosty wind is blowing and it is snowing. The prison kitchen gives us a little coal every day for our stove. But the amount suffices for only an hour or two.

Packages now frequently arrive for neutral citizens who have long since been sent away. The senders of these packages do not know that these people have been deported and are perhaps no longer alive. Mr. S. manages to get hold of these packages—for German efficiency is a greatly exaggerated legend. He distributes their contents to those who need them most. The Germans are not quite clear about our names. Very often these packages contain potatoes and carrots, and other vegetables that we can cook on our stove.

Our friend, Zofia K., sends us a package of bread, potatoes, and onions every week. Packages arrive also for the women who have been released because of ill health and who are now living in a hotel on the Aryan side. They have got in touch with some Jews hiding there whose families are interned in the Pawiak. They have rescued Mrs. P. and her little daughter. Dita W. managed to do this by bribing some Gestapo officials with a considerable sum of money. Now the unfortunate Mrs. P. is out of danger.

Recently she also obtained the release of her mother and her sisters Tusia and Noemi, as well as of Mrs. S. with her sixteen-year-old son Martin, sixty-year-old Mrs. R., and Mr. K., his wife and his three-year-old son, Richard.

A Paraguayan passport has arrived for Mr. D., who is at present in our building. Today he told us horrible stories about what is happening in the cells of the Pawiak.

Bürckel carries out the executions personally. This sadist takes great pleasure in his work. In the larger cells, where more than a dozen prisoners are locked up, he hangs one of them in front of the others, after having tortured him for a long time, and then he orders one of the cellmates to take the body to the refrigeration room of the Pawiak, which is now filled to overflowing. Later he hangs the man who has carried out the corpse, and thus one by one empties an entire cell. Mr. D. also told us of the horrible pain he inflicts on the prisoners. He applies fantastic tortures, burns various parts of their bodies, pierces them with pins, etc.

DECEMBER 1, 1942

Today Rutka came with Uncle Abie and his wife to our window in the Pawiak. Rutka does not look badly at all, and as usual her face was wreathed with smiles. During the lunch hour they came out of the door of the house opposite the prison where they work, and asked the German guard for permission to speak with their interned family. This German was an elderly man. He granted their request, and even kept watch to warn them if another German patrol should approach.

We were very happy to see them so close and to speak to them. Rutka told us that her father was still working as one of the chief overseers at Aschman's factory. Unfortunately she could not stay long, for she had to return to her work, as did Uncle Abie and his wife. Later I saw them marching in ranks after work. Rutka smiled at us and disappeared at the corner of the snowbound street.

The German who directs the work of sorting in the house opposite the prison tortures his workers. Sometimes I see him order someone to leave the ranks and to throw himself on the ground twenty times. The victim must fall with his face in the snow or in the mud. To keep him in a state of terror, the German holds his revolver pointed at him. People tired from work and in a hurry to get home are kept in the cold street by this Nazi, who orders them to march back and forth, stopping them now and then to count them.

The workers employed in the houses opposite and adjoining the prison know all the internees. When their overseers are absent for a while, they exchange a few words with us. They ask us when we will leave for America and tell the world what is going on here. And we look on helplessly, unable to do anything for them.

Mr. S., our representative, who is now living on the Aryan side, is very active. He makes all sorts of efforts to rescue at least a few more Jews from the ghetto. Now this resourceful man is trying to marry several interned young men to women from the ghetto, so as to enable these women to be interned on the strength of their marriage certificates. He is asking a number of interned girls to do the same thing so that they can take a few men out with them.

The date set for our departure is still December 16, and I still do not believe it. Our rooms are now very sad. Many of our friends have been released. The evenings are quiet, and we read books. A few days ago a package of books came from the ghetto for the interned Jews. They were sent here by Mr. S., one of the most active leaders of the community.

All of us threw ourselves on the books with the same impatience with which we throw ourselves on food. My joy was

great when I discovered among them Adrienne Thomas'
Catherine, the World is Aflame! the second volume of *Catherine Becomes a Soldier.*[2] Although I have read this book several
times, I began to reread it with the same interest. I have
learned a great deal from the story of Catherine, my favorite
heroine, who has remained my ideal to this day.

This book brought back to me a piece of my past. It was in
1938, during the Munich conference, when it seemed that war
was about to break out. The streets of my native Lodz were
agitated, there were several demonstrations, and my parents
whispered to each other in a peculiar manner to prevent me
from hearing what they said.

One of those autumn nights, when the sky was heavily
clouded and rain was monotonously drumming at my window,
I sat in my warm, brightly lighted room, snugly curled up in a
chair, swallowing page after page of this novel. Then I made
my acquaintance with its heroine, Catherine. I forgot all reality; I lived with Catherine, I loved and saw the world through
her eyes. Late that night, when I turned the last page of the
book, it seemed to me that my name was Catherine. Later I
dreamed a great deal about what the world would look like
when I was as old as Catherine. I thought that when a war
broke out I, too, would have my Lucien Quirin, that there
would be shootings and bombardments and epidemics, and
endless trains of wounded soldiers. Perhaps I, too, would be at
the Metz station, helping to give food to the wounded heroes.
My Lucien, too, would fall, and I after him. But no... I did not
want to die. The following morning I awoke in a state of dejection. At school all my friends put down the name of Adrienne
Thomas' book on their "must" lists. I had only one desire—to
write such a novel myself one day.

In 1939, shortly before the war, I read this book again.
When we were locked up in the ghetto, I tried to find it everywhere, but could not. Now it was like a miracle: here it was in
the Pawiak! And when I received it, my mattress ceased being

dirty, I no longer felt the fleas or the hunger. I read the life of Catherine, who was a real heroine and behaved with great courage in difficult circumstances.

DECEMBER 10, 1942

We are spending much time studying languages. Marysia S. and Guta E. are studying Spanish. The W. family, Adam, Rose, Esther, and I, study English.

Amidst all this nightmare we have some amusement. Tadeusz R., a well-known designer, has made a few humorous posters, which hang in the room of the male internees. Adam W. and I wrote a number of satirical songs describing various aspects of our life together, about the women who quarrel in the kitchen, our impressions of the air raids, and our patriotic attachment to the various American countries. An anthem has even been composed in honor of our "nation of internees," made up of citizens of various distant countries which these citizens have never seen. This anthem, written by Adam W., runs as follows:

> There is in the Pawiak a brand-new nation
> From every country and every city.
> They live together in great unity
> In great cold and great starvation.
> Most of them are from the land
> Which lies near the Paraguay;
> There the life is especially gay
> For the fowl and flies in the sand.
> The most aristocratic group
> Comes from Costa Rica;
> Among them there is the blackbeard
> Who is the leader of our troupe.
> There is the prospective wife
> Of a citizen of Bolivia.
> Little she knows what to expect

From her future married life.
And our only Mexican
Has proposals without number.
All the girls are raving mad
To get hold of this rare man.
Two brunettes from Nicaragua—
One is quiet and one loud,
One is modest and one proud,
But both fighting mad *pro domo sua*.
Three Carmens and a toreador,
An old woman and granddaughter
With lots of bags and heavy bundles
Dream of their "native" Ecuador.
Those whose flag has stars and stripes
Are the proudest of them all;
Though locked up behind these walls
They are the lords and masters.

(In the second stanza the author refers to the Paraguayan citizens, who are in the majority here. Blackbeard is the pseudonymous name of our representative. The fourth stanza refers to Marysia S., whom we tease unmercifully about the probable unfaithfulness of her Bolivian husband. The United States citizens are regarded as "lords and masters" because they are the only real foreign citizens in contrast to the others whose citizenship or passports are of recent origin.)

DECEMBER 17, 1942
Our departure has again been postponed, this time till next year. Our rooms are terribly crowded, because all the internees who were released because of ill health returned with their bundles before the date originally set for our departure. The prison commandant was forced to give us two additional rooms, for in the meantime new internees had been brought here from the provinces, among them several

members of the W. family, and Rabbi R. of Pinczow with his family. All of them have South American passports. These people were at the last moment removed from a transport going to Treblinka. When the Pawiak commissioner led them through the yard they looked terrible, their clothes were ragged and dirty, and the shadow of death lay on their faces. The Rabbi came first, followed by his wife, his two unmarried daughters, another daughter with her husband, and his son, whose wife held their six-month-old child in her arms.

It was a dreadful procession, and I felt as though they were following a funeral. The newly arrived women were put in our room. When they entered I burst into tears and thought of my uncles, Percy and Abie. Why could we not save them? I threw myself on my mattress and wept for a long time.

Dita W., one of yesterday's arrivals, told us last night what she had heard about the camp at Treblinka. During her frequent visits to Gestapo headquarters at Aleja Szucha, she became acquainted with a German who was an official in this death camp. He did not realize that she was Jewish, and told her with great satisfaction how the deported Jews were being murdered there, assuring her that the Germans would finally "finish off" all the Jews.

At the Umschlagplatz, the cattle cars are loaded with one hundred and fifty people each, after their floors have been covered with a thick layer of lime. The cars have no windows or other openings. The people lie on top of each other without sufficient air to breathe, and without food or water. The cars are often left for two or three days at the Stawki station. The locked-up people must perform their natural functions in the closed cars and, as a result, the lime dissolves, filling the cars with poisonous fumes. The survivors are unloaded at Treblinka station and divided according to their trades. Shoemakers, tailors, etc., are grouped separately in order to make the victims believe that they are going to be employed in workshops. The real purpose is to make them go to their deaths more obediently. The women are separated from the men.

The actual death house of Treblinka is situated in a thick wood. The people are taken in trucks to buildings where they are ordered to undress completely. Each is given a cake of soap and told that he must bathe before going to the labor camp. The naked people, men, women, and children separately, are led into a bathhouse with a slippery tile floor. They tumble down the moment they enter it. Each small compartment is so filled with people that again they must lie on top of one another. After the bathhouse is entirely filled, strongly concentrated hot steam is let in through the windows. After a few minutes the people begin to choke in horrible pain.[3]

After the execution, the dead bodies are carried out by Jews—the Nazis specifically select the youngest and most vigorous for this purpose. Other Jews are compelled to sort out the shoes and clothes of the victims. After each transport, the Jews employed to bury the dead or sort their belongings are relieved by others. They are unable to stand this work for more than a week. Most of them lose their minds and are shot. Even the Ukrainian and German personnel are often relieved, because the older German soldiers begin to complain of their tasks. Only the chief German authorities remain the same.

Escape from Treblinka is impossible, yet two young Jews managed to do the impossible.[4] After long wanderings in the woods they arrived in Warsaw and related other details. According to them, the Germans employ various gases as well as electricity in certain execution chambers. Because of the enormous number of the murdered, the Germans have constructed a special machine to dig graves.

People who have traveled in trains past Treblinka say that the stench there is so poisonous that they must stop up their nostrils.

After Dita's accounts none of us could sleep.

We have also heard with distress Dita's stories about the sufferings of the Jews who are hiding on the Aryan side. The ocean of blood in which the Jewish population of Poland is being drowned still has not washed away the existing anti-Semitic poison. Certain Poles, especially workers and radical intellectuals, often risk their lives to save their Jewish friends, but cases of a shameful attitude toward Jews are also frequent in Warsaw. In the first place, Dita W. told us, many Polish landlords refused to rent her a room. Some Poles told her politely that they were forbidden to rent rooms to Jews, and others abused her and slammed the door in her face. Finally she managed to find a refuge with some Polish friends whom she had known before the war. She stayed with them for some time, and they were exceptionally kind, but then she had to move out in a hurry because another Pole, their neighbor, informed the Gestapo that they were giving lodgings to Jews. Dita W., being an American citizen,[5] was entitled to stay on the Aryan side, but in order to avoid unpleasantness for her friends, she moved to a hotel.

Similar stories are told by other internees who have returned from a stay on the Aryan side. There are a number of Jews hiding there, but they live in constant terror. Many are blackmailed by the Poles with whom they are staying. After their money and jewels are all gone, their hosts deliver them to the Germans.[6] All this goes on in spite of the fact that the Polish population, like the Jews, is bitterly persecuted by the invaders. Enormous transports of Poles constantly leave for East Prussia and Central Germany.[7] On the Aryan side, too, people are afraid to go out into the street because of the daily manhunts.

A thick layer of snow has covered the pavements, but I cannot forget that under this clean white blanket the stones are stained with human blood. Day after day I can see the workers in the houses across the street pass under my windows. Rutka smiles and Uncle Abie waves at us. Sometimes, when the old

German guard happens to be on duty, Uncle Abie tosses me a letter. Yesterday he threw me a piece of string to which a package was tied. In the package was found a loaf of bread, a jar of honey, and a number of letters for the internees. Today Uncle Abie repeated his performance of yesterday. But I wonder what has happened to Romek—I have not heard from him in a long time.

All the Gentile women among the foreign nationals have been transferred from the "Serbia" to the rooms in our buildings, which were formerly occupied by the male internees. Mothers with children have been released.

We have a new attendant, a young woman in her early twenties, a refined anti-Semite. She openly discriminates against the Jewish internees. When she leads us to our bath she calls out, "Gentiles first!" When one of us asks to be taken to the prison office, she always answers, "I have no time, the Jews are always bothering me."

A new group of American citizens from Radom has arrived. They have been put in the first room in our apartment, the one formerly occupied by Mrs. Sh. and her daughter and grandsons.

DECEMBER 26, 1942

It looks as though our departure is really imminent. The Nazis are making great efforts to impress us favorably. The day before Christmas, all the internees' quarters were scrubbed, even the rooms occupied by the Jews. On Christmas Day we had an exceptionally good meal that consisted of a thick pea soup, a portion of sauerkraut, potatoes, and two pounds of bread.

At nine in the evening Commissioner Nikolaus, accompanied by his aides Jopke and Fleck, and three SS men in uniform, entered our room, saluted us, and assured us that we would surely leave in the very near future.

This morning we received a visit from the hangman, Bürckel. He wore his gala uniform and, probably on account of the holiday, did not carry his riding crop. He had had a good dose of liquor and was in an exuberant mood. He approached old Rabbi R., took him by the hand and, shaking with laughter, wished him a merry Christmas. "We Germans can be kind, too!" he snickered as he staggered out of our room.

DECEMBER 31, 1942

This is the last day of 1942. It is empty and sad here. I have read and reread Romek's letter which Zelig slipped to me today. A year ago I was with him. Just as now, it was a dark, cloudy dusk, and snow was falling outside. This is what Romek writes:

"You must have been surprised at not hearing from me for so long, but I have almost been in the other world. On December 14, I was leading my group of workers to their daily job of removing the ruins of houses. At one point I climbed to the third floor of the house to see how the work was going. Suddenly I felt the wall shaking and a few seconds later I was buried under a mass of rubble. By a miracle my head and one of my arms stuck out. I remained fully conscious and called for help. My workers rushed over to me and began quickly to remove the bricks and stones under which I was buried. I was almost free when suddenly the workers began to run away. I raised my head and saw that a crane was moving over my head with a full load of bricks and stones. I thought that now my last moment had come. I do not know how long this anguish lasted because I fainted, and when I came to I saw the machine motionless, with its load suspended in the air. The workers then returned and finally dug me out. I could not stand on my feet, but I had to stay on the job, for if the German guards had realized that I was unable to work they would have sent me to Treblinka with the next transport. Two of my workers were sent there that night. I could not get up the next day. My mother took me to a doctor, who found severe contusions all over my body. A few days later water began to form in my knee. At present I am lying hidden, with my legs held up between boards. If the Germans discovered me here they would finish me off at once. I am praying God to be able to return to work as soon as possible. I will try to write you again soon, if I am alive."

We received two letters from our father at the same time. He is in the internment camp for American citizens at Titmoning, twelve miles from Laufen, and is well. The Red Cross supplies them with food, and the internees are treated kindly. They are staying in an old castle set in a picturesque countryside. He writes that after all he has gone through in the last few years, he feels as if he were in paradise.

JANUARY 1, 1943
New Year's Eve for me was full of nightmares. I fell asleep and woke up several times, for I was tormented by horrible dreams; I relived all the scenes I had witnessed during these years of war. Again and again the little children of Janusz Korczak's home passed before my eyes. I knew that they were dead and I wondered why they kept smiling and smiling. Each time I fell asleep these children came before me. Then I was awakened by shouts and laughter coming from the direction of the prison yard. The Nazi officials were gaily welcoming the New Year. From time to time I heard the sound of shots, followed again by laughter and the noise of broken glass. Then came roaring drunken voices.

The first day of 1943 is cloudy and snowy. As I write these lines I cannot stop thinking of Dita W.'s stories of Treblinka. I see before me the tiled bathhouses filled with naked people choking in the hot steam. How many of my relatives and friends have perished there? How many young, still-unlived lives? I curse the coming of the New Year.

JANUARY 17, 1943
We are about to leave. Our suitcases are packed. We are sitting in our coats, waiting.

Early this morning *Obersturmführer* Fleck came to take us to Gestapo headquarters at Aleja Szucha to say farewell to our friends on the Aryan side. Permission to say goodbye to our Gentile friends was obtained by our representative, Mr. S., who had to negotiate with Commissioner Nikolaus for a long time before he would agree.

At ten in the morning, we left the Pawiak in trucks. The streets of the ghetto were empty and dead. In many houses the windows were wide open despite the cold, and the curtains fluttered in the wind. Inside one could see the overturned furniture, broken cupboard doors, clothes, and linen lying on the floor. The looters and murderers had left their mark.

The doors of many stores were ajar, and merchandise chaotically littered the counters. Some streets were strewn with furniture and broken china. At the ghetto exit on Nalewki Street, I saw a Jewish policeman adding coal to a little stove. A German guard was warming his hands at it.

On the Aryan side, few people could be seen. Here and there a passer-by hurried along a deserted thoroughfare. When such passers-by saw our truck filled with people under a Nazi escort, they sadly shook their heads. They surely thought that we had been rounded up to be sent to labor camps in Germany.

At Aleja Szucha , we found Mrs. Zofia K., our Gentile friend who had been so helpful to us. She brought us a package of bread, cookies, and candy, and wept as she bade us farewell. The Nazis did not allow us to stay long, and an hour later we were taken back to the Pawiak. We were told to be ready to leave at a moment's notice. But we waited endlessly. I passed the time rereading my diary and rewriting parts of it in abridged form. I must not forget anything. In his last letter Romek wrote, "Remember, there are still 40,000 Jews left in Warsaw, and they are waiting for help from outside. Don't forget them." Mr. D., who had been released from the Pawiak for a few days and reported back this morning, told us the sad news that the ghetto is in a panic because, according to reliable information, the Germans are to resume their deportation campaign on January 18.[8]

While we are waiting here we can see transports of people being sent out of the Pawiak to the Oswiecim camp. Is that where the Nazis intend to send us, too?

CHAPTER XVI

INTERNMENT CAMP

JANUARY 18, 1943

A few minutes ago I awoke from my sleep. I cannot believe my eyes, and I still do not know whether I am dreaming or waking. Our train is moving in the direction of Poznan, not of Oswiecim. It seems now as though I have been traveling for a very long time. At 2:00 a.m. Commissioner Nikolaus and his assistant Fleck arrived at the Pawiak in an elegant limousine, which was followed by a dozen closed police cars. We were ordered to go to the yard, where we have taken our walks during the last six months. A thick layer of snow covered the ground. The Ukrainian soldier who stood on guard in a long fur coat with his rifle on his shoulder, said to us "*Do Svidania!*" (Goodbye.) The women attendants also came out to say goodbye. From the sad expression on their faces we felt that they thought we were being sent to our death. Not one of them believed that we were really being sent to an internment camp.

Commissioner Nikolaus read the names of the internees in alphabetical order. Armed soldiers led the persons named to the police cars. By three o'clock we had left the gates of the Pawiak behind and, for the last time, traversed the streets of the ghetto.

It was dark everywhere, except for the little fires of the stoves near the sentry posts. I felt choked by tears when we drove down Leszno Street. How much Jewish blood has been shed here. We were silent, and our Gentile companions sympathized with us.

My own feelings were mixed. Of course, I was glad to be rescued from this valley of death, but I could not help reproaching myself and wondering whether I really had the right to run away like this, leaving my friends and relatives to their fate.

Our train was not at the station but on a siding some distance from the city.[1] When we finally got on board, day had begun to break. We sank exhausted on the hard seats and fell asleep at once.

We are now approaching Zbaszyn on the former Polish-German frontier. There are new faces among my fellow travelers. Mr. S. managed to save a few Jews at the last moment. He himself is traveling with a young woman whose life he has saved. Her name is Mimi K. Mr. B., the Haitian citizen, saved his niece, Dosia. Among the new internees whom I had seen at the Pawiak there is also the newborn son of Mrs. L., who came into the world on the Aryan side. The baby is so tiny that we fear he will not survive the trip. All the women help to take care of him.

JANUARY 20, 1943
Yesterday we traveled across Germany all day long. We took a detour in order to avoid passing through Berlin. The most beautiful part of our trip was along the winding river Rhine, with its verdant hills and rich vineyards. In the afternoon we reached Saarbruecken, where, for the first time, we saw traces of ruin, caused, probably, by Allied bombs.

At six o'clock we were at Metz. The German Red Cross gave us a plate of good potato soup. I looked at the German nurses in their gray aprons with the red cross, and I had a strange feeling that I had been here before, that I had already seen all this. This is true, for I have been here in fancy with my favorite heroine in Adrienne Thomas' book; she was here in 1914. Everything looked exactly as it was described in the book—there was the big station with many marks of shrapnel and bullets. When the train left the station, I imagined that I saw Catherine's ghost, and heard her say, "I have given my life in vain."

Late at night we arrived in Neuburg, where we were again given a meal, this time better and more abundant than the previous one. There was a white tablecloth on the table, and, in addition to a tasty broth, we received bread and sausage. Apparently, the Nazis want us Americans to tell everyone that Germany is not lacking in anything.

We have just passed Nancy. In twenty minutes we will be at Vittel. The landscape is entirely new. Not a trace of the snow that covered Warsaw. Here everything is sunny and spring is in the air.

JANUARY 25, 1943

I feel as though I have been in Vittel[2] for a long time. We are fenced off with barbed wire, but we are living in paradise as compared with our three years in the ghetto. We have a separate room on the fourth floor of an elegant hotel. It is clean, and each one has a bed for himself. What more could one ask for?

I am slowly getting acquainted with my new surroundings, with the people and the conditions in the camp. For the first three days I did not leave my bed, I could not have enough of the pleasure of lying in the clean sheets. Only yesterday did I go out for my first walk in the park. Everyone looked at us with curiosity. No wonder, for we are the first transport of Americans from outside France.

Once, when I was lost in the park, I approached another internee who was walking by and asked her in English to show me the way to the Hotel Central. The woman answered in French that she could not understand English. It turns out that many of the British internees do not understand their own language—they are people who were born in England but came to France as little children.

It is very pleasant to walk in this park. In one of the lanes I noticed a number of American nuns, handsome young girls. They smiled at me with great kindness, and began to question me as to how we had lived in Poland, whether we had been in a camp, and how we had been treated there, whether we had received packages from the Red Cross and whether it was true that the Germans had perpetrated atrocious crimes against the Jews. When I told them that for six months I had been starving in prison, some of them gave me chocolate tablets. Then they asked me to wait a moment while they went back to their rooms. Soon they rushed out again, their hands full of canned food and sweets. I did not dare bite into the chocolate tablet I held in my hand. One of the sisters, seeing my confusion, broke off a piece and put it into my mouth. It was the first chocolate I had had in four years.

The children who came with us are practically buried in sweets and surrounded with much kindness. Most of them are much too mature and intelligent for their age. Three-year-old Krysia W. and four-year-old Stefanek K. walk in the park like grownups and greet everyone they meet with the Polish word *czekolada*, which sounds enough like chocolate to be understood by anyone. They always come back with their faces and hands smeared with chocolate.

This is a large camp. In the park there are three hotels, the Grand Hotel, the Vittel Palace, and the Ceres. Two thousand Englishmen are living in the two latter—they were interned immediately after the capitulation of France. At first they were kept in the military barracks at Besançon, but for a year now they have been at Vittel. These two hotels are very comfortable, and in the Ceres there is a fine library with books in many languages. The Vittel Palace has been transformed into a hospital, and the medical service here is excellent. The doctors are French war prisoners. On the ground floor of the Grand Hotel there are many stores. One of them, the *Bon Marché*, has wooden shoes (rationed), needles, thread, old-fashioned dresses of 1920, collars, artificial flowers, and similar dry goods. In another store can be found brooches, pins, boxes with the inscriptions, *"Souvenir de Vittel"* and *"Nous Reviendrons."* The pins with the inscription *"Nous Reviendrons"* ("we shall return") have become a patriotic badge, which almost every Frenchman now wears.[3]

On Saturdays and Sundays there are moving-picture shows, mostly of old French films. During the week the screen is pulled up and the cinema is changed into a theater. Excellent plays, revues and concerts are given here.

The three hotels are connected, and all together they form an enormous block situated on a hill. From the Grand Hotel, stairs lead to the park in which are situated the mineral water springs. They are being operated even now. The park is surrounded by three barbed-wire fences, and outside, armed guards walk back and forth. In the middle of the park there is a little lake with the inevitable swan.[4] There is also a little pavilion in which several shoemakers are working. They, too, are internees, and each of us is entitled to have his shoes repaired by them once a month. Behind the pavilion there is a church and the magnificent villa of the camp commandant. To the left of the commandant's building, there is a narrow path leading to the Hotel de Source, which is also inhabited by English people. Beyond is the Hotel Continental for people over sixty. The English and American nuns, too, are staying there; they take care of the old men.

On the other side of the camp is the Hotel Central, reserved for the Americans, whose number is not very large. They arrived in Vittel in September, 1942. Only women are here; their husbands are at Compiègne.

FEBRUARY 3, 1943

Today, for the first time, we received packages from the American Red Cross—Series Number 8. My mother had tears in her eyes when she opened her package, and all of us admired the care with which some unknown American hands had packed everything. Each little item reflected human warmth. All of us felt that the people who had sent us these things were thinking sympathetically of the starved people of Europe.

Lucia G., the pretty seventeen-year-old blonde who was with us at the Pawiak, shared the feast we organized after opening these packages. We found in each a can of condensed milk, margarine, cheese, corned beef, sugar, crackers, chocolate, cocoa, coffee, dehydrated orange juice, prunes, two packages of cigarettes, a package of tobacco, and powdered soup. We placed all these things on the table, and danced around out of sheer joy. Then we prepared for our feast. And we thought all the time, how could we send some of these things to Warsaw?

FEBRUARY 24, 1943

There is no more wonderful feeling than freedom. In Vittel I have a taste of it for the first time in three years. Although I can see the barbed wire and the Nazi guards a few steps away, I feel myself under the protection of the American flag. My only grief is the thought of my relatives and friends in Warsaw, from whom I have not received any news so far.

Spring is approaching. I spend whole hours in the park, reading and dreaming. I breathe the sharp odor of the pine trees, and feel happy when I am alone. I wish I could always be alone. I watch the passers-by. Some of them wear French army uniforms, which the Germans have given them instead of coats.

The days pass quickly. The food the Germans give us is insufficient, and without the Red Cross packages we would starve. The internees try to make the time pass by organizing all sorts of entertainments, dramatic circles, sports clubs, educational groups, etc. But we do not share in all these games. My thoughts are constantly in Warsaw. What is happening there? Every day I scan the papers, but I do not find anything in them about the Polish capital.

FEBRUARY 28, 1943

We have two important guests in our camp: the former Brazilian consul in Katowice, Poland, Paulo J., and his son Hilmar. Father and son met in the train after several months of separation, during which the Nazis had sent them from one German prison to another. Twenty-two-year-old Hilmar told me of his experiences. The Nazis accused him of all sorts of crimes that he had never even dreamed of, and on the pretext that he was doing espionage work for some European country they locked him up and tortured him. He still has unhealed wounds on his body and a broken rib which did not grow together well. He looks like a skeleton. Before he and his father received their first Red Cross packages, all the other internees gave them food. These Brazilians are overjoyed at being in the camp. They think it is a veritable Paradise, although the English and Americans never stop complaining about the food and the camp conditions. One must have gone through what we went through in Poland in order to appreciate our present existence.

In a few days we are to be transferred to the newly opened Hotel Nouvel, which will be occupied by families. The men now interned at Titmoning are due here soon to join their wives and children.

MARCH 15, 1943

We have been staying at the Hotel Nouvel for two weeks. The men from Titmoning and Compiègne have not arrived yet, but a group of men has arrived from Gleiwitz to rejoin their families after a long separation.

Our new rooms are pleasant and clean. My mother was given a separate room, which she will share with my father when he arrives. My sister, Rosa W., and I have a separate room too. Almost all the former internees of the Pawiak are lodged on the second floor. There are also Americans and English in our hotel. The relations between them are not of the best, for the English are rather snobbish. But no one really worries about this, since we have other and much more pressing problems.

MARCH 17, 1943
The longer I remain in Vittel, the clearer and sharper in my mind are the faces of the friends and relatives with whom I lived in the ghetto. I have many nightmares.

Yesterday we received two letters, one from Romek and one from Uncle Abie. Romek wrote to me on the blank for internees that I had sent him. This is what he said: "Every word from you gives me great joy. I am happy to know that at least you are safe. Do not worry about me, it is not worth it; we shall never see each other again."

Uncle Abie writes that if we can do something for him to do it as soon as possible, because he does not know whether he will be able to remain at the same address very long. My mother wept bitterly when she read these ominous words. She began to rush around to various people in the camp who have connections abroad, but she has not been able to arrange anything.

MARCH 29, 1943
All the male American citizens more than sixteen years old were suddenly sent away from here to Compiègne. The Nazis gave the ridiculous excuse that German war prisoners are being badly treated in America. The camp authorities exempted from this order only Mr. D., who was recently operated upon and is still in the hospital, Rabbi R., as a clergyman, and the consul and his son. It is very lonely here without the

men. We were all so close to each other, almost like one family, during the tragic months in the Pawiak.

APRIL 18, 1943

It is now late at night. I can hear Anna's and Rosa's regular breathing. They are sound asleep, but I am restless. The wind outside shakes the trees. I feel that somewhere horrible events are taking place. The weather is strange—the sky is clear and full of stars, there is not a trace of a cloud, and yet a strong wind is blowing. I am thinking of Romek and the sad letter I received from him yesterday. "I am working without ceasing," he wrote, "because work makes me forget all my troubles... The number of our friends is growing smaller and smaller. My foot is much better; I do not limp any more. Of our old acquaintances I still see only Tadek; no one else is left. Dolek is with Janek [this means that he escaped to the Aryan side].[5] Recently I saw Rutka; she has become very serious. Do not think about me, my dear. I know my days are numbered. I wish you all the best. Your Romek."

This letter was written on March 21. The wind outside is growing wilder and wilder, and my restlessness does not subside. There is something ominous in the air...

APRIL 25, 1943

Lehar's musical comedy, *The Land of Laughter*, was performed at our camp theater with tremendous success.[6] The famous English actress, Miss L., directed the performance, and the YMCA supplied the materials for the costumes, which were made by the seamstresses among the internees. Kendall T., an English internee, painted the settings. We also gave a revue directed by Morris S., a young English musician who has organized an orchestra here. Niusia W. played a special Polish number in this revue, and eight couples, dressed in colorful regional Polish costumes, danced. We danced Polish dances and sang many Polish songs.

Mary Berg (far right) in a performance of The Russian Harvesters
at Vittel internment camp, 22–23 March, 1943. Photo courtesy of
the Stella Gumuchian Collection, James Fox archives.

The success of this number was outstanding. The Americans
and the English were enthusiastic about it. The day after the
opening we heard remarks all over the camp: "Those Polish
girls were so colorful…" *"Ces Polonaises sont admirables…"*

Before the performance, our announced intention to give a
Polish number caused us much unpleasantness on the part of
our own Polish Gentile internees, who were offended by the
idea that Jewish girls were to dance Polish dances. When she
first heard about it, Niusia W. declared during one of the
rehearsals that she would have nothing to do with the whole
show. But a reasonable Gentile Polish woman admonished her
not to become the tool of the bigots and to continue her work.
In the end, the same Polish women who had agitated against us
attended the performance and applauded the Polish number,
which was òne of the most successful in the whole revue. It is
sad to think that after all our common sufferings, there is still
so much racial antagonism between us.

We are greatly comforted by the wonderful attitude of the nuns, who show great devotion toward the Jewish children. They have organized a school, and give lessons in Polish, English, and French. The mothers of the children help in this work. The soul of this undertaking is a nun of the *Les Auxiliatrices* order, whom we all call Mother Saint Helen. She is a tall, majestic woman with a magnificent figure. She emphasizes her sympathy for the persecuted Jews on every occasion.

CHAPTER XVII

THE BATTLE OF THE GHETTO

I have not written anything here for a long time. What good does it do to write; who is interested in my diary? I have thought of burning it several times, but some inner voice forbade me to do it. The same inner voice is now urging me to write down all the terrible things I have heard during the last few days.

We, who have been rescued from the ghetto, are ashamed to look at each other. Had we the right to save ourselves? Why is it so beautiful in this part of the world? Here everything smells of sun and flowers, and there—there is only blood, the blood of my own people. God, why must there be all this cruelty? I am ashamed. Here I am, breathing fresh air, and there my people are suffocating in gas and perishing in flames, burned alive. Why?

Toward the end of May, a group of women and children arrived here from Liebenau. I almost jumped for joy when I suddenly ran into Bola. We could not believe that we were

really together; it was like a story out of the Arabian Nights.
The first few days we were absolutely inseparable. I told her
about our friends in the ghetto, and the events there after
April, 1942, when she was interned, and she in turn told me
about her life in Liebenau. Bola arrived in our camp at the
same time as Roza W.'s cousin, Erna W., another girl of our
own age. We were as happy as children and, for a while,
entirely forgot the terrible reality around us.

Suddenly the news spread throughout our camp that the
Warsaw Ghetto had been set afire and that all the remaining
forty thousand Jews had been burned alive. The origin of this
report was a letter received from Warsaw by one of the
interned American nuns. The letter said that Nalewki Street
was aflame, but the writer obviously meant the whole ghetto.

At first there was panic among the interned Jews, but later
we simply refused to believe that the story was true. Then a
new transport of internees arrived from Warsaw, and they
brought a detailed story about the latest events in the ghetto.

The newly arrived people were put in the Hotel Providence, which was immediately fenced off with barbed wire in
order to prevent the old internees from communicating with
them. But the Germans apparently failed to take into account
the fact that the windows of the Hotel Providence give onto
the grounds of the Hotel Nouvel. That day and for several
days afterward conversations, interrupted by weeping, were
carried on through the windows of the two hotels. Among the
new internees we saw many familiar faces. There was Mr. K.,
for instance, who had been in the Pawiak with us and had been
released shortly before our departure because he was ill. He
gave us most of the details about the tragic last days of the
Warsaw Ghetto.

We learned that the campaign of extermination was
renewed on the very day we left the Pawiak for Vittel: that is
to say, on January 18, 1943. Incidentally, the Jews had long
since expected something of the kind. We left the Pawiak at

2:00 a.m. A few hours later strong detachments of SS guards, Lithuanians, Ukrainians, and a special regiment of Latvians entered the ghetto and began a pogrom. But to their surprise, these beasts met with armed resistance. Many Jews barricaded themselves in their houses and fired at the manhunters. It turned out that the underground movement in the ghetto had collected considerable stores of guns and ammunition.

The Nazis and their helpers withdrew from the ghetto. Five days later they returned with tanks and armored cars. Every house which offered resistance was set afire, and the people who tried to rush out were thrown back into the flames and perished. Nearly a thousand people died in this battle. Then, for the space of several days, huge human transports were sent from the ghetto to Treblinka.

There was a breathing spell of several weeks after this, but this time the survivors in the ghetto no longer had any

Jews captured during the Warsaw Ghetto Uprising are marched to the assembly point for deportation, May 1943

illusions. They knew that their fate was sealed, that the Nazis had decided to exterminate the Jewish population completely.

The final liquidation of the ghetto began in March. The German owners of the ghetto workshops were ordered to inform their employees that they must report to a registration center to be sent to Trawniki.[1] As upon previous occasions, they assured the employees that they need not fear anything, that the people remaining in the ghetto were considered a valuable element, that they would be given work under good conditions, that they would live in the factories and would not be separated from their families.

Only a small group of Jews, the most dejected and resigned, the hungry ones who could no longer live in their underground hideouts, reported. The majority did not believe the German promises. They knew that the labor camps of Trawniki were only bait intended to lure them to Treblinka.

The young people and all the other able-bodied men and women joined the underground movement and procured arms with their last funds. Feverish preparations for armed resistance began. The small underground cells now formed a large, well-disciplined organization. The Jewish working-class groups combined, and with the help of the Polish Socialist Party and other Leftist Polish groups, smuggled food and ammunition into the ghetto through tunnels dug under the walls. The Germans were well aware of these preparations, but they needed no pretext for opening their attack on the ghetto. Since only a small group of Jews had reported to go to Trawniki—barely two hundred persons—the Nazis decided to transport the others, nearly forty thousand Jews, by force.

On the night between April 18 and 19, 1943, on the eve of Passover, which is for the Jews a feast of liberation, armored units of SS guards, Ukrainians, Latvians, and Lithuanians surrounded the "Big Ghetto" area bordered by Leszno, Nowolipie, Bonifraterska, and Smocza Streets. By daybreak of April 19, the German guards in armored cars entered the ghetto through Zamenhofa Street and began to bombard the houses. The barricaded Jews replied with hand grenades and gunfire. After a few hours, the Nazis withdrew from the ghetto.

From every window and roof, from every ruined wall, the Nazis were met with a hail of bullets from automatic rifles. The signal for the fight was given by a group of young people who pelted the approaching German tanks with hand grenades. The Nazis returned after lunch with field artillery, and opened a barrage on Nowolipie, Bonifraterska, and Franciszkanska Streets. Then the pitched battle began.

The Jewish women took an active part in the fighting, hurling heavy stones and pouring boiling water on the attacking Germans. Such an embittered and unequal battle is unprecedented in history. The Germans finally decided to use their heavy artillery.

The bombardment was particularly heavy on the nights of April 23, 24, and 25, when the whole ghetto was turned into an enormous conflagration. The burning houses formed an impenetrable wall of fire which made escape impossible, and thus the heroic fighters were doomed to perish in the flames. Those who, by a miracle, managed to get through were shot by Nazi guards outside the ghetto walls. The shooting also found many victims among the Polish population on the Aryan side, adjoining the ghetto walls.

The streets of the ghetto were an inferno. Shrapnel burst in the air, and the hail of bullets was so dense that anyone who put his head out of a window was hit. The Germans used more firing power during the Battle of the Ghetto than during the siege of Warsaw. Nalewki, Nowolipie, Franciszkanska, Karmelicka, Smocza, Mila, Nizka, and Gesia Streets and Muranowski Square were completely destroyed. Not a single house remained in those streets. Even the bare walls of the burned houses were later blown up with dynamite. For many nights, the fire of the ghetto could be seen for miles around

SS troops walk past burning buildings during the
suppression of the Warsaw Ghetto Uprising, May 1943

Warsaw. "When we left the Pawiak," one of the newly arrived
internees told us from a window of the Hotel Providence, "we
saw an enormous mountain of fire and the houses on Dzielna
Street shook from the explosions."

Many Jews who had hidden in specially built cellars perished in the fire and smoke. One Jew who managed to escape
during the battle said that the SS guards pulled out women
and children (who were hiding in sewers) by their hair, and
shot them. They swept the deeper sewer pipes with machine-
gun fire and in many cases pumped in poison gas.

Under the ghetto there was a network of secret corridors
and tunnels. It seems that the Germans knew of this fact and
blew up all the cellars with dynamite. Thousands of people,
men, women and children, young boys and girls, who had
taken refuge there, fought till their last breath.

Even the Germans were amazed at the heroic resistance put
up by the defenders of the ghetto. They could not understand

where these starved, exhausted people drew so much courage and strength from in their fight for the last citadel of Polish Jewry.

From the former "Little Ghetto," where the Toebens and Schultz factories and several smaller workshops were situated, the last Jews were removed by force.

Among the newly arrived internees in the Hotel Providence there is Esta H., a good friend of mine from Lodz. She told me from her window about her tragic experiences before she was finally interned in the Pawiak. She was then working at Toebens' and was in the factory when the Germans began to transport the workers to Trawniki. At that time, the Battle of the Ghetto had already begun.

"We were herded into the yard," she related. "I was in a state of complete panic and thought we would be shot immediately. When I came downstairs, armed Germans had surrounded a large number of workers. The sounds of shooting and explosions came from all sides, and the windowpanes of the factory were shaking. When all of us were gathered together in the court, the Nazis ordered us to stand against the wall and raise our hands. The men among us were repeating prayers, and I bitterly regretted that I did not know any. But in my own words I prayed for a quick death.

"But fate spared me. After a while a high-ranking German arrived in the yard and gave orders that we be sent to the Umschlagplatz. I thought this meant Treblinka. I was in a complete daze, and came to only in the freight car, where I found myself crowded against a dense mass of people. All that time I had not even noticed that my husband was beside me. I was terribly thirsty. At one of the stations where the train halted for a long time, he bought a bottle of water from one of the Ukrainian guards who escorted us. He paid one hundred and fifty zlotys for it. These Ukrainian guards made a fortune during that trip. They charged six hundred zlotys for a small loaf of bread. We gradually realized that the train was not moving in the direction of Treblinka; after a trip of twelve hours we arrived in Trawniki.

"This camp occupies a very small area. We were put in an old barn. There was no water nor latrines. Only some of us received straw bags, the others lay on the bare ground. On the following day, three of the deportees fell ill with typhus, and the number of the sick increased from day to day. They were not separated from the others. Every day at six we were awakened to go to work; at six in the evening we returned to our barn, completely exhausted. The food we received was just sufficient to keep us alive. The nearest village was a few miles away, but no one dared sneak out of the camp to get food there, for the bayonets of the Lithuanian and Latvian guards bristled all around us.

"But even in this camp there were smugglers. Every day while going to work we met peasants carrying fruit and bread which they tried to sell to the workers. Sometimes we succeeded in getting some food that way, but in several instances the Ukrainians shot both the peasant and the Jews who were trying to buy from him. Once a Gentile from a nearby village tossed a piece of bread across the barbed wire to a young Jewish boy of about twelve years of age. With a face shining with joy the boy picked up the bread and began to eat it. At that moment, the Ukrainian guard from the nearest post ran to the boy, and with one blow knocked the bread out of his hands. Then he began to beat the poor child with the butt of his gun. He continued beating him even when he lay on the ground. He beat him to death.

"I almost went insane. Other people witnessed this scene in complete helplessness.

"However, a few people managed to escape. Once, late at night a group of guerrillas attacked our camp, disarmed the guards, and freed a few dozen internees. Some of the Ukrainian guards even joined the guerrillas and helped to disarm other guards. There were also cases of guards who ran away from the camp to join the underground groups.

"Near Trawniki, in the woods, there is a mass grave of several thousand war prisoners. They had been interned in our camp. All the peasants in the neighboring villages know about this mass grave, for they witnessed the execution of the Russian war prisoners by the Germans and were forced to dig this enormous grave.

"I do not know how long I would have been able to stand it," Esta concluded, "but, fortunately, after a few weeks we received our foreign passports and from that moment on everything went well. We were sent to Gestapo headquarters in Warsaw, then we spent three days at the Hotel Royal with a large group of internees from South American republics. Finally we were taken to Vittel with the last batch of Pawiak internees. But I cannot be happy, for my parents are still at Trawniki.

"A large number of documents like ours recently arrived in Warsaw. But most of the people to whom they were sent died long ago, in Treblinka or during the Battle of the Ghetto."

The Battle of the Ghetto lasted for five weeks. Its starved, exhausted defenders fought heroically against the powerful Nazi war machine. They did not wear uniforms, they had no ranks, they received no medals for their superhuman exploits. Their only distinction was death in the flames. All of them are Unknown Soldiers, heroes who have no equals. How horrible it is to think of all this—so many relatives and friends among them, Uncle Abie, Romek, Rutka... I have been standing at my window for the last few days, talking with the newly arrived internees in the Hotel Providence. I drank in their words avidly, and my thoughts carried me over there, to the burning houses of the ghetto where I had lived for three years with all these heroes. Every now and then I felt faint, as if my very heart had withered, and I would leave the window to drop down on my bed.

The wallpaper in our rooms is covered with a complicated, dark red design. Once I stared at this paper, and fancied that the red lines on it were merging into long red streams of blood... Thus *their* blood streamed, merging with the flames. Our blood, our bones, burning to ash. God, why do we have to suffer all this? Uncle Abie, Romek, and the others... Perhaps some of them have escaped?

On the day I spoke with Esta W., I gathered various foods from the internees of our hotel and, at eleven that night, Hilmar J. went stealthily across the barbed wire to the Hotel Providence. He distributed the food among the new internees, and received personal greetings from the ghetto, as well as a number of letters they had brought for certain people in our hotel.

One of these letters was for Felicia K., from a relative of hers who had remained on the Aryan side for a long time with the help of forged identification papers. Mrs. K. had obtained papers for him from Switzerland, and she had been unable to understand why he had not come to Vittel. The letter explained why. "My conscience does not allow me to save myself," he wrote, "now that I have seen so many of my nearest die a horrible death. Am I better than they were? I have no courage to leave the ruins. No, I will not leave Warsaw. This is my place, I must stay here. What is the value of my life in comparison with these heroes who shed their blood for our people? As I write you this letter I can still hear explosions from the ghetto. The last cellars are being blown up with dynamite. Under the ruins my brothers and yours are buried. Judge for yourself, can I run away from them? Last night I went by the ghetto gates and I still could hear shooting. The last Jews are still resisting. Posters in the Warsaw streets announce that 'Poland has at last gotten rid of the Jewish Communist elements.' After all I have gone through in the last few weeks I have not the courage to take the slightest step to save myself. Life has lost all value for me."

Mrs. Felicia K. and the others who read this letter wept bitterly.

The stories about the attitude of certain Poles toward the Jewish tragedy are also revolting. It is true that the underground publications of the Polish working class parties appeal to the Poles to help and give asylum to Jews who escape from the burning ghetto, but the number of Poles who heed this appeal is very small. The courageous Poles who risk their lives to hide escaped Jews in their homes are often denounced by anti-Semitic hooligans, and thus others are deterred from doing their very human duty to our martyred people. Under these circumstances, there is not much hope that a large number of Jews will succeed in saving themselves.

JULY 15, 1943

I do not know how to express my overwhelming joy—no, joy and sadness. Today I received several letters from Rutka. She is alive and well. On April 17, her parents got her out of the ghetto by paying a considerable sum of money. They were supposed to join her the next day, but on April 18 the Nazi extermination squads surrounded the whole ghetto, and now sixteen-year-old Rutka is alone on the Aryan side.

Her letter contains many dark hints, and I am surprised that it passed the censor. She says that in the end she will surely commit suicide. She saw Romek the day she left the ghetto, and on the same day she saw our Gentile friend, Zofia K., who gave her my address. Her four letters, which arrived today, bear different dates. Her second letter contains a note from Dolek. He and his relatives obtained foreign passports and were interned. In this letter Rutka says, "The days I spent with Dolek were the happiest of my life. I had a feeling that I was under someone's protection."

Today a certain Mr. R. arrived from Warsaw. There is a suspicion that he is connected with the Gestapo. He came all alone, without any police escort. He says that nearly two thousand people who had foreign passports were recently sent to the camp of Bergen-Belsen near Hanover. According to him, the last internees of the Pawiak and the Hotel Polski are there. There are many relatives of these internees among us, who are worried about their fate. So far all our inquiries about this camp at the Swiss commission have remained unanswered.[2]

JULY 18, 1943
In these bestial times, it is a comfort to meet people whose hearts are full of real love for the persecuted and needy. That is why I like to watch our wonderful Mother Saint Helen. I feel less dejected when I am near her. I admire her patience, her industry, and her love for little children. No labor is too hard for her. This magnificent woman gets down on her knees to scrub floors with her delicate hands. She wipes the children's noses and dries their tears. Despite the long black dress she wears, she has much practical common sense in solving all the worldly conflicts which arise here among people of various races and faiths.

She directs the school, and I take great pleasure in helping her. I make signs, paint toys for the children, and have also illustrated ten copies of the only children's book we were able to get for the whole class.

AUGUST 6, 1943
My father has finally arrived with a transport of men from Titmoning. We are at last reunited after a long separation. The meetings of the various families were very moving; people wept for joy. But there are still many women and children who have not seen their husbands and fathers for more than two years.

Transports also came from Compiègne and from other camps in Germany, such as Tost and Kreuzberg.[3] This concentration of internees from so many camps gives us hope that the exchange is near.

I have again received letters from Rutka containing tragic allusions. Her last letter describes how Tadek died. I was convinced that Tadek would survive us all, for he had the best chance. But he is no longer alive. The unfortunate boy committed suicide. I could gather from Rutka's letter that his father was killed by the underground groups. Tadek could never bear this disgrace; he must have felt that he would never be able to wipe the stain from his name. His father was killed at his home on April 17, a day before the outbreak of the insurrection. The next day Tadek killed himself. Poor boy, he loved me so much.

AUGUST 22, 1943
People die and are born in our camp. Recently we had two funerals for old Englishmen from the Hotel Continental. Three new babies have come into the world. The mothers are surrounded by great care, and receive special packages through the nuns. Pregnant women, too, receive extra packages and are under the supervision of French physicians who are war prisoners.

One of these physicians, Dr. L., is a famous surgeon. His situation is pathetic. His wife and child are in a camp near Paris, whence transports are constantly sent to Poland. He keeps asking us whether all that is said about Treblinka is true. He refuses to believe that people are killed there by the thousands with poison gas and steam.

Our camp is a little world in itself. We even have cells of the French underground movement. The internees know that somewhere in our camp there is a secret radio. Every day the latest news is spread by word of mouth with the greatest speed. It seems that the Germans suspect something of the kind, for yesterday they searched the hotel, but they could not find the radio. It is said that while the Germans carried on their search someone was walking in the park carrying the radio in a suitcase.

The Germans now make searches in a different hotel every day, but the radio continues to function and informs us of events. The news is good. The Russians are approaching the Polish border, Germany is being bombed constantly by air, the Allies have landed in Italy, and the African campaign was concluded long ago.

From Africa, I received a letter from my cousin, Henry W., who is an officer in De Gaulle's air force. To receive letters is now a great privilege in Europe, and I enjoy it thanks to the American flag. I correspond constantly with Rutka, who is on the Aryan side in Warsaw. The internees are allowed to send only one blank a week, but I use the blanks of my whole family and, in addition, several friends in camp give me theirs. The censors have quite a bit of work to do reading my mail.

The work at school gives me great joy, and provides me with an opportunity to practice my English and French. I now direct the artwork in two classes. We use the cardboard from the Red Cross packages as material, and for glue we use dissolved powdered milk. The majority of the children are from Poland; many of them arrived in the two last transports, which came here after the liquidation of the ghetto. They have learned French and English very quickly, and are a great comfort to all of us.

OCTOBER 2, 1943

During the two days of Rosh Hashana, the men prayed in one of our rooms. We set up a table with candles, just as we did in the Pawiak, and Madame Sh., the wife of the Grand Rabbi of Warsaw, stood near the altar. A sad and solemn mood prevailed.

On the second day of Rosh Hashana, I received a letter from Rutka, informing me that Uncle Abie is alive. Zofia K. told her that he is working in the suburb of Praga. My parents think it is a good omen that the letter arrived on Rosh Hashana. But Rutka still has not answered my questions about Romek. What she does say about him is not clear. I am afraid that she does not want to tell me the truth. He must have perished with thousands of other heroes in the ghetto.

SEPTEMBER 5, 1943

Today we received a letter from our uncle in Toulouse. He writes that he must change his address frequently, and that his daughter, my cousin, was forced to give her one-year-old child to a Gentile family in order to hide it from the Nazis. The situation of the French Jews is getting worse from day to day. Thousands of Jews are being sent from Paris to the camp at Drancy, which is only a stage on the journey to Treblinka.

In other Nazi-occupied countries, too, the Jews are being gathered together in provisional camps called *Durch-gangslager* (transit camp), before being sent to the various death factories in Poland. These Jews do not know what a terrible fate awaits them. They have no idea of what has happened to the Polish Jews.

The largest transports of Jews are now being sent from the Dutch camp of Westerborg.[4] We were told about this by some British citizens who came here from Holland a few days ago. An American woman who recently came from there told us about the admirable attitude of the Dutch people toward their Jewish co-citizens. They not only hide the Jews in their homes, but several times Dutch underground groups have attacked trains carrying deported Jews and liberated them. In some towns the Dutch population burned the civil registers, thus making it difficult for the Nazis to find out who was Jewish. In other towns the Gentile population organized protest strikes against the persecution of the Jews, and in some cases, forced the Germans to stop the deportations.

OCTOBER 10, 1943

Yesterday was the Day of Atonement, and today is my birthday. I feel very old, despite the fact that I am only nineteen. My mother prepared a surprise party for me and invited all the young people in the camp. They tried to create a cheerful mood, but their artificial gaiety only saddened me.

NOVEMBER 15, 1943

Today we took a wonderful walk outside the camp to a nearby village. We obtained permission for it after long and wearisome negotiations. Our group comprised thirty persons, and the German who escorted us changed his severe tone as soon as we gave him a few packages of American cigarettes and other valuable articles.

For the first time in eleven months, we left the area fenced by barbed wire. The path led between the green hills of the Vosges. At certain points it was so narrow that we had to walk in single file. The sun shone brightly, and a light, cool breeze was blowing. We did not meet a living creature on our way. Then we went around a tiny village. Dirty, emaciated children were playing in front of the huts, and a horse tied to a fence picked monotonously at the grass.

The larger village, which was our goal, did not look much better. The houses were dilapidated, the people thin and weather-beaten. Soon we were surrounded by a band of children who begged us: "*Avez-vous quelque chose à manger?*" We gave them bread and chocolate. They stuffed it in their mouths with trembling little hands.

In the center of the village there was a little inn. A few women who were sitting near the fireplace rose to serve us. Bottles of red wine and Kirsch appeared on the long table. The German guard sat down to drink, and gave us permission to walk about freely, after admonishing us to be back at a certain time. Together with Erna, Bola, Rosa, and Harold, a young Englishman, I went to look for flour, which cannot be had in the camp at any price. After a long search we found a bakery which made rationed bread. The poor baker hesitated a long time, but when he saw our tins of canned food he poured flour into our bags. We also bought long French loaves of bread at seven francs a loaf, but it was black bread quite unlike the good pre-war bread of France. A peasant woman gave us a few eggs, and thanked us over and over again for the cake of soap and piece of American cheese we gave her in return. Wherever we went we were greeted with joyous exclamations: "*Les Anglais! Les Américains!*"

Upon our return to the inn we had a great surprise. On the table there was a radio, which had previously been hidden. The German guard had drunk heavily and was asleep on a bench outside. Harold dialed a foreign station, and for the first time in four years, I heard a radio broadcast.

We happened to tune into a program sent from America to Europe. The broadcast was in German, followed by an English translation. We heard the latest news. Paris was being heavily bombed, as well as the Normandy coast. The Russians had recaptured a number of cities, and had taken many thousands of German prisoners. The broadcast concluded with a salute to all the oppressed peoples of Europe. We listened with bated breath. Suddenly our German guard came in. Fortunately, he was too drunk to realize what was going on. I quickly turned the dial to get a Paris station, and we heard gay music.

Late in the afternoon we returned home with our trophies. Each of us had a little bag with a few pounds of flour. There was a little hole in Erna's bag, and flour marked our path. One of the English girls declared triumphantly that she had the best trophy of all—she had a rabbit in her bag! All these treasures went unnoticed by the supervisor who checked us in at the camp entrance, because it was dark when we returned.

NOVEMBER 17, 1943
It is ten o'clock. A little lamp is burning in my room. I have hung a blanket over my door to prevent any light from showing through the cracks. Officially we are supposed to turn the lights out at ten, but the night is the only time I can read or write. Special black shades are on the windows, but I have hung a coverlet on them, too, and I am sitting in a corner at my little lamp.

I like to hear the drone of the British and American planes that pass by here every night at the same hour. I listen to the hum of the heavy bombers as if it were the purest music. The melody of the propellers is my best lullaby, and I fall asleep with a growing hope that in the end the dark forces of Nazism will be defeated. The following morning I read the German war bulletins informing us that Paris was heavily bombed, and that, of course, only hospitals and children's homes were hit. Perhaps my cousin Henry W. is among the fliers who pass overhead at night. How I wish he would drop me a letter!

NOVEMBER 21, 1943

The first exchange of prisoners between England and Germany has taken place. About one hundred persons have left Vittel, mostly the sick and those over sixty. The farewells were very moving. We all envied them, and the fortunate ones smiled as though seeing the gates of paradise after a long martyrdom.

Last Saturday, we saw a travelogue of New York in our cinema. First the Statue of Liberty emerged from the mist— a gigantic woman with a torch in her hand. Then the lofty skyscrapers came into view. I saw the streets of New York and people hurrying about. Cars rushed at an enormous rate of speed. Then came Broadway with its neon lights. The travelogue ended with a ship entering the port of New York. At that point applause swept the hall. Apparently everyone thought of the moment he himself would arrive at New York aboard a ship. My mother, who sat beside me, could barely control herself. "Look," she said to me with enthusiasm, "that's Radio City and that's Fifth Avenue, and there's Broadway..."

The applause lasted a long time, and the film aroused the deepest emotions in all those who knew New York. I cannot understand why the Germans showed it.

NOVEMBER 27, 1943

The first transport of Italian war prisoners has come to Vittel. They are Italians who went over to the Allies after Benito's capitulation. They were put up at the Hotel des Colonies outside the area of our camp.

We had an unexpected letter from my cousin Henry W. He has been in London for two months and is still serving under De Gaulle.

DECEMBER 18, 1943

There is a terrible panic among the Jewish internees. The Germans have suddenly ordered Americans and British of Jewish origin to register. We do not know what this means, but various rumors are circulating. Some say that the Jews will be sent to Palestine in exchange for Germans interned there. Others maintain that we will be sent back to Poland. The Jews sit in their rooms in despair and do not know what to do. It looks as though something serious is afoot, for a special commission composed of high officials from the German Foreign Office has arrived in camp.[5] The Gentile internees sympathize with us, especially the nuns. Mother Saint Helen declared that should we be sent back to Poland she would not permit the children to go. "I will not give them the children," she said resolutely. "I will hide them in the church, and I defy them to go there."

DECEMBER 26, 1943

This time we got away with only a scare. The Nazi commission has vanished and the whole camp, Jews and non-Jews, breathed with relief.

This year our Chanukah feast coincided with Christmas, and many Jews and Gentiles felt that this fact was symbolic. Chanukah candles are lit in many of the rooms occupied by Jews, while the Christmas tree in front of the church is decorated with tinsel. Perhaps our common suffering and persecutions will finally eradicate blind race hatred?

JANUARY 1, 1944

New Year's again! What will it bring us? Last night we had a
celebration. For a while I, too, forgot myself and danced. But
suddenly I fancied that shadows were dancing around me.
Then I felt a strong ringing in my ears, which soon changed
into a wild laughter. I felt dizzy and asked my partner to take
me home.

JANUARY 12, 1944

There is again a wave of uneasiness in the camp. A rumor has
it that in Vittel, too, the Jews will soon be isolated in a kind of
ghetto. Many Gentiles are indignant and declare they will not
permit it. But, strange as it may seem, even here there are
Aryans who are pleased at this prospect, who maintain that
the Jews should be separated from the Gentiles, just as they
were in the camp at Titmoning. It is possible that the same
anti-Semites are responsible for these rumors.

JANUARY 30, 1944

A few days ago, the camp administration ordered the
Americans to be ready to leave at a moment's notice. The
English are skeptical, and maintain that the exchange will not
take place for another year, because that much time elapsed
before the departure of the first batch of English. The possessors of the American green passports that were issued before
the war will have preference, at least, according to the
Germans.

I have been waiting impatiently, and have been so restless
for the last few days that I have spent almost all my time
walking in the park.

FEBRUARY 16, 1944

I have received a desperate letter from Rutka. She writes that
her identification papers and money were stolen from her. She

is now alone, lost in the midst of a world of hatred and man-hunts. "The thought of you is my only comfort. I live in hope that I shall see you again." Poor Rutka, how much she has gone through, and how much still lies ahead of her!

FEBRUARY 27, 1944
At last a date has been set! The exchange will take place in Lisbon on March 5. Wounded American soldiers and civilian internees are scheduled for exchange. But it is not clear yet what the ratio of the exchange will be—five Germans for one American, or vice versa, five Americans for one German. Various rumors are circulating on the subject. The camp administration organizes a new registration every hour; new people are put on the lists, old ones are crossed off. We are all at a terrible pitch of tension and nervousness. Our family was on the first two lists, but now we have been taken off them. My mother is rushing around from one office to another. Only about thirty persons are supposed to go with the first batch, while there are one hundred and fifty candidates for exchange in Vittel.[6] All these shifts and rumors have completely shattered our nerves.

FEBRUARY 28, 1944
The lists have been closed. We are not going. My mother constantly visits the commandant, only to be told again and again that we cannot go because my father is of military age, and because it is against his principles to separate families. If this is true, most families cannot go, because their men are less than fifty-five years old. Meanwhile, all the nuns and possessors of green passports have received confirmation that they will be in the first batch. But the commandant says that changes may take place at the last moment. This reminds me of the Nazi tactics in the Pawiak. There, too, they changed their minds every minute, apparently for the sole purpose of torturing us.

FEBRUARY 29, 1944

The list of Americans to be exchanged has been definitely confirmed. We are not going. The fortunate ones have received orders to pack their bags. From my window I can see suitcases piling up in their rooms. Outside it is snowing. Sometimes I imagine that I am back in the Pawiak.

CHAPTER XVIII

JOURNEY TO FREEDOM

MARCH I, 1944

We are in the train! We are going despite everything. During the last twelve hours we have been through the most heart-rending experiences. Every half hour there were changes. At 6:00 p.m. the camp administration called out, over the loud-speaker, the names of all those who were not on the list. A few persons were lacking to make up the transport, so we hoped that we, too, would be taken. My mother rushed to the commandant, but soon returned with a downcast face; it was too late. But she did not give up hope, and kept praying that something would happen at the last moment.

And it did happen. At 10:00 p.m. transports arrived from Titmoning and Liebenau, and it turned out that there would be room for some more internees. The administration summoned the native Americans, and my mother was accepted at once. At first my father was supposed to remain in Vittel, and my mother agreed to this, because she was convinced that at the last moment there would be another change, and that my father would be allowed to go with us. Meanwhile she packed all our things. Just as in Warsaw, a number of people visited us and gave us the addresses of their American relatives. They helped us to pack and bustled around us. Niusia W. prepared our food for the trip, while Bola lay weeping in her room.

At seven in the morning, my mother went to the camp administration office and, a few minutes later, she came running back, crying, "We're all going!"

I shall never forget the moment when we said farewell to the people with whom we had suffered so much, constantly suspended between life and death. Everyone said, "Please don't forget us, all our hopes are pinned on you. Don't be silent. See to it that we are rescued..." All without exception, men, women, and children, wept. Hundreds of hands waved to us from the windows beyond the barbed-wire fence. In the distance I could see Erna wiping her eyes. Beside her stood Rosa, Harold, and many others, friends and strangers.

Our compartment is the one adjoining our German escorts. They are in a state of extreme nervousness. I have never seen Germans so upset. They keep checking the number of their prisoners against a list in their hands.

MARCH 2, 1944
We have been in Biarritz for several hours. The train halted two miles from the main station. Among the passengers there is a growing fear. According to some rumors, a number of the internees will be sent back to Vittel, because there are allegedly too many of us to exchange.[1]

MARCH 3, 1944
A few minutes ago we exchanged all our money for dollars. This has finally reassured us; we really believe we are going to America now. All the men were made to sign a pledge that they would not fight against Germany in any army. When they left the cars to sign this pledge we saw a train with German internees arrive on another track. They have come from America to be exchanged for us. All of us actually pitied these Germans.

MARCH 4, 1944

Our train is now on Spanish territory. At the stations some people greet us with the "V" sign. The poverty of Spain strikes one at once. Ragged children stretch out their hands, begging for a coin. There are many soldiers, especially smartly dressed officers. The civilian population is dressed in rags, and the people have hollow cheeks.

Many of the Germans who escorted us have remained on the French side of the border, and those who still accompany us now are dressed in mufti. With their uniforms, they have shed their insolence.

MARCH 5, 1944

We have just crossed the Portuguese border. The uniformed Spanish police have been replaced by Portuguese secret police. We are still in the same train. Here, too, people greet us with "V" signs.

Our train is approaching Lisbon. I can see the sails of various ships. Someone in our car has just shouted the word, "Gripsholm!" This unfamiliar Swedish word means freedom to us.[2]

I was awakened by the sound of the ship's engine. The *Gripsholm* was on the open sea. I went out on deck and breathed in the endless blueness. The blood-drenched earth of Europe was far behind me. The feeling of freedom almost took my breath away.

In the last four years I have not known this feeling. Four years of the black swastika, of barbed wire, ghetto walls, executions, and, above all, terror—terror by day and terror by night. After four years of that nightmare I found it hard to enjoy my freedom at first. I constantly imagined that it was only a dream, that at any moment I would awaken in the Pawiak and once again see the aged men with gray beards, the blooming young girls and proud young men, driven like cattle to the Umschlagplatz on Stawki Street to their deaths.

The exchange ship *SS Gripsholm* entering
New York Harbor

I even fancied sometimes that I heard the cries of the tortured, and the salty smell of the sea suddenly changed into the
nauseating, sweetish odor of human blood, which had often
entered our windows in the Pawiak.

Below in the lounge someone had begun to play the piano,
and this reminded me of Romek, who used to play the same
Schubert melodies. I saw his long, delicate fingers before me.
I went to my cabin and threw myself on my bed, weeping
bitterly.

I had thought that on the ship I would forget the nightmare
of the ghetto. But, strangely enough, in the infinity of the
ocean I constantly saw the bloody streets of Warsaw.

On deck I made friends with American soldiers and fliers
who had been shot down on missions over Germany, and who
had been exchanged together with us. Some of them had

empty hanging sleeves. Others walked on crutches. Two young officers had horribly disfigured faces, and others had had their faces burned. One of them had lost both legs, but a smile never left his lips.

I felt close to these Americans, and when I told them about what the Nazis had done in the ghetto, they understood me.

Aboard ship I saw the first American film in four years. It was *Yankee Doodle Dandy*. The soldiers and officers had tears in their eyes when they saw it.

By nightfall of March 14, the outline of the American coast began to emerge from the mist. The passengers went out on deck and lined the railings. I was reminded of the Biblical story of the flood, and of Noah's ark, when it finally reached dry land.

All that day I felt completely broken, as though I had to bear the burden of many, many years. I did not take part in the entertainment that night. I lay in a corner of the deck, listening to the sound of the waves that were growing stormier and stormier.

On March 15, our ship approached New York.[3] People who had gone through years of common misfortune began to say farewell to each other. A mood of fraternal affection prevailed among us. On everyone's face there was an expression of restless expectation. I saw the skyscrapers of New York, but my thoughts were in Warsaw and I was talking with Rutka. For a moment I fancied that I was taking her by the hand and pulling her aboard ship.

Dear Rutka, I miss you very much. I wish I could share my good fortune with you. How wonderful it would have been to step on American soil with you. I wish I could give you at least a little part of the freedom and happiness that are in store for me. I am with you now. The Statue of Liberty, that proud woman with a torch in her hand, which I see before me, is looking toward you as much as toward me. She greets you, too, you and all our friends who are still alive and also those whom we shall never see again.

Rutka, look with my eyes, let your heart beat with mine. We are approaching freedom. Each of us will find bread here, a home, freedom. No one will ever appreciate freedom as much as we who once lost it.

My Rutka, tell all of those who are still alive that I shall never forget them. I shall do everything I can to save those who can still be saved, and to avenge those who were so bitterly humiliated in their last moments. And those who were ground into ash, I shall always see them alive. I will tell, I will tell everything, about our sufferings and our struggles and the slaughter of our dearest, and I will demand punishment for the German murderers and their Gretchens in Berlin, Munich, and Nuremberg who enjoyed the fruits of murder, and are still wearing the clothes and shoes of our martyrized people. Be patient, Rutka, have courage, hold out. A little more patience, and all of us will win freedom!

NOTES

INTRODUCTION

[1] "Thousands Mourn Victims of Ghetto," *New York Times*, 20 April 1944, p. 10.

[2] Transcript of "Woman of Tomorrow."

[3] S. P. has a few photocopied pages of the original Polish manuscript, but the full Polish manuscript as well as Mary Berg's original diary are apparently no longer extant.

[4] S. P. thanks Fabian Fuerste at the Wiener Library for establishing the exact dates and issues that the diary appeared in German.

[5] Among others, "The Extermination of 500,000 Jews in the Warsaw Ghetto: the Day to Day Experience of a Polish Gentile" was published by the American Council of Warsaw Jews and the American Friends of Polish Jews in New York in 1942.

[6] After the war, the *Oneg Shabbat* archives of the ghetto, organized by Emanuel Ringelblum, were recovered in Warsaw, and the diaries and chronicles of Adam Czerniakow, Janusz Korczak, Chaim Kaplan, Abraham Lewis and Emanuel Ringelblum, who perished in the Holocaust, came to light. Several memoir accounts appeared over the next four decades, including those of Alexander Donat and Helena Szereszewska, and survivors of the Warsaw Ghetto Uprising, like Yitzak Zuckerman and Vladka Meed. The memoir of the ghetto policeman Stanislaw Adler, who survived but killed himself in 1946, was also published in English in 1982 by Yad Vashem. Since only one per cent of the ghetto inhabitants survived the war, even accounts written after 1945 are rare.

[7] Review, *New Yorker*, 1945.

[8] Review, *Kirkus*, 1945.

[9] Young, M. *New York Times Book Review*, 1945.

[10] Weiskopf, F. review, *Saturday Review*, 1945.

11 In 1945, a Hebrew translation of the diary appeared in Tel Aviv, and a Spanish edition came out in Buenos Aires. In 1946 an Italian edition appeared in Rome and in 1947 a French translation in Paris. Several decades later, Shneiderman edited a Polish translation of the original English, which appeared in Poland on the fortieth anniversary of the Ghetto Uprising in 1983. A Hungarian translation followed in 1991, as well as a new Italian translation.

12 In 1986, *A Bouquet of Alpine Violets*, a play based on the diary, was staged in Warsaw. See Kaufman, M. T. "Warsaw Play Dramatizing Ghetto Diary," *New York Times*, ProQuest Historical Newspapers, 18 May 1986, p. 13. More recently, *Tempesta*, a production inspired by Mary Berg's diary, appeared in five countries as street theater in an adaptation directed by Cora Herrendorf. The production was by the Teatro Nucleo company, which began in 1974 in Argentina and finds its home in Italy today. (See Teatro Nucleo's website at http://www.teatronucleo.org.) In 1991, Heinz Joest's documentary film, "A Day in the Warsaw Ghetto: A Birthday Trip to Hell," directed by Jack Kuper in Canada, featured text from Mary Berg's diary.

13 Lucy Dawidowicz (1975); Nora Levin (1973); Yisrael Gutman (1982); Martin Gilbert (1985).

14 Letter from Eckhardt to Pentlin, dated 1995.

15 Rosenfeld, A. H. (1980).

16 Quoted in Elbaum, E. (1945).

17 Mary Berg's father was born on 19 July 1893 in Pultusk, Poland and died in the United States in 1970, where he had continued his antique business after the war; her mother Lena died in the United States in 1989.

18 Israel Gutman, *The Jews of Warsaw, 1939–1943, Ghetto, Underground, Revolt* (Bloomington, Ind.: Indiana University Press), 1982, p. 108.

19 Wiszniewicz, J. *And Yet I Still Have Dreams*, trans. R. Grol (Evanston, Il: Northwestern), 2004.

20 He is identified in "Minutes of the Second Plenary Session of the Jewish Education Council in Warsaw," PH/ 9–2–7 in Kermish (1986), pp. 464, 466.

21 [A Preliminary Study in Teaching People during the War.] PH/ 13–2–4 in Kermish (1986), p. 469.

[22] Lewin, A. *A Cup of Tears: A Diary of the Warsaw Ghetto*, A. Polonsky, ed. (Oxford: Blackwell), 1988, p. 84.

[23] "The Profile of the Jewish Child," #ARI/47 in Kermish (1986), p. 383.

[24] Mary Berg gives the address as 16 Sienna Street. It seems likely that is in error. The address of the school is given in this essay as Sienna 34, which would have been closer to her home. See ARI/341 in Kermish (1986), pp. 515–16.

[25] [Jewish Youth in the War Years.] ARI/46 in Kermish (1986), pp. 516–19.

[26] Ringelblum, E. (1958).

[27] Ringelblum, E. (1958), p. 329.

[28] Hilberg, R., Staron, S. and Kermisz, J., eds. *The Warsaw Diary of Adam Czerniakow: Prelude to Doom* (New York: Stein and Day), 1972, p. 295.

[29] Sternbuch, G. and Kranzler, D. *Gutta, Memories of a Vanished World, A Bais Yaakov Teacher's Poignant Account of the War Years* (NY: Feldheim), 2005.

[30] Steinberg, M. (2004), pp. 341–2.

[31] Ringelblum, E. (1974), pp. 249–50.

[32] See Wyden, P. (1992), p. 307.

[33] Reich-Reinicki, M. (1999), p. 186.

CHAPTER I: WARSAW BESIEGED

[1] Mary [Miriam] Wattenberg was born in Lodz on April 20, 1924. It is likely that she changed her birth date during the German occupation because Jews could not have the same birthday as Adolf Hitler. Perhaps she used the new date, October 10, in her published diary to protect family who might be alive in wartime Poland, just as she used the pseudonym Berg rather than her family name Wattenberg for that reason.

[2] Yom Kippur. During the war, the Germans often chose Jewish holidays for actions in the ghetto, such as pogroms and deportations.

[3] Edward Rydz-Śmigły (March 11, 1886–December 2, 1941). In November 1939 Rydz-Śmigły followed Józef Piłsudski as the Marshal of Poland and Commander-in-Chief of the Polish armed

forces. He fled with the Polish government to Romania during the siege where he was interned. Later he returned to join in the resistance, but shortly thereafter he died of heart failure in Poland.

4 Nicolas Poussin (1594–1665) was a French painter in the classical style during the Baroque period. Eugène Delacroix (1798–1863) painted in the French romantic style.

5 The neighbor was a *Volksdeutsche*, a person who had lived in pre-war Poland and whose family may have lived in Poland for generations. *Volksdeutsche* chose to sign a *Volksliste* establishing themselves as ethnic Germans during the occupation. This neighbor most likely got a financial reward or other privileges for denouncing the Wattenbergs.

6 Jan Matejko (1838–1893), a Polish painter born in Cracow, was beloved for his military and patriotic portraits, and particularly for paintings protesting the partition of Poland.

7 Officially Lodz had already become a part of the Third Reich on November 9, 1939.

8 The American Consulate moved to the Embassy building in Warsaw and remained open until the spring of 1940. It is possible that one reason the Wattenbergs had come to Warsaw in 1939 was to be near it.

9 The border between the new General Government and the Soviet Union was closed.

10 41 Sienna Street is still standing in Warsaw.

11 This was known as the Bałuty area.

12 At this time America was neutral and Germany did not want them to enter the war. It is therefore likely that this woman was paid for diplomatic reasons.

13 Galicia is an area in south-eastern Poland. Prior to 1918, it was part of the Austro-Hungarian Empire. He was telephoning from an area which the Soviet Union occupied in 1939.

14 About 250,000 to 300,000 Jews fled Poland to the Soviet Union after the German invasion. It is generally estimated that about half of them survived the war.

15 These were documents likely forged in Warsaw. See Eck (1957), p. 139.

16 The American Embassy in Berlin, located on the Pariser Place, was destroyed in 1939 and the Embassy worked out of temporary buildings near the Tiergarten in Berlin thereafter. Roosevelt

had recalled the American Ambassador, Hugh R. Wilson, in 1938. A Chargé d'Affaires remained in Berlin until December 1941.

[17] Sienna Street was one of the elegant streets of pre-war Warsaw. Located in the Little Ghetto, houses on the odd-numbered side of the street backed onto the ghetto boundary. Berg's Graphic Arts School was located here, in addition to a food kitchen, a café, and Korczak's orphanage.

[18] In the first months of the occupation secret schools began and by the summer of 1940, they took a more organized form. See Rosenthal (1979), p. 19.

[19] These are Adam Mickiewicz (1798–1855), Julisz Slowacki (1809–1849), and Stanislaw Wyspianski (1869–1907). "The Wedding" (*Wesele* in Polish) was a drama first staged in Cracow in 1901.

[20] The American Joint Distribution Committee, often called "the Joint" for short, was represented in Warsaw and played an important welfare role in the ghetto. It provided funding through the Jewish Social Self-Help committee.

CHAPTER II: THE GHETTO BEGINS

[1] There were about 2,000 members of the Jewish police in 1940. Many of the police were attorneys or other professionals and the majority of the leadership were refugees from Lodz. Although the police did not receive salaries, they had advantages in food rations and housing. In the final days of the ghetto, they assisted the Germans in "actions," rounding up people and marching them to the Umschlagplatz for deportation to Treblinka.

[2] KSP probably stands for Komendy Stolecznej Policji (Municipal Police Department).

[3] These rickshaws were a ghetto invention. One driver rode a bicycle behind an attached basket cart for two passengers. The work was so arduous for the drivers that they did not live long.

[4] At night there was a curfew so residents could not move freely about the ghetto. Housing committees organized music hours and skits, social circles, reading groups and bridge clubs. Youth clubs and circles were also organized in the large apartment blocks.

[5] "Pull" means knowing the right people, but it is likely that bribes, at least in some instances, were expected. The ghetto slang for "pull" was "to play the organ" or "to play the music box."

CHAPTER III: LIFE GOES ON

[1] By February 1941, hunger was an everyday reality. The official German ration allowed for the ghetto was 184 calories, while for Poles it was 699 calories and Germans could receive 2,613 calories a day (Roland [1992], p. 102). Having money to buy food on the black market was the only sure means of preventing starvation.

[2] According to the official ORT web site (www.ort.org), the name ORT was coined from the acronym of the Russian words Obshestvo Remeslenofo zemledelcheskofo Truda (Society for Trades and Agricultural Labor) in 1880. The ORT committee distributed money to Jewish schools for new handicraft and agricultural training. It also gave loans to artisans and purchased small acres of farmland for families to work. Today it is a non-profit organization with its world headquarters in Geneva.

[3] This was the Berson and Bauman Children's Hospital. Dr Anna Braude-Heller was the head doctor in the ghetto. See Roland (1992), pp. 94–6; Szwajger (1990), p. 19.

[4] The Haggadah contains text and rituals for the Passover Seder meal.

[5] A comedy by Jozef Polaczek [Polacek or Polatshek].

[6] An operetta about Baron von Kimmel written by Walter Kollo [Elimar Walter Kollodzieyski].

[7] Adam Czerniakow had the only automobile permitted in the ghetto. The day before the deportations began on July 22, 1942, the Germans took the automobile from him. This was clearly an omen of the beginning of the end of the ghetto.

[8] ToPoRol is derived from the Polish words "Towarzystwo Popierania Rolnietwa," meaning Society for the Support of Agriculture. One of the organization's aims was to plant food in the ghetto, hoping not only to counter starvation but also to get people outside and raise morale.

[9] Zionist youth movements in the ghetto organized these farm workers with the assistance of Toporol. So many Polish farm workers had been sent to Germany that the farms and estates

outside of Warsaw did not have enough farm labor. The work was hard, but the workers did not go hungry.

10   There are two small sections of the original wall remaining in Warsaw today near 55–59 Sienna Street.

11   The German translation is "Closed Epidemic Area—Only Through Traffic Permitted."

12   Pierre-Jean de Béranger (1780–1857). The "Alleluja" is from Mozart's motet "Exultate, Jubilate."

CHAPTER IV: UNDERGROUND

1   The *Gazeta Zydowska* was published in Cracow from July 1940 to summer 1942. Dobroszycki sees it as a German "tool" to deceive the ghetto inhabitants and many ghetto residents avoided the paper since it was an official German publication. Judenrat officials of various ghettos in Poland edited it. There were fifty titles of the underground press in the Warsaw Ghetto, including nineteen in Polish, such as the assimilationist *Zagiew* (Ember), and twenty-eight in Yiddish, such as the *Bundist Biuletin*, the Zionist *Dror* (Hebrew, Generation), and the Communist *Morgn Frayhayt* (Yiddish, Tomorrow Freedom, 1942). The Yiddish-language *Geto-Tsaytung* published in Lodz in 1941 was the only Jewish paper besides the *Gazeta Zydowska* permitted by the Germans in Poland.

CHAPTER V: RUSSIAN BOMBS

1   This paper was forbidden in the ghetto. It was an official German newspaper, which explains its viewpoint.

2   The Judenrat made the appointments. After Poles were forced to leave the Jewish district, Jews fought hard to receive these coveted positions. There were cases where lawyers were working as caretakers. "You had to have a whole heap of friends in the right places to obtain the position" (Szereszewska [1997], p. 21).

3   Italian citizenship might have given him some protection at that time. Although Italy was a German ally, Mussolini did not deport Italian Jews. Once Italy surrendered to the Germans in 1943, Italian Jews were subject to deportation (Hilberg [1973], p. 291).

[4] Robert Schumann's "Träumerei," Opus 15, Number 7. Since Schumann was a German composer, the inhabitants of the ghetto were officially forbidden to play his works. On April 30, 1942, another memoirist noted that it had been forbidden to use any German literary work, music or art in the ghetto for some time, but the Germans had begun to rigorously enforce this (Kaplan [1973], pp. 321–2).

CHAPTER VI: TYPHUS

[1] *Das Reich* was edited and published by Joseph Goebbels, German Minister of Propaganda, from 1940–45. *Der Völkische Beobachter* was the official newspaper of the National Socialist Party. It appeared from 1920 through 1945.

[2] After December 7, 1941 American journalists would not have been allowed to continue their work in Warsaw, so it is not clear to whom Mary Berg is referring. She may have seen either an article by an English-language journalist such as Otto Koischwitz, who had American citizenship but was working in Berlin in the Foreign Ministry, or a reprint, perhaps out of context, of an American publication, or simply a Nazi fabrication.

[3] Polcia is an equivalent to the name Paula or Pola in Polish. It is a woman's first name, which has a Latin derivation, meaning small. Mops in Polish means a pug dog, so this was perhaps a mild way of making fun of her or her name. Fuchs in German is the word for fox.

CHAPTER VII: "VIOLENCE AGAINST THY BROTHER"

[1] This occurred in Bialystok on June 28, 1941. Between 1,000 and 2,000 Jews perished in the fire.

[2] Mary Berg was right. This was probably another rumor among many which ran rampant in the ghetto, fuelled by the atmosphere of fear and desperation among the ghetto inhabitants as well as their isolation from outside news. Milejkowski hypothesized that the epidemic was caused by the food supply, which arrived in the ghetto contaminated by the delivery wagons that were also used to haul human excrement (Roland [1992], p. 180).

[3] Stefan Zeromski (1864–1926) was one of Poland's foremost writers.

4   This is the shortest chapter in the Christian Old Testament and is named for the prophet Obadiah. It comes from the oral tradition in the Jewish faith and is part of the laws of the Mishnah text of the Talmud.

5   German orders forbade the teaching of religion and public worship in the ghetto. Also, it is the Hebrew letter, which represents knowledge and learning.

6   Stawki Street was near the railroad shipping tracks. Less than a year later, Stawki Street became the entrance to the Umschlagplatz, the deportation site to Treblinka and later to Majdanek.

7   This is the song "Sto Lat" in Polish. The words are translated as follows: "For a hundred years, for a hundred years, May he/ she live for us. For a hundred years, for a hundred years, May he/she live for us. One more time, one more time, may he/ she live. May he/she live." The musical score, the Polish text and a sound clip are available at the University of Texas: www.utexas.edu/courses/polish/media/stolat.htm.

8   The play is by Jerzy Jurandot who was born Jerzy Glejgewicht in Warsaw, Poland in 1911. He was the artistic and literary director at the Melody Place in the ghetto. He survived the war and died in 1979 (Turkow [1995], pp. 167, 174, 201).

9   Joseph Pilsudski was founder of the Polish legion in World War I and he was a primary force in the establishment of an independent Poland after the war. He was mourned as a national hero at his death in 1935.

10 According to Ringelblum, thirteen assassinations of Jewish Gestapo collaborators by underground groups in the ghetto took place in the period from September 1942 through April 1943, including Alfred Nossig (1974, pp. 250–1), Gurman, and Milek Tine, among others (1958, p. 280). For details of how the ghetto underground made their decisions before issuing death warrants see Zuckerman (1993), pp. 319–23.

11 This was the only place that goods could pass into the ghetto legally, i.e. with German oversight and permission.

CHAPTER VIII: HORROR STALKS THE STREETS

1   The collection began in the Judenrat offices on December 25 in the bitter cold of winter 1942; this was a great loss for people (Czerniakow [1979], p. 308). Ironically, few of the furs were used

on the Russian front. In January 1943, the underground burned the SS warehouses at 31 Nalewki where some of the furs were stored.

[2] It was not until early 1942 that this tall footbridge was built crossing from the "Little Ghetto." It was located at the corner of Chlodna and Zelazna streets, near Czerniakow's home at 20 Chlodna, so the traffic for the Aryan side could pass through on the street below. According to Litai (1966), "The Jews called this place 'Gibraltar' " because German patrols could swoop down on passers-by (p. 23).

[3] Perhaps Szajer wanted to believe this. However, many scholars and memoirists describe this service as a sham, a way for young men with connections to avoid labor details. The address, 13 Leszno, is in itself, an indication that it was connected to the "13." See, for example, Mazor (1993), pp. 184–5; Ringelblum (1958), pp. 200, 332; Adler (1982), p. 234.

CHAPTER IX: ANOTHER YEAR

[1] Berg believes that Szajer's act was charitable and perhaps he believed this as well, but other sources indicate that the jobs were highly sought after and the mills were operated by the ghetto underworld.

[2] The medicines available were very limited and those drugs the Judenrat-run pharmacies did carry cost a high price.

[3] Julius Tuwin (1894–1957) was born in Lodz to Jewish parents. He fled Poland in 1939 and came to the United States in 1942. "Polish Flowers" is a lyrical, epic poem, full of his compassion for his homeland and for the poverty of its people. He returned to Poland in 1946.

[4] Many diaries and memoirs of the Warsaw Ghetto describe "Frankenstein" and his cruelty. On May 30, 1942, Ringelblum wrote: "Last week was a bloody one ... particularly around the Small Ghetto, where a policeman who has been dubbed 'Frankenstein' is on service. He was given this nickname because he looks and acts like the monster in the film of that name" ([1958], p. 283). Edelman describes him as "... a Schutzpolizei gendarme by the name of Frankenstein, [who] had on his conscience over 300 people murdered in one month, more than half of whom were children" ([1988], p. 28). See also Czerniakow (1979), p. 365;

Mazor (1993), p. 117; Szwajger (1990), p. 47; Turkow (1995), p.108.

CHAPTER X: SPRING IS CRUEL

[1] This was probably a trick to reduce the number of medical personnel in the ghetto and Dr. Miechowski was murdered on arrival or worked to death soon thereafter. A forced labor camp was established at Treblinka in 1941 for Jewish men. By 1942, this camp became Treblinka I and the death camp, which began operations in July 1942, was called Treblinka II.

[2] Zaklikow was a *shtetl* located in the Sub-Carpathian Mountains. Jewish existence came to an end there in November 1942 when the Jewish residents were deported to Belzec death camp. Between March and August 1942 more than 65,000 Jews had been deported from the Lwow ghetto and murdered. The final liquidation of the ghetto took place in early June 1943 (United States Holocaust Memorial Museum).

[3] It is unclear why Mary Berg thought her mother was "hiding" and why Mrs. Berg had not registered in April. Perhaps she was waiting for correspondence from Switzerland. Mary Berg explained in the "Woman of Tomorrow" interview that "knowing that she was going to be interned, Mother wrote to the Swiss legation in Switzerland, asking permission to take her family with her, which was granted."

[4] The community received permission to open public schools in the fall of 1941 and the school year began in January 1942 with six schools open. By spring of that year, nineteen schools were open with 6,700 pupils (Rosenthal [1979], p. 19). There were no secondary schools permitted legally. Perhaps Mary Berg is referring to the new Yiddish-language schools, which had been opened in May.

CHAPTER XI: THE GERMANS TAKE PICTURES

[1] Undoubtedly the Germans had propaganda aims in mind with the filming. The documentary, "Asien in Mitteleuropa," was filmed by Willi Wist, beginning on May 2, 1942 and ending June 2, 1942. Most ghetto diarists and memoirists remember this event, and a fragment of the original film, without sound, is in the Bundesarchiv in Koblenz, Germany. See the Fritz Bauer Institut at www.cineholocaust.de for a partial listing of the scenes in the film.

[2] The killings at Gesia Street took place in mid-May 1942 (Edel-man [1988], p. 30). One hundred and ten prisoners of the so-called Central Jail ("Gesiowka") were executed for "illegally" crossing to the Aryan side. Special proclamations signed by Auerswald were posted in the ghetto about the "just" punishment received by these "criminals."

[3] American and British Commonwealth citizens had been required to register for the first time on April 14, 1942. This was part of the plan laid out at the Wannsee Conference to remove all non-Aryans from the German Reich (Eck [1957], p. 36).

[4] Ruth Lawrence worked with Rev. Gaither Warfield at the Methodist mission in Warsaw. He established the American Colony with Gestapo permission. Lawrence was secretary.

[5] In March 1943, workers in the ghetto were transferred to Plaszow Labor Camp. On March 14, the remaining non-workers were murdered in the ghetto (see Spector, S., vol. 1, p. 280).

CHAPTER XII: THE PRIVILEGED GO TO PRISON

[1] This change in the attitude of the Germans toward those with foreign papers should be noted. Early testimony and scholarship suggested that the Germans were luring Jews to come forth with papers in 1942 (and later) as a trick and planned all along to murder them. More recent scholars such as Friedman argue that the Germans were doing so primarily for purposes of exchange as a means of bringing Germans abroad back to the Reich.

[2] The Polish name of the film is *Dziesieciu z Pawiaka*. It was directed by Ryszard Ordynski and premiered in 1931.

[3] Mexico declared war against Nazi Germany on May 22, 1942, so it was an Allied nation at this time.

[4] This was not the orphanage known as Korczak's, which was in the Little Ghetto.

CHAPTER XIII: THE CHILDREN GO FOR A WALK

[1] It is very likely that Mary Berg is mistaken here. Dzielna Street ran along the side of Pawiak prison where "Serbia" was located. At Pawiak, Mary Berg had probably heard people refer to 39 Dzielna as the "Korczak home" and assumed that Korczak's orphanage

THE DIARY OF MARY BERG

had moved there from Sienna Street. When she saw children led out by German guards from 39 Dzielna Street, she assumed she was seeing Korczak being led away with the children.

CHAPTER XIV: THE END OF THE JEWISH POLICE

[1] Historically, there are at least six towns named Sosnowiec in Poland, all in the proximity of Warsaw. Perhaps this is a veiled reference to Sosnowiec near Auschwitz in Katowice province. If that is the case, then Mary Berg is perceptive: she means the English and neutral citizens have been murdered.

[2] Oswiecim is the Polish name for the city of Auschwitz and for the concentration camp established there for Poles in 1940. Gassing began there in 1941 and the first Jewish transports arrived in the spring of 1942. People in the ghetto knew the methods of killing at Auschwitz as well as at Belzec and Chelmno. An *Oneg Shabbat* bulletin in early 1942 reported that eyewitnesses were saying that conductors in trains passing near Belzec were told to close the windows to keep out the smells from the murders occurring there (Kermish [1986], AR/I/1382, p. 32). By the spring of 1943, the four gas chambers at Birkenau were in full operation, but already in the fall of 1941, the Germans had initiated the gassing of victims at the main Auschwitz camp.

CHAPTER XV: BLOODY DAYS AGAIN

[1] The cows had probably been in a secret dairy in the ghetto. Perhaps these cows had provided milk for the infants of wealthy people and for the restaurants and clubs that operated in the ghetto that served the underworld and those who still had wealth from pre-war days.

[2] Adrienne Thomas (Bertha Adrienne Strauch) served from 1914–1916 as a nurse on the front at Metz in the First World War, after which she became a pacifist. Her first book, *Catherine Becomes a Soldier*, appeared in 1931. It was soon translated into fifteen languages and was popular worldwide. *Catherine, the World is Aflame!* appeared in 1938. Thomas was in Vienna when the Nazis annexed Austria. She came from a Jewish family, so she fled to France and, in 1940, arrived in the United States, where she spent the war years. She was born in the Alsace in 1897 and died in 1960 in Vienna.

3 Contemporary accounts of the methods used in Nazi camps vary, although many report the use of "steam." See, for example, Ringelblum (1958), p.321, who, like Mary Berg in her original shorthand, refers to the killing center as "Treblinki."

4 Several witnesses with firsthand knowledge of Treblinka had returned to the ghetto by December 1942. See Ringelblum (1958), pp. 320–1; Edelman (1988), p. 32.

5 Mary Berg does not distinguish here between U.S. citizens and internees who held citizenship or protective papers from Latin and Central American countries.

6 It has been estimated that about 28,000 Jews were in hiding in Warsaw at some time and of them about 41% (11,500) survived to see liberation (Paulsson [2002], pp. 199–248).

7 They were going to Germany as forced labor and farm workers. One estimate is that nearly two million Polish workers were forcibly deported, most from the General Government (Davies [2003], p. 106).

8 Early morning on January 18, 1943 armed Germans and Ukrainians entered the ghetto and called for the ghetto workers to come from their apartments to be sent to the Umschlagplatz. To their surprise, people went into bunkers they had prepared and underground fighters met the Germans with armed resistance. In four days of fighting, about 4,000 to 5,000 Jews were murdered in the ghetto or deported. The number of German casualties is uncertain. Gutman believes it was less than "several dozen" (Gutman [1994], pp. 179–84).

CHAPTER XVI: INTERNMENT CAMP

1 The train left in the middle of the night and it departed from a siding outside of Warsaw so that the internees would not witness the Germans re-entering the ghetto to deport the remaining 30,000 to 40,000 Jews.

2 Vittel is a health resort in France. The internment camp was officially called Frontstalag 142. The camp was composed of the resort hotels and the spa park. Although barbed wire surrounded the whole area, the internees were able to walk around in the park during the daytime.

3 The shops were in a separate building close to the Grand Hotel. During the war, the arcade was open to the detainees and so were

a few shops and boutiques under the supervision of people from the town. In pre-war years, the Galerie des Curs was open to non-residents of the hotel. At the end of it was the limit of the access to the grounds where detainees could exercise; it was also a kind of "lovers' lane" for young detainees.

4   The guards sometimes rode bicycles around the perimeter. The park was 2.5 hectares and 2,500 meters long and was enclosed by barbed wire. It was open to the internees from the hotels except from 8:00 in the evening to 7:00 in the morning.

5   The letters were censored, so the internees often wrote in a kind of code, using English words that had double meanings. Correspondence from Poland had to be in German, so often correspondents wrote in a Germanized Yiddish, using Roman letters.

6   An operetta by Franz Lehar (1870–1948), "Das Land des Lächelns" (The Land of Smiles). The operetta was first performed at Vittel in November 1942 on the stage of the theater in the Casino building. Stella Gumuchian, who ran the entertainment committee and was an accomplished musician, had only one music score of Lehar's production and it was for the piano. From this she worked out the various scores for other instruments of the orchestra.

CHAPTER XVII: THE BATTLE OF THE GHETTO

1   Trawniki, a labor camp, opened in the fall of 1941. It was also used for training SS recruits from the Soviet Union and the Baltic states. Beginning in the spring of 1942, Jews from Western Europe were deported to Trawniki. In August 1943, it became a sub-camp of Majdanek. On November 3, 1943, 10,000 Jews from the camp were executed and buried in nearby pits. It also served as a transfer camp to the Belzec death camp (Aktion Reinhard, www.deathcamps.org).

2   Of the 2,500 to 3,000 persons from the Hotel Polski who were sent to Bergen-Belsen, only approximately 250 who held papers for Palestine survived (Eck [1957], pp. 142–3).

3   These were civilian internment camps. The Tost Camp Ilag VIII was at Gleiwitz, Poland from 1941–1942.

4   Mary Berg means Westerbork, a transit camp outside of Amsterdam, where the Otto Frank family were sent after they were discovered in hiding in the secret annex.

[5] Their foreboding proved true for those Polish Jews who held Central or South American papers. In August 1943, Alois Brunner in Paris asked Adolf Eichmann in Berlin to send a commission to Vittel to examine the documents of the Polish Jews in the camp who held Central and South American papers. When the commission arrived on September 8, it was an ominous signal of what was to come (Rutkowski, p. 47). On September 8, 1943 the Jews with South American papers had to surrender their documents (Katzenelson, p. 30).

[6] Berg's estimate of 150 people who were eligible for exchange may be low. Shortly after her departure, the Polish Jews at Vittel who held South and Central American papers were deported to Drancy Camp in France in two transports and from there to Auschwitz.

CHAPTER XVIII: JOURNEY TO FREEDOM

[1] Fortunately, this did not occur. The train was delayed at Biarritz to wait for some 350 American civilians to join the group from Vittel and be exchanged with them.

[2] The *SS Gripsholm* was chartered by the United States State Department from the Swedish American line and used to repatriate American citizens from the Far East, South America, Belfast and Algiers as well as from Europe and South Africa. In the period from 1942–1946 it made twelve roundtrip voyages of mercy. Painted in the blue and yellow of the Swedish flag, the ship ran with its lights on to identify it as a diplomatic ship.

[3] See *New York Times*, "128 Still Aboard," March 17, 1944. The *Gripsholm* docked with 662 passengers.

BIBLIOGRAPHY

Contemporary Reviews of Berg's Diary

Review, *Kirkus*, **13** (February 15, 1945), p. 24.

Library Journal, **70** (February 15, 1945), p. 162.

Young, Marguerite. "First Hand Report of a Nightmare," *New York Times Book Review*, February 18, 1945, p. 6.

New Yorker, **21** (February 24, 1945), p. 77.

Weiskopf, F. *Saturday Review*, **28** (March 3, 1945), p. 34.

Horn Book, **21** (May, 1945), p. 210.

References

Adler, Stanislav. *In the Warsaw Ghetto, 1940–1943: An Account of a Witness. The Memoirs of Stanislav Adler*. Jerusalem: Yad Vashem, 1982.

Czerniakow, Adam. *The Warsaw Diary of Adam Czerniakow, Prelude to Doom*. Eds. Raul Hilberg, Stanislaw Staron and Josef Kermisz. New York: Stein and Day, 1968, 1979.

Davies, Norman. *Rising '44: The Battle for Warsaw*. London: Penguin, 2003.

Dawidowicz, Lucy. *The War Against the Jews, 1933–1945*. New York: Bantam, 1975.

Dobroszycki, Lucjan, ed. *Reptile Journalism, The Official Polish-Language Press under the Nazis, 1939–1945*, trans. Barbara Harshav. New Haven: Yale, 1994.

Eck, Nathan. "The Rescue of Jews with the Aid of Passports and Citizenship Papers of Latin American States." *Yad Vashem Studies on the European Jewish Catastrophe and Resistance* **1** (1957), pp. 125–52.

Edelman, Marek. "The Ghetto Fights." In *The Warsaw Ghetto, the Forty-Fifth Anniversary of the Uprising*. Warsaw: Interpress, 1988.

Elbaum, Esther. "She Lived in the Warsaw Ghetto, An Interview with Mary Berg." *Hadassah Newsletter*, March–April 1945, pp. 420–1.

Gilbert, Martin. *A History of the Jews of Europe during the Second World War*. New York: Holt, Rinehart and Winston, 1985.

Gutman, Israel, et al. *Encyclopedia of the Holocaust*. 4 vols. New York: Macmillan, 1990.

——. *The Jews of Warsaw, 1939–1943: Ghetto, Underground, Revolt*. Bloomington (IN): Indiana, 1982.

——. et al. *Rescue Attempts during the Holocaust: Proceedings of the Second Yad Vashem Internatonal Historical Conference, April 1974*. Jerusalem: Yad Vashem, 1977.

——. *Resistance, The Warsaw Ghetto Uprising*. New York: Houghton Mifflin, 1994.

Heinemann, Marlene E. *Gender and Destiny: Women Writers and the Holocaust*. New York: Greenwood, 1986.

Hilberg, Raul. *The Destruction of the European Jews*. New York: New Viewpoints, 1973.

Kaplan, Chaim. *Scroll of Agony, The Warsaw Diary of Chaim A. Kaplan*. Trans. and Ed. Abraham I. Katsh. London: 1966; *The Warsaw Diary of Chaim A. Kaplan*. Trans. and rev. edn Abraham I. Katsh. New York: Colliers, 1973.

Katzenelson, Yitzhak. *The Song of the Murdered Jewish People*. Israel: Ghetto Fighters' House, 1980.

——. *Vittel Diary*. Ghetto Fighters' House, n.d.

Kermish, Joseph (Ed.). *To Live with Honor and Die with Honor!... Selected Documents from the Warsaw Ghetto Underground Archives "O.S."* Jerusalem: Vad Yashem, 1986.

Kranzler, David. *Thy Brother's Blood, the Orthodox Jewish response during the Holocaust*. Brooklyn (NY): Mesorah, 1987.

Levin, Nora. *The Holocaust: The Destruction of European Jewry, 1933–1945*. New York: Schocken, 1973.

Lewin, Abraham. *A Cup of Tears, A Diary of the Warsaw Ghetto*. Ed. Antony Polonsky. Oxford: Blackwell, 1988.

Litai, Chaim Lazar. *Muranowska 7, The Warsaw Ghetto Rising*. Tel Aviv: Massada, 1966.

Mazor, Michel. "The House Committees in the Warsaw Ghetto." In *The Holocaust as Historical Experience, Essays and a Discussion*. Eds. Yehuda Bauer and Nathan Rotensteich. New York: Homes & Meier, 1981, pp. 95–108.

——. *The Vanished City, Everyday Life in the Warsaw Ghetto*. Trans. David Jacobson. New York: Marsilio, 1993.

Paulsson, Gunnar S. *Secret City, The Hidden Jews of Warsaw, 1940–1945*. New Haven (CT): Yale, 2002.

Pentlin, Susan. "Community in a World of Chaos, Life in the Warsaw Ghetto." In *The Century of Genocide*. Eds. Daniel J. Curran, Jr., Richard Libowitz and Marcia Sachs Littell. Westfield (PA): Merion, 2002, pp. 63–75.

——. "Holocaust Victims of Privilege," in *Problems Unique to the Holocaust*. Harry James Cargas, Ed. Lexington: University of Kentucky, 1999, pp. 25–41.

——. "Mary Berg," in *Encyclopedia of Holocaust Literature*. Eds. David Patterson, Alan Berger and Sarita Cargas. Westport (CT): Oryx, 2002, pp. 19–21.

——. "Mary Berg," in *Holocaust Literature, An Encyclopedia of Writers and their Work*. Ed. Lillian Kremer. New York: Routledge, 2003, pp. 138–41.

——. "Mary Berg's *Warsaw Ghetto, A Diary*" in *Bearing Witness to the Holocaust 1939–1989*. Ed. Alan L. Berger. Lewiston (NY): Edwin Mellen, 1991, pp. 255–71.

——. "Mary Berg," and "Warsaw Ghetto: A Diary," in *Reference Guide to Holocaust Literature*. Ed. Thomas Riggs. Detroit: St. James Press, 2002, pp. 29–30 and 617–81.

Reich-Reinicki, Marcel. *The Author of Himself*. Trans. Ewald Osers. Princeton (NJ): Princeton, 1999.

Ringelblum, Emanuel. *Notes from the Warsaw Ghetto, The Journal of Emanuel Ringelblum*. Trans. and ed. Jacob Sloan. New York: Schoken Books, 1958.

——. *Polish-Jewish Relations during the Second World War*. Eds. Joseph Kermish and Shmuel Krakowski and trans. Dafna Allon, Danuta Dabroska and Dana Keren. Evanston (IL): Northwestern, 1974.

BIBLIOGRAPHY

Roland, Charles G. *Courage under Siege, Starvation, Disease, and Death in the Warsaw Ghetto*. New York and Oxford: Oxford University Press, 1992.

Rosenfeld, Alvin H. *A Double Dying: Reflections on Holocaust Literature*. Bloomington: Indiana University, 1980.

Rosenthal, David. "The Unvanquished Sector of the Warsaw Ghetto, its School System." *Jewish Frontier* 46 (April 1979) 4, pp. 18–21.

Rutkowski, Adam. "Le camp d'internement et d'éxchange pour Juifs de Vittel." *Le Monde Juif*, Paris, 102 (April–June 1981), pp. 35–70.

——. "O Agenturze Gestapowskiez W. Getcie Warszawskim." *Biuletyn Zydowskiego Instytutu Historycznego*. Warszawa: Jewish History Quarterly, 1956, pp. 38–59.

Spector, Shmuel et al. *The Encyclopedia of Jewish Life Before and During the Holocaust*, 3 vols. New York: Washington Square, 2001.

Steinberg, Madeleine. "Une Internee Civile Britannique Témoin Indirect de la Fin au Ghetto de Varsovie." *Le Monde Juif*, Paris, **180** (January–June 2004), pp. 315–60.

Szwajger, Adina Blady. *I Remember Nothing More, The Warsaw Children's Hospital and the Jewish Resistance*. New York: Pantheon, 1988, 1990.

Szereszewska, Helena. *Memoirs from Occupied Warsaw 1940–1945*. London: Vallentine Mitchell, 1997.

Turkow, Jonas. *C'était ainsi, 1939–1943 la vie dans le ghetto de Varsovie*. Trans. Maurice Pfeffer. Paris: Editions Austral, 1995.

Wiszniewicz, Joanna. *And Yet I Still have Dreams*. Trans. Regina Grol. Evanston (IL): Northwestern, 2004.

"Woman of Tomorrow." Interview with Mary Berg by Nancy Craig. WJZ radio, 8:30 a.m. February 21, 1945. Transcript, S.L. Shneiderman Archives, Diaspora Research Institute, Tel Aviv.

Wyden, Peter. *Stella*. New York: Simon & Schuster, 1992.

Zuckerman, Yitzhak. *A Surplus of Memory. Chronicle of the Warsaw Ghetto Uprising*. Trans. and Ed. Barbara Harshav. Berkeley: University of California, 1993.

Newspaper Articles

"96 New Yorkers in List of 524 Americans Returning Home aboard the Gripsholm." *The New York Times*, ProQuest Historical Newspapers. March 12, 1944, p. 26.

"128 Still Aboard Liner." *The New York Times*, ProQuest Historical Newspapers. March 17, 1944, p. 5.

"312 Repatriates Arrive in Lisbon." *The New York Times*, ProQuest Historical Newspapers. February 26, 1944, p. 3.

"500 Americans Freed from Camp in Germany." *The New York Times*, ProQuest Historical Newspapers. September 14, 1944, p. 3.

"663 Due Here Today on the Gripsholm." *The New York Times*, ProQuest Historical Newspapers. March 15, 1944, p. 1.

"2,000,000 Murders by Nazis Charged." *The New York Times*, ProQuest Historical Newspapers. August 8, 1943, p. 11.

Adams, Frank S. "35 Soldiers, Ill but Happy, First to Leave Gripsholm." *The New York Times*, ProQuest Historical Newspapers. March 16, 1944, p. 11.

Douglas, Francis. "Vittel and the Jews." Trans. James Fox. *L'Arche*, **298** (January 1982), pp. 77–9.

Gleiser, Edith. "Free Again, Describes 3½ Years' Internment." *Christian Science Monitor*. August 15, 1944, p. 10.

"Gripsholm Sailing Delayed Few Days." *The New York Times*, ProQuest Historical Newspapers. March 4, 1944, p. 7.

"Gripsholm Quits U.S. on Exchange Mission." *The New York Times*, ProQuest Historical Newspapers. February 16, 1944, p. 1.

"Internees Gripped by Fury of Battle." *The New York Times*, ProQuest Historical Newspapers. September 16, 1944, p. 3.

"Last Repatriates leave Gripsholm." *The New York Times*, ProQuest Historical Newspapers. March 18, 1944, p. 3.

"More Americans to be Exchanged." *The New York Times*, ProQuest Historical Newspapers. February 13, 1944, p. 9.

"Others to Join Wounded." *The New York Times*, ProQuest Historical Newspapers. February 26, 1944, p. 3.

"Repatriates on Gripsholm Tell of Europe under Nazi Hell." *Christian Science Monitor*. March 17, 1944, p. 11.

Spraggs, Melita. "Woman Internee Tells of Days in Germany, 'Prayed for the Men who were Bombing Us.' " *Christian Science Monitor*. August 17, 1944, pp. 1–2.

"Thousands Mourn Victims of Ghetto." *The New York Times*, ProQuest Historical Newspapers. April 20, 1944, p. 11.

"Underground Press gives Details of Battle: Jews Fought for Their Lives in Warsaw." *The New York Times*, ProQuest Historical Newspapers. September 25, 1943, p. 6.

"US Wounded Taken Aboard Gripsholm." *The New York Times*, ProQuest Historical Newspapers. March 5, 1944, p. 17.

"War Prisoners being Exchanged. 17 Disabled Americans are on List." *The New York Times*, ProQuest Historical Newspapers. October 19, 1943, p. 10.

Warren, Lansing. "Freed Americans Dazzled in Lisbon." *The New York Times*, ProQuest Historical Newspapers. February 27, 1944, p. 19.

——. "Nazis' Arrests Hit Red Cross." *The New York Times*, ProQuest Historical Newspapers. March 6, 1944, p. 8.

"Warsaw Casualities Include an American." *The New York Times*, ProQuest Historical Newspapers. October 7, 1939, p. 3.

Audio-visual Sources

Joest, Heinz. "A Day in the Warsaw Ghetto, A Birthday Trip to Hell." Director Jack Kuper. Canada, 1991. 30 minute video, black and white.

Pasatieri, Thomas. "Letter to Warsaw [poems by Pola Braun]." Music of Remembrance; Mina Miller, artistic director; Jane Eaglen, soprano; Gerard Schwarz, piano. Seattle: CD, Naxon, American Classics, 2004.

Polskie Tango 1929–1939. Wiera Gran. "Gdy odejdziesz" ["When You've Gone Away"] Old World Tangos, vol. 3. Oriente Musik, 2005.

Web Research Sites and Databases

Aktion Reinhard. http://www.deathcamps.org

Architektura przedwojennej Warszway. Ryszard Maczewski. http://www.warszawa1939.pl

Central Database of Shoah Victims' Names. Yad Vashem.
   http://www.yadvashem.org
Culture pl. Directory. http://www.culture.pl/en/culture
Film Polski. Polish Film Database. http://www.filmpolski.pl
Forum Zydow Polskich. http://fzp.jewish.org.pl/
Fritz Bauer Institut. http://www.fritz-bauer-institut.de/
Historical Sites of Jewish Warsaw.
   http://jewish.sites.warszawa. um.gov.pl/wstep_a.htm
Jewish Berlin online. "Wieder das Vergessen." Database of 55,000
   victims. http://jewish-weblife.com/m1_engl.html
JewishGen. Holocaust and Poland databases.
   http://www.jewishgen.org/
Jewish Women's Archive. http://www.jwa.org/
Jews of the Old Lodz Biographical Directory.
   http://www.lodzjews.com/indexus.htm
Library of Congress Online Catalog. http://catalog.loc.gov/
Memorial de la Shoah. Centre de documentation juive contempor-
   aine, Paris. http://www.memorialdelashoah.org
Moses Schorr Center in Warsaw. http:www/schorr.edu.pl.
National Library of Poland.
   http://alpha.bn.org.pl/screens/opacmenu.html
ORT World Headquarters. http://www.ort.org/
Polish Jews. http://polishjews.org
Shtetl Links. JewishGen. http://www.shtetlinks.jewishgen.org/
S.L. and Eileen Shneiderman Collection of Yiddish books at the
   University of Maryland Libraries.
   http://www.lib.umd.edu/ SLSES/index.html
Tribute to the Swedish American Line. *S.S. Gripsholm.*
   http:// www.salship.se
United States Holocaust Memorial Museum (USHMM). Photo
   Archive and Library. http://www.ushmm.org
Warsaw Ghetto Database. [Getto Warszawskie. Internetowa Baza
   Danych O Warszawskim Getcie], http://warszawa.getto.pl/
Warsaw Voice. Polish and Central European online Review.
   http://www.warsawvoice.pl
Yivo Institute. http://www.yivo.org/downloads/Cinema.pdf

CHRONOLOGY OF EVENTS

1933

January 30   Hitler appointed Chancellor of the German Reich

March 20   Dachau Concentration Camp opened

1935

September 15   Nuremberg Laws defined "a Jew;" German Jews lost citizenship

1938

October 28   17,000 Polish Jews expelled from German Reich

November 9   Crystal Night pogrom began against Jews in German Reich

1939

September 1   German troops invaded Poland

September 23   Judenrat (Jewish Council) appointed in Warsaw

mid-October   Hitler ordered T-4 Euthanasia program (backdated to September 1)

October 28   First closed ghetto established in Poland in Piotrokow Trybunalski

1940

April 30   Lodz Ghetto sealed

June 14   German troops entered Paris

November 26   Warsaw Ghetto sealed

1941

June 22   Germany invaded Soviet Union

December 7   Chelmno Death Camp in western Poland began operation

1942

January 20	Wannsee Conference in Berlin outlined Final Solution
July 17	Foreigners in Warsaw Ghetto interned in Pawiak prison
July 22	Deportation of Warsaw Ghetto population to Treblinka began
July 23	Czerniakow, head of Warsaw Ghetto Judenrat, committed suicide
September 21	Major deportations from Warsaw Ghetto to Treblinka ended

1943

January 18	Warsaw foreigners sent to Vittel; first armed resistance in the Warsaw Ghetto occurred
April 19	Warsaw Ghetto Uprising began

1944

February 25	*SS Gripsholm* exchanges from Lisbon recommenced
April–May	300 Polish Jews deported from Vittel to Drancy and to Auschwitz
August 1	Polish Uprising in Warsaw began
September 12	Vittel Internment Camp liberated

1945

January 26	Auschwitz Death Camp liberated
February 19	English-language edition of Berg's diary published in America
April 30	Adolf Hitler committed suicide in bunker in Berlin
May 8	Victory in Europe declared by Allied Forces

INDEX